ABSTRACTS *of* WILLS

Carroll County Maryland

1837–1852

I0129357

Jennifer Shipley-Sullivan

HERITAGE BOOKS
2009

HERITAGE BOOKS
AN IMPRINT OF HERITAGE BOOKS, INC.

Books, CDs, and more—Worldwide

For our listing of thousands of titles see our website
at
www.HeritageBooks.com

Published 2009 by
HERITAGE BOOKS, INC.
Publishing Division
100 Railroad Ave. #104
Westminster, Maryland 21157

Copyright © 2009 Jennifer Shipley-Sullivan

International Standard Book Numbers
Paperbound: 978-0-7884-5041-9
Clothbound: 978-0-7884-8295-3

For my parents, Gary and Dorcas Shipley, and for my husband – Jack.

ABOUT THE AUTHOR

JENNIFER SHIPLEY-SULLIVAN is a native Texan who has been conducting genealogy research in Maryland for over ten years. Most recently, she published "Konrad Zeul 1754-1830 Hessian Soldier, Maryland Farmer" in *The Hessians: Journal of the Johannes Schwalm Historical Association.*

Cover Art

❧

The subject matter for the cover art image is the cemetery at St. Thomas Episcopal Church in Owings Mills, Baltimore County, Maryland. My father's grandparents, the Bluchers, are buried at St. Thomas. It is also the church my grandmother, Grace Blucher Shipley, attended in her childhood.

My father, Gary Shipley, a native Baltimorean, created the image in pen and ink and contributed it specifically for this publication. I believe him to be one of the best artists that I know, and I admire him greatly.

Foreword

Like many of you, I have been bitten by the genealogy bug. That coupled with a love of early American history has turned a hobby into a passion. Over the past ten years, I have been able to trace my father's family back through six generations.

My research has been successful due to the vast amount of resources available for Maryland. Of course, the Maryland State Archives in Annapolis is a treasure trove but so are many publications like the seven volume series of cemeteries by the Carroll County Historical Society, the seventeen volume series of Maryland German church records by Frederick Weiser, works by individuals such as Mary Ann Ashcraft, Bill and Martha Reamy, Henry C. Peden and Robert Barnes.

I would like to be able to contribute to the community that has given me so much. I decided to write this volume, in particular, as:

- Wills reveal many facts about relationships, professions, property holdings and lifestyles

- Much of my own family research has been conducted in Carroll County and I have a familiarity with many of the families

- The time period 1837-1852 bridges the 1850 census which will, hopefully, help fellow researchers "connect the dots"

My Maryland ancestors were both English and German immigrants who came to the Americas across a time frame that spans from the late 1600s to the early 1800s. They carved out a meager, but industrious, life for themselves which has allowed me the opportunities I have today. In transcribing this small piece of history, I pay homage to them, and to those I became briefly acquainted with during this effort: the slave recently released from bondage facing a world railed against them; a daughter hoping to find a husband with her dowry; the entrepreneur who waits for the final settlement for a ship lost at sea decades ago; a son wishing to make good on the land that his father has given him; the spinster who meticulously bequeaths out her belongings to her loved ones; the priest who wishes to provide for his flock and hopes that he will not be forgotten after death; the husband who gives everything to a wife with small children in the hopes that all will be well without his presence; the homeless man who attempts to maintain civility even in death; the brother whose time has come too early; the grandmother who continues to rule the roost and the purse strings and the father that desires only the best for his children.

I have enjoyed my time transcribing these wills. They have given me a small window into the private lives of these individuals and a broader insight into the ways of life at the time. I hope that you enjoy reading them as much as I did.

However, I could not have done this effort alone and I would like to thank those who helped me along the way. I would like to thank my parents and my husband. They not only edited this volume but also have accompanied me over the years on many outings to libraries, archives, court houses and cemeteries which were not always entirely at their will.

Many of the wills contained German signatures which were easy to interpret with the clerk's subsequent entries in English. I did run into a will written entirely in German (the will of John Reiszle on page 173). I was able to enlist the help of a fabulous translator who not only produced solid work but returned the request at lightning speed. I would like to thank Esther Bauer

Ph.D. of Genealogy Translations for her translation. Thank you, Esther.

Thanks to the staff at the Maryland State Archives, especially Jill Ludlum. I only have the opportunity to visit the archives once or twice a year, but Jill is always responsive to my remote requests from Texas. Thank you, Jill.

Jennifer Shipley-Sullivan
Grapevine, Texas
July 2009

Introduction

Abstracts of Wills, Carroll County, Maryland 1837-1852 is transcribed from holdings at the Maryland State Archives in Annapolis, Maryland. Specifically, microfilm titled "Carroll County, Register of Wills (Wills) 1837-1975 WK 847-848". The 381 wills herein represent the first will book for Carroll County subsequent to the county's creation in 1837 from the joining of parts of Frederick and Baltimore Counties, Maryland.

Records are listed in alphabetical order by testator. All spellings have been replicated as in the original document. Each abstract includes:

- Testators name including alternative spellings

- Residence of testator at the time the will was written as well as other personal information given by the testator such as marital status or occupation

- Date that the will was written (there are some instances where only a month or year was given, this is indicated by comments in brackets)

- Date the will was filed

- Date the will was proved or probated (to note, if the date the will was filed is different from the date it was probated, the filed date will help give a better approximation as to the death date of the testator since wills often would be filed before proven)

- The will number and folio (page) number

- Abstract of the will (there are several instances where the testator bequeaths items to a wife or children but does not explicitly name them, this is indicated by comments in brackets)

- Abstract of the codicil to the will (only where applicable)

- Abstract of any renunciations to the will (only where applicable)

- Witnesses to the will and codicil

- Executors (denoting their relationship to the testator if indicated within the will)

- Whether or not the will was signed (to possibly determine if the individual was literate)

Table: Example of Format

Surname, First Name	residence / occupation
	date will written
	date will filed
will number, page number	date will probated

Abstract: includes items such as names and relationships, will bequests, household possessions, land tract names, etc.

Codicil: if any exists

Renunciation: if any exists, also includes date and witnesses

Witnesses: names listed
Executor(s): names listed (relationship to testator)
Signed by either the testator's mark or signature

Care was taken to include items that might be of interest to both historians and genealogists. All counties mentioned are assumed to be in Maryland unless otherwise stated. No other sources were used to supplement the abstracts. The index includes all individual's names and the names of land tracts. Please direct any requests for copies of the original records to the Maryland State Archives

Abstracts of Wills
Carroll County, Maryland
1837-1852

Addelsperger, Eleanor   widow of Westminster, Carroll County

August 16, 1843
August 3, 1846

Number 232, Folio 426   August 3, 1846

To my daughters, Elizabeth Addelsperger and Margaret Addelsperger, all of my estate to be shared equally. I desire that my daughters, Elizabeth and Margaret, reimburse Jacob Mathias for acting as executor of my husband's estate (which was settled in the orphan's court of Frederick County, Maryland). My daughters, Elizabeth and Margaret, have received an additional inheritance above and beyond my other children [not named] as they took care of me and comforted me in my old age. My other children have been provided for in my husband's will.

Witnesses: James Raymond, John F. Reese, William N. Hayden
Executor(s): Elizabeth Addelsperger (daughter)
Signed by her mark

Alben, George   of Carroll County

July 31, 1844
September 9, 1844

Number 186, Folio 333   September 9, 1844

To my wife, Mary Alben, all my estate for her natural life. After her decease, my estate should go to my son, Joseph Alben. Upon receiving my estate, Joseph should pay my other children forty seven dollars each, namely: Zachariah Alben, Eli Alben, Henry Alben, Hannah Hate, George Alben, Mary Harris and Sarah Harris.

Witnesses: Caleb Hoshal, Richard Stansbury, Robert Morrison
Executor(s): Zachariah Alben (son), Joseph Alben (son)
Signed with his signature

Algier, Henry   of Carroll County
                                        June 30, 1845
                                     November 10, 1845
Number 212, Folio 390   November 10, 1845

To my son, Melchor F. Algier, my dwelling plantation in Carroll County called Lot No. 1 bounded by the lands of Nicholas Algier, Richard Ware, Francis Elseroad, John Algier, George Ebaugh, George Reese and "George's Purchase." To my beloved wife, Mary, one half of the dwelling house on above mentioned Lot No. 1 for the rest of her natural life. I desire that my son, Melchor, "provide a sufficient and genteel maintenance for his mother during her life time." To my daughter, Nancy Algier, Lot No. 2 in Carroll County which adjoins the above described Lot No. 1 and is bounded by the lands of Jacob Hildebrand and Zachariah Ebaugh. To my daughter, Nancy Algier, two cows, one spinning wheel and one feather bed with furniture. To my son, Joshua Algier, all my lands in Carroll County Lot No. 3 adjoining above mentioned Lot No. 1 and No. 2 and bounded by the lands of the Helderbrands, Creighs, Brown's Mill Lot and Francis Elseroads (on condition that my son, Joshua, does not marry Barbary Hilderbrand). To my daughter, Rachel Houck, all the land in Carroll County called "Georges Purchase" lying on the east side of the public road leading from Hampstead toward Browns Meeting House. To my daughter, Rachel Houck, the promissory note between myself and her husband, David W. Houck, dated May 3, 1841. To my wife, Mary Algier, two cows, two feather beds with bedding, one table and one chest. I desire that my son, Melchor, dig a ditch so that my son Joshua will have benefit of water from Springs Branch. All my other personal goods should be equally divided amongst four of my children, namely: Amon, Rachel, Lucinda and Nancy.

Witnesses: Amon Richard, Moses Shaffer, Reuben A. Troyer
Executor(s): Melchor F. Algier (son)
Signed with his signature

2

Angel, Anna Marie   of Carroll County
                                               July 19, 1846
                                           August 10, 1846
Number 234, Folio 428   August 10, 1846

To my sister, Rebecca Marshall, all my goods and chattel.   My Executor should collect money owed me from William Lawyer for services to him and his family.   My Executor should collect the money owed me from the estate of my half-brother, David Byers (the same David Byers late of Lancaster County, Pennsylvania).   To my brother, William Henry Angel, and to my sister, Rebecca Marshall, all the cash left from my estate.

Witnesses: Daniel Baumgardner, John H. Baumgardner, David Circle
Executor(s): J. Henry Hoppe (my friend)
Signed with her signature

Appler, Jacob (senior)   of Uniontown, Carroll County
                                                August 1, 1839
                                       January 6, 1842 (codicil)
                                                 April 17, 1843
Number 151, Folio 258   April 17, 1843

My executors should sell my real estate in Uniontown, Carroll County including a dwelling house, three and a half lots in town and several lots outside of town.   My executors should also sell my farm on Little Pipe Creek in Carroll County providing that a road is available for access to the grave yard on the property.   I give to each of my six sons the sum of one thousand dollars, namely: David, Jonathan, Abraham, Jacob, Isaac and Jesse.   I give each of my five daughters the sum of one thousand dollars, namely: Nancy Linsney (widow of Christian Linsney), Eleanor King, Mary Winters, Margaret Weaver and Elizabeth Christ.   If any of my children creates a disturbance or brings suit against the provisions set forth in my will then their portion shall be equally divided amongst my other children.

Codicil

Whereas I have since loaned eleven hundred dollars to my son, Jesse Appler, this amount should be taken from his share. The legacy for my daughter, Mary Winters, should be kept in trust by my executors and the interest paid to her. After the death of my daughter, Mary Winters, the principal should be equally divided among her children.

Witnesses: James L. Billingslea, John Roberts, John Gore, Moses Shaw
Executor(s): Isaac Appler (my son), John Hyder, William Roberts
Signed with his signature

Arbaugh, Mary   of Carroll County
                                      October 22, 1846
                                      March 1, 1847
Number 245, Folio 451   March 1, 1847

To my cousin, Mary Wickert, the first choice of my blankets, all of my quilts, my silk shawl and rocking chair. To Margaret Crabster my linen table cloth. To Eliza Golley one table cloth. To my brother in law, Baltzer Arbaugh, my large German Bible. To my nephew, William Arbaugh, my English Bible. To Matilda Lockard my iron kettle. All my clothes are to be equally divided between Mary Wickert, Elizabeth Ramby and Elizabeth Arbaugh. The proceeds from the sale of my estate should be equally divided between Mary Wickert, Elizabeth Ramby, William Arbaugh and Elizabeth Arbaugh.

Witnesses: Stephen Oursler, Jacob Wickert
Executor(s): William Lockard
Signed by her mark

Arbaugh, Peter   of Carroll County

October 14, 1838

October 29, 1838

Number 41, Folio 71   October 29, 1838

To my wife, Mary Arbaugh, all my real estate and personal property for her use during her natural lifetime. After my wife's death, my estate should be sold and the proceeds should be equally divided between John Bowman and Sarah Ann Switzer.

Witnesses: Solomon Woolvy, William Lockard, Stephen Oursler
Executor(s): Mary Arbaugh (wife)
Signed by his mark

Armacost, David   of Carroll County

June 27, 1851

September 22, 1851

Number 364, Folio 617   September 22, 1851

To my wife, Susannah, all my personal property and real estate including a tract of land called "Petersburgh Resurveyed" which was conveyed to me by Mary Ann Harrison in September 1850. I also direct that one half of my estate should go to my heir when it comes of age should it be a boy. If my heir is a girl, then my wife, Susannah, should decide what the appropriate legacy should be. If my wife, Susannah, should remarry, then the profits from my estate should be saved for the benefit of my child when it comes of age.

Witnesses: James Kelly, James Marshall, Alexander Fowble
Executor(s): Susannah Armacost (wife)
Signed with his signature

Arnold, Joseph   of Carroll County
                                      November 28, 1837
                                      February 12, 1838
Number 23, Folio 39   February 12, 1838

I desire that my negro, Samuel, and his wife, Cass Anna, and
their children (Polly, Lydia, Rebecca, Zacharias, William, Cass
Anna and any additional children that they should have in my
lifetime) are to be freed upon my death. I give to my negro
man, Samuel, my property in Carroll County that adjoins the
lands of David Leister, George Crowl and David Everly which
is by the stone formerly dividing Frederick and Baltimore
Counties. To my negro man, Samuel, and his wife, Cass Anna,
I give two cows, one horse, six sheep, one breeding sow and
kitchen furniture. To my niece, Hester Hickinger (daughter of
my brother Samuel Arnold), three hundred dollars. To my
nephew, Joseph Arnold (son of my brother Samuel Arnold), the
balance of my estate providing that (1) my nephew follows my
previously expressed desires with respect to my negroes, (2)
that my nephew, Joseph Arnold, allows the family of Samuel
and Cass Anna the use of my home for one year after my death
including use of the kitchen, garden, wood, ability to make hay
from my pastures, and (3) that my nephew, Joseph Arnold,
gives my negro, Samuel, the sum of seventy five dollars.

Witnesses: David Leister, George Crowl, John Baumgartner
Executor(s): Joshua Smith
Signed by his mark

Arthur, Catherine   widow of Solomon Arthur, late
                                      of Carroll County
                                      March 12, 1849
                                      June 25, 1849
Number 302, Folio 535   June 25, 1849

The balance of my estate should be equally divided between my
three children, namely: Solomon, Lydia and Catherine. If my

daughter, Lydia, should die then her portion should be divided equally between my other children, Solomon and Catherine.

Witnesses: Jacob Mathias, David Orendorf
Executor(s): Solomon Arthur (son)
Signed by her mark

Arthur, Joseph   of Carroll County
                                         January 17, 1843
                                         February 13, 1843
Number 14, Folio 253   February 27, 1843

To Lydia Leister, my house keeper, all my estate of every description.

Witnesses: Jesse Reifsnider, Joseph Mathias, J. Henry Hoppe
Executor(s): Lydia Leister (housekeeper)
Signed with his signature

Arthur, Solomon   of Carroll County
                                           May 7, 1847
                                         February 19, 1849
Number 291, Folio 521   February 26, 1849

To my beloved wife, Catherine Arthur, the whole of my estate of every description whatsoever.

Witnesses: John Mathias, Jacob Mathias
Executor(s): Catherine Arthur (wife)
Signed with his signature

Atlee, Isaac   of New Windsor, Frederick Co.
                                                                  April 10, 1832
                                                            December 10, 1849
Number 312, Folio 548   December 10, 1849

All my lands on Pipe Creek (where my youngest son now resides) adjoining the lands of Isaac Hyde, Steve Williams and Henry Fulkes, should be divided between: my wife, Mary, my eldest son, Samuel J. Altee, and my son, James C. Altee. To my daughter, Margaret Amelia Gist, the plantation in Baltimore County where she and her husband, Joshua C. Gist, now reside. I also exonerate my daughter, Margaret Gist, from the payment of any account of charges I may have made against her and her husband. To my wife, Mary, the house and lot in New Windsor where I now reside including all contents. I direct that my son, James C. Atlee, should provide his mother with pasture for two cows, a horse and chopped wood during her natural lifetime. To my son, Samuel J. Atlee, the saw mill provided he allows his brother, James C. Atlee, use of the mill. It is my desire that my son, Samuel, lives with his mother and maintains her. Lastly, it is my desire that my two colored men, Gabriel and Frank, to be freed and clothed. It is also my desire that the passage to Liberia be paid for Gabriel and Frank as it is their desire to go to Liberia.

Witnesses: Jacob Landes, Robert Lods, Archibald Love
Executor(s): James C. Atlee (son)
Signed with his signature

Babylon, Andrew   of Carroll County
                                                                  March 17, 1849
                                                            November 3, 1851
Number 367, Folio 621   November 3, 1851

To my wife, Susanna Babylon, all my household property and a third of my real estate. And after my wife's death, my estate should be sold and the proceeds equally divided among my children [not named]. One hundred dollars to each of the children of my deceased daughter, Mary Morelock. The residue of my estate to my sons, namely: Michael Babylon, Jacob Babylon, Jesse Babylon, David Babylon and John Babylon.

Witnesses: Henry H. Harbaugh, John Nusbaum, Abraham Myers
Executor(s): Michael Babylon (son), John Babylon (son), Jesse Babylon (son)
Signed by his mark

Babylon, Philip   of Carroll County
                                       December 28, 1841
                                       January 31, 1842
Number 119, Folio 196   January 31, 1842

"Whereas the property which I now possess hath been chiefly acquired by the joint industry of my wife Elisabeth Babylon and myself and thinking some addition to her dower or thirds necessary the better to enable her to live with convenience and comfort I do will and give to my wife Elizabeth Babylon the following articles to wit" one bed with bedstead and bedding, floor carpet, chest, cow, rocking chair, six of my best chairs, table, iron kettle, two iron pots, the stove and pipe in the new house and all my cupboard ware. The residue of my personal property is to be sold. From the proceeds of my personal property, I give to my daughters, Eliza Myers and Mary Ann Baugher, each four hundred dollars. My son, Jacob Babylon, may stay on the farm where I now reside for the term of one year after my death on condition that he provides my wife ten bushels of wheat, ten bushels of corn and ten bushels of potatoes. After one year, I ask that my executor sell all my real estate and from the proceeds give my daughters, Eliza Myers and Mary Ann Baugher, each two hundred dollars and to my wife, Elizabeth, one third of the proceeds from the sale of my real estate. The residue of my estate should be equally divided among my three sons, namely: Jacob, John and William Babylon.

Witnesses: Daniel Zollickoffer, John Smith
Executor(s): John Babylon (son)
Signed by his mark

Bachman, Peter   of Carroll County
                                      December 1, 1841
                                      April 6, 1842
Number 129, Folio 216   April 6, 1842

To Joshua Wilderson, all of my clothes. My executors should purchase a pair of gravestones and set them at my grave. To, Joshua Wilderson, one bed with bedstead and bedding, two chests, one trunk, one mantle clock and all my other goods and chattel. The balance of my estate is to go to Joshua Wilderson.

Witnesses: George Fieser, Frederick Lohr
Executor(s): David B. Earhart (my friend)
Signed by his mark

Baker, William   of Baltimore County
                                      October 1, 1825
                                      December 10, 1839
Number 67, Folio 124   February 17, 1840

To my beloved wife, Naomey Baker, all my real and personal property during her natural life. After my wife's decease, I give to my son, Jesse, and to my daughter, Elener, fifty acres of land to be equally divided between them. The remainder of my land should be equally divided among my four sons namely: Charles G., Moris, William and Simeon.

Witnesses: Samuel Phillips, Rezin Bennett, Uriel Phillips
Executor(s): Morris Baker (brother)
Signed with his signature

10

Barnes, Archibald   of Baltimore County
                                        March 8, 1836
                                        January 22, 1838
Number 22, Folio 38   January 22, 1838

To my nephew, Alfred Barnes, all of the land south of the Liberty Road that was conveyed to me by Jacob Tener. I also give to Alfred Barnes one cow and one bed with bedstead and bedding. To my niece, Louisa Buckingham, one hundred dollars after one year of my death providing that she and her child are still living. To my nephew, Archibald Barnes, my little horse called Trifle, along with the saddle and bridle. To my brother, Thomas Barnes, the residue of my estate provided that he maintains my sister, Airey Barnes.

Witnesses: Joshua C. Gist, Joshua Franklin, Benjamin Bennett
Executor(s): Thomas Barnes (brother)
Signed with his signature

Barnes, Thomas   of Carroll County
                                        June 3, 1843
                                        June 19, 1843
Number 157, Folio 272   June 19, 1843

To my dear wife, Violette E. Barnes, all the land that I own south of the New Liberty Road. After the death of my wife, the land should be equally divided between my two children, Archibald and Sally Elizabeth Barnes. I desire that the ten acres north of the New Liberty Road (the land adjoining the land I sold to James C. Atlee) should be sold to pay my debts. All my remaining land north of the New Liberty Road is to be equally divided among my two children, Archibald and Sally Elizabeth Barnes. All my household furniture is to be equally divided among my wife and two children. To my son, Archibald Barnes, my two year old colt called "Fib" with saddle with bridle. To my wife and two children, the following: horse carriage and harness, two cows, one brown mare called "Kit", the old horse called "Fix", all my wagons, ploughs and farming utensils and my indentured colored boy called William. To my niece, Louisa Buckingham, ten dollars after five years of my decease. I ask that my executor sell my young mare called "Primrose" and sell "thirteen or fourteen hundred chestnut rails which are already made." The residue of my estate is to be equally divided between my wife, Violette, and my two children, Archibald and Sally Elizabeth Barnes.

Witnesses: E. L. Crawford, Richard A. Kirkwood, Thomas Ingels
Executor(s): Joshua C. Gist
Signed with his signature

Barnes, Zadock   of Carroll County
                                                    October 7, 1840
                                                         May 21, 1849
Number 301, Folio 534   May 21, 1849

To my wife, Elizabeth Barnes, all my estate both real and personal for her natural life. After the death of my wife, I direct that all my property should be sold and distributed as follows: to my daughter, Prudence Barnes, forty dollars; to my son, Levi T. Barnes, fifty dollars; to my daughter, Rachel Barnes, forty dollars; to my son, Slingsby L. Barnes, fifty dollars; to my daughter, Narcissa Barnes, forty dollars; to my granddaughter, Elizabeth P. Conaway (of my daughter Amelia who is now deceased), forty dollars to be paid to her when she arrives at the age of eighteen. The balance of my estate is to be equally divided among all my living children, namely: Elvira Condon (wife of Thomas Condon), Andrew P. Barnes, Prudence Barnes, James P. Barnes, Levi T. Barnes, Rachel Barnes, Slingsly L. Barnes, Thomas E. F. Barnes and Narcissa Barnes.

Witnesses: Samuel Evans, Stephen Gorsuch, Josiah S. Cover
Executor(s): Andrew P. Barnes (son), James P. Barnes (son)
Signed with his signature

Bartholow, Michael   of Carroll County
                                                    May 17, 1842
                                                    January 30, 1843
Number 145, Folio 249   January 30, 1843

To my beloved wife, Nancy Bartholow, during her natural life
or widowhood one horse of her choice of my estate and if that
horse dies or becomes useless she is to be furnished with
another horse from my estate. I also give to my wife, the
following: my family carriage and harness which is to be kept
in good repair; all my household and kitchen furniture; all my
goods, wares and utensils; also as much good family flour, pork
and firewood as she may need; the use of one fresh milk cow at
all times; the sum of twenty five dollars of cash given to her on
an annual basis in order for her to pay clergy or other charitable
purposes; all the rights and privileges of the house where I now
dwell including the garden, stable, spring and spring house;
"and to be furnished with all necessary clothing and support,
medicine and medical attendance that may be required for her
comfort, all, of which the aforesaid bequest is to come out of
the farm and premises whereon I now dwell." To my daughter,
Elizabeth Hooper, during her natural life the interest annually
of one thousand dollars at six percent to come out of the
properties in the City of Baltimore (one house and lot on Union
Street, and one on the corner of Pine and Fayette Street). Upon
the death of my daughter, Elizabeth, her legacy should be
shared equally among her brothers and sisters. The balance of
my property in the City of Baltimore, I give to the
grandchildren by my daughter, Sarah Penn (by her late husband
John Hooper), namely: Michael Hanson Hooper, John Thomas
Hooper, Uritha Hooper and Ann Bartholow Hooper (wife of
William K. Glassge). To my granddaughter, Francina Barnes,
my maple bureau. To my daughter, Sarah Penn, a silk dress
and ten dollars. To my son in law, Jacob W. Penn, a leather hat
and five dollars. To Samuel White (a colored man), ten dollars

13

only if he may be found and if not then equally divided among his brothers and sisters. All my personal property should go to my wife, Nancy Bartholow, during her natural life or widowhood. The residue of my estate is to be equally divided among my following children, namely: Thomas Bartholow, John Bartholow, Michael Bartholow, Elizabeth Weaver and Mary Barnes.

Witnesses: Michael Smith, Jesse Lambert, Samuel Ecker
Executor(s): Thomas Bartholow (son), John Bartholow (son), Michael Bartholow (son)
Signed with his signature

Baumgardner, Jacob   of Carroll County
                                September 3, 1846
                                September 28, 1846
Number 238, Folio 435   September 28, 1846

To my daughter, Mary Magdalene Baumgardner, one bed with bedstead and bedding, one breakfast table, one bureau, one spinning wheel, two iron pots, one set of ladles and flesh fork, one cow and six chairs. The rest of my personal estate should be sold and the proceeds should pay my debts and be used to purchase two pair of gravestones, one pair for myself and the other pair for my deceased wife, Magdalene. All my real estate in Carroll County should be sold and the proceeds divided as follows: to my daughter, Mary Magdalene Baumgardner, two hundred dollars; to Matilda Sullivan, as payment for services rendered, fifty dollars; to Peter Kals, my son in law (who was married to my daughter Elizabeth), one dollar. The residue of my estate should be equally divided among my children, namely: Jacob, John, Samuel, Josiah and Mary Magdalene Baumgardner.

Witnesses: Joseph Wivell, Abraham Zentz, Henry Orndorff
Executor(s): John Baumgardner (son)
Signed with his signature

Baumgartner, Jacob (senior)   of Carroll County

                                    May 26, 1838
                                    September 7, 1840
Number 84, Folio 146   September 7, 1840

To my son, Jacob Baumgartner (junior), all my personal and real estate in Carroll County. My real estate in Carroll County includes a tract of land called "Chestnut Ridge" which was deeded to me by George Stump, a tract of land called "Heller Noell" deeded to me by Peter Mikesell, and a tract of land called "Philipsburgh" deeded to me by George Lingerfelter. I ask that my executor purchase a pair of tombstones for myself and my beloved wife, Elizabeth (who is now deceased). To my daughter, Ann Mary (wife of Nicholas Garret), ten dollars. To my son, John Baumgartner, five hundred dollars.

Witnesses: Jacob Mikesell, John Reineman, David B. Earhart, Henry Houck
Executor(s): Jacob Baumgartner (junior)
Signed with his signature

Baumgartner, Peter   of Mountjoy Township, Adams
                                    County, Pennsylvania
                                    November 8, 1835
                                    February 19, 1844
Number 168, Folio 295   February 19, 1844

To my dear wife, Elizabeth, the new end of my dwelling house for her use during her life time as well as one bed, bureau and eight hundred dollars. To my son, Peter, ten dollars. My property both real and personal should be sold and the proceeds should be equally divided amongst my eight children, namely: Jacob, Catherine Ohler (wife of Thomas Ohler), Daniel, John, Margaret Martin (widow of David Martin), Rosannah Clutz (wife of Jacob Clutz), and Mary Hawk (wife of Samuel Hawk), and Henry Baumgartner.

Renunciation
Jacob Clutz refuses to act as executors and defers the role to the other co-executor named in the will, Daniel Baumgartner. Witnessed February 15, 1844 by Daniel Haffner.

Witnesses: William Paxton, Jonas Spangler, John Eltz
Executor(s): Daniel Baumgartner (son), Jacob Clutz (son in law)
Signed with his signature

Beasman / Baseman, Sarah   of Carroll County
                                        April 11, 1837
                                        August 4, 1845
Number 206, Folio 378   August 4, 1845

To my daughter, Sarah Murray, one feather bed and my negro woman called Phebe.   To my granddaughter, Ruth Kemp, one feather bed with furniture.   To my daughter, Eliza Ann Beasman, one small bureau, one walnut breakfast table, one looking glass, pewter plates, silver spoons, two hundred dollars, a horse and one feather bed.   To my granddaughter, Caroline Prugh, two silver spoons.   The residue of my cupboard furniture should be equally divided among my two granddaughters, Caroline Prugh and Eliza Ann Beasman.   To my grandson, Joshua Beasman, my negro women called Patience and Charity (along with their children), one eight day clock and one silver watch when he arrives at the age of twenty one.   To my grandson, Thomas B. Conaway, one gun.   The residue of my estate should go to my executrix, Mary Beasman (my daughter in law and widow of Johnze Beasman) for the use of herself and her three children.

Renunciation
Thomas B. Conaway refuses to act as executor and asks that the letters of testamentary be transferred to Mary Beaseman (the other executor mentioned in the will).   Witnessed August 4, 1845 by Jacob Mathias.

Witnesses: Nicholas Dorscy, Obadiah Buckingham (junior), Abraham Prugh
Executor(s): Mary Beasman (daughter in law), Thomas B. Conaway (grandson)
Signed with her signature

Beaver, Nancy   of Carroll County

August 22, 1842

October 3, 1842

Number 136, Folio 233   October 3, 1842

To my mother, Susannah Beaver, all my lands and real estate in Carroll County as well as all my personal property. After the death of my mother, I give all my real estate to my niece, Susannah Lampert (on condition that she remains living with my mother until my mother's death). Should my niece leave my mother before my mother's death, I then ask my executors to sell my estate and distribute the proceeds equally among my brother and sisters [not named].

Renunciation
William Beaver (of Adam) refuses to act as executor and defers such right to Jacob Beaver. Witnessed October 3, 1842 by Joshua Yingling.

Witnesses: Michael Sullivan, Lewis Trumbo, Jacob Fringer
Executor(s): Jacob Beaver (brother), William Beaver (brother)
Signed by her mark

Bechtel, Samuel   of Carroll County

October 15, 1846

December 28, 1846

Number 241, Folio 440   December 28, 1846

One third of my cash should go to my wife, Mary Ann Bechtel, and the remaining cash should be equally divided among my children. I give my land in Carroll County (which was conveyed to me by Charles Slingluff and James L. Billingslea) to my wife for her to hold until my youngest child reaches the age of twenty one. My grist mill and saw mill should be turned into rental properties with one hundred dollars a year from rent going to my wife and the residue of rent profits equally divided among my children. My executors, in due time, should build a home for my wife on my property one that she will call her own. After the death or marriage of my wife, all my property should be sold and the proceeds should be equally divided among my children [not named].

Witnesses: Jacob Cassell, Augustus Stonesifer, John Baumgartner
Executor(s): Joshua Metcalf (my trusty friend and neighbor)
Signed with his signature

Beggs, Eleanor   of Carroll County
                                                            March 1, 1841
                                                            April 26, 1841
Number 100, Folio 168   April 26, 1841

To my sister, Jannett Byers, my tract of land called "Rochester" containing about five and three quarters of an acre. To my sister, Jannett Byers, two tables, two looking glasses, two beds and bedsteads, stove, two cupboards, chairs, candles and candlesticks, my queens ware and utensils.

Witnesses: John Robertson, Joshua Lockard
Executor(s): John Beaver
Signed with her signature

Beho, Mary   of Westminster, Carroll County
                                                            March 1, 1851
                                                            December 1, 1851
Number 369, Folio 623   December 1, 1851

"... to be decently buried at the discretion of my of my executor herein after named or my good and faithful husband if then living." To my dear husband, William Beho, my part of the interest in a house and two lots in Westminster on the road leading to Littlestown. This one half acre of land, called "Pigmans Addition", is situated opposite the residence of Isaac Shriver and adjoins the lands of Jacob Reese and Joseph Mathias. This is the same land where I reside today and have resided at for the past eighteen or twenty years.

Witnesses: Joshua Yingling, Horatio Price, Alfred Troxel
Executor(s): Dr. Samuel L. Swormstedt (my worthy and trusty friend of Westminster)
Signed by her mark

Bennett, Belinda   of Baltimore County
                                     April 16, 1833
                                      June 1, 1840
Number 75, Folio 134   June 1, 1840

To my loving sister, Nancy Hewit, my negro woman called Fanny. To my loving sister, Sarah Bennett, all my live stock and household furniture. To my loving brother, Benjamin Bennett, one hundred dollars. To my niece, Sarah Bennett (the daughter of my deceased brother Robert Bennett), fifty dollars. Should my niece, Sarah Bennett, not live long enough to enjoy the said fifty dollars, the money should be divided equally among the children of my brother, Larkin Bennett. I also give fifty dollars to be used for educating the orphan poor children of my neighborhood. To the children of my brother, Larkin Bennett, all the rest of my estate to be equally divided among them.

Witnesses: Elijah Robesson, Uriel Phillips, William Loving
Executor(s): Rezin Bennett (cousin)
Signed with her signature

Bennett, Benjamin   of Carroll County
                                         March 25, 1844
                                         June 3, 1844
Number 178, Folio 317   June 3, 1844

To my son, Thomas Jackson Bennett, five hundred dollars and during his life a decent maintenance should be paid and provided to him by my two sons, Allen Bennett and Benjamin Franklin Bennett. To my daughter, Kitty Helen Bennett, one thousand dollars with four hundred dollars to be paid by the fair market equivalent of goods from my personal property and the remaining six hundred dollars to be paid by my two sons, Allen Bennett and Benjamin Franklin Bennett. To my two sons, Allen Bennett and Benjamin Franklin Bennett, the residue of my estate in equal amounts. It is my will that neither my house nor my negroes shall be sold and it is my desire that my negroes should be freed at the age of thirty.

Witnesses: Elias Brown, William Ewings, Wesley Bennett
Executor(s): Allen Bennett (son)
Signed with his signature

Bennett, Eli   of Carroll County
                                         March 3, 1840
                                         March 27, 1840
Number 73, Folio 132   April 27, 1840

To my dear wife, Rachel Bennett, the plantation where I now reside on a tract of land called "Bachelors Refuge" containing three hundred acres. After my wife's death, this property is to be equally divided among my nieces and nephews, namely: to the children of my brother, Elisha Bennett; to the children of my deceased brother, Benjamin Bennett; to the children of my brother, Thomas Bennett; to the children of my deceased brother, Samuel Bennett (provided that my nephew, Samuel Bennett, who is the son of Samuel Bennett is excluded as he has already received his share); to the children of my sister, Mrs. Margaret Brown. My land called "Polly's Habitation" where John Pickett now resides should be sold and the proceeds are to go to my sister, Mrs. Margaret Brown. My negro man called Ben should be freed on September 1, 1840 and my executors should give him fifty dollars at that time. To my wife, Rachel Bennett, my negroes called Alice, Mijak, Ann, Charles, George and Emma. To my niece, Mrs. Margaret Mercer, my negro boy called Wesley, one mare called Sal and a bed with bedstead and bedding. To my wife, Rachel Bennett, the residue of my estate.

Witnesses: Nathan Brown, Samuel Lindsay, Samuel Gore
Executor(s): Rachel Bennett (wife)
Signed with his signature

Bennett, Elisha   of Carroll County
                                        March 26, 1842
                                        April 9, 1845
Number 199, Folio 367   April 9, 1845

To my sons, Jesse Bennett, Wesley Bennett, Charles W. Bennett and Perry Bennett, each one quarter of a dollar. To the children of my daughter, Elizabeth H. Johnson, six hundred and fifty dollars which is owed to me by George Bramwell. To the children of my son, Charles W. Bennett, the tract of land (with the house where my son Charles currently resides) that was conveyed to me by George Bramwell which is on the south side of the "road leading from Ely's Mill to the late residence of Doctor Elisha Hall." To my grandchildren, Charles Wesley Taylor and Matilda Taylor, twenty five cents each and my executor should pay them four dollars and ninety five cents with the latter being the balance due to them from my brother Benjamin's estate. Also to my grandchildren, Charles Wesley Taylor and Matilda Taylor, seven dollars being the balance of the legacy bequeathed by Davis Warfield to their mother. To my daughter, Sarah Ann Taylor, one hundred dollars. Also to my daughter, Sarah Ann Taylor, the five hundred dollars that was bequeathed by my brother, Benjamin Bennett, to my daughter, Mary Ann, the latter who is now deceased. To my daughter, Elizabeth W. Johnson, the residue of my estate.

Witnesses: Nicholas Dorsey, Samuel Bennett, Jacob Frederick
Executor(s): Wesley Bennett (son)
Signed with his signature

Bennett, Elisha   of Carroll County
                                                June 13, 1845
                                          November 16, 1846
Number 239, Folio 436   November 16, 1846

To my wife, Rachel Bennett, fifty dollars to be paid to her annually along with her bed, bedstead and bedding, her table and bureau, her black horse and a cow for her use during her widowhood. To my daughter, Minerva Shreeve, four hundred dollars. To my grandson, Elisha Prugh, the plantation where I now reside on which is known as the Home Farm containing one hundred and fifty six acres and also a small tract of land that was conveyed to me by William H. Ogg that contains seventy acres. To my grandson, Francis Lewis Bennett, two hundred dollars. The plantation and lands that was conveyed to me by John Smith known by the names of "Property Arnolds Desire", "Oggs Discovery" and "Arnolds Desire" should be sold and the proceeds should by equally divided between my daughters, Honour Prugh and Minerva Shreeve. The balance of both my real and personal estate should go to my daughter, Honour Prugh.

Witnesses: Joshua C. Gist, Washington Nicodemus, Charles Allen
Executor(s): Abraham Prugh (son in law)
Signed with his signature

Bennett, Margaret   of Carroll County

April 14, 1845

May 26, 1845

Number 203, Folio 374   May 26, 1845

To my daughter, Kitty Helen Bennett, I give my negro girl called Ann and my negro boy called Aaron along with two of my best feather beds, three cows, the side board and bureau. To my son, Benjamin Franklin Bennett, my negro girl called Harriott and one of my best feather beds. To my son, Thomas Jackson Bennett, one of my best feather beds. The residue of my estate should be equally to be divided among my three sons, namely: Allen Bennett, Thomas Jackson Bennett and Benjamin Franklin Bennett.

Witnesses: Samuel Moreton (junior), Wesly Bennett, Elias Brown
Executor(s): Allen Bennett (son)
Signed by her mark

Bennett, Sarah   of Carroll County

August 26, 1841

September 6, 1841

Number 112, Folio 187   September 6, 1841

To my niece, Saran Ann Bennett (daughter of my brother, Robert Bennett), the sum of fifty dollars. The residue of my estate should be equally divided among the four children of my brother, Benjamin Bennett, and the four children of my brother, Larkin Bennett, namely: Thomas Jackson Bennett, Allen Bennett, Kitty Hellen Bennett, Benjamin Franklin Bennett, Silas Bennett, Rezin Rufus Bennett, Eleanor Ann Bennett and Lewis Henry Bennett.

Witnesses: Elias Brown, N. Brown, Wesley Bennett
Executor(s): Allen Bennett (nephew)
Signed with her signature

Biggs, Frederick   of Carroll County

                                  March 17, 1840

                                  March 30, 1840

Number 74, Folio 133   March 30, 1840

To my beloved wife [not named] my "negro Pariss and the same amount that one of the children gets." To my son, Frederick, the young bay mare with saddle and bridle. The money I have already given to my children William, Joseph M., Mary Ann and Susan should be taken from their shares. The residue of my estate should be equally divided among my eight children, namely: William, Joseph, Catherine, Amy, Mary Ann, Susan, Frederick and Julian.

Witnesses: Joseph Trosill, John Shealey, Benjamin Biggs, Isaac Dern
Executor(s): William Biggs (son), Solomon Rusi (son in law)
Signed with his signature

Biggs, Joseph   of Carroll County

                                  January 23, 1841

                                  April 26, 1841

Number 101, Folio 169   April 26, 1841

To my dearly beloved wife, Mary, my negro slaves and the residue of my personal and real estate. When my son, Edmond, reaches the age of twenty one, all my personal and real estate should be sold and the proceeds divided as follows: one third to my wife and the balance to be equally divided among my children [not named].

Witnesses: James Bunting, Frederick W. Biggs, Benjamin Whitmore, Isaac Dern
Executor(s): Joseph Biggs (son), Mary Biggs (wife)
Signed with his signature

Biggs, Mary   of Carroll County
                                             January 20, 1842
                                             January 31, 1842
Number 121, Folio 201   February 7, 1842

To my children, Catherine, Amy, Julian and Frederick, my colored woman called Pricilla as well as one bed, stove, two cows, corner cupboard and all my kitchen furniture to share equally. To my daughter, Julian, one mare and fifty dollars with the money to be paid out of the fund in the hands of William Biggs and Solomon Crire (executors of the estate of William Biggs). To my son, Frederick Biggs, the sum of fifty dollars out of the fund previously mentioned. I ask that my executors pay the sum of fifty dollars to Levi Whitmore as rent money for the home that my son, Joseph Biggs, currently occupies. To my grandchildren, Thomas, Amenious and Marcella (all children of my son Joseph), the sum of fifty dollars each to be invested in real estate or some productive stock as deemed by my executors with the interest from said investments going to my son, Joseph.

Witnesses: William Biggs (of J), John Thealey
Executor(s): William Biggs (my son)
Signed by her mark

Biggs, Mary   widow of Joseph Biggs, late of
                                             Carroll County
                                             April 7, 1848
                                             June 12, 1848
Number 282, Folio 507   June 12, 1848

To my daughter, Elenora, my two negroes slaves called Hannah and Charlotte. To my daughter, Adelaide, my negro boy called Harry for the term of twenty two years and nine months at which time he will be thirty years old and should be freed. None of my slaves should be sold out of the state. The estate left to me by my husband's will which was dated January 23,

1841 should be equally divided among my two daughters, Elenora and Adelaide. To my son, Edmon, fifty dollars.

Witnesses: Jacob Veant, Daniel Utz, Joseph Utz, Dorus Groff
Executor(s): Dorus Groff
Signed with her signature

Birnie, Clotworthy   of Carroll County

March 24, 1845

June 23, 1845

Number 204, Folio 375   June 23, 1845

To my son, Clotworthy Birnie (junior), my fowling piece, powder flask, shot pouch and mathematical instruments (he has already received his full portion of my patrimonial estate). To my son, Roger Birnie, my pistols and bullet mould. The residue of my estate should be equally divided between my daughter, Margaret Birnie, and my son, Roger Birnie.

Witnesses: James McKillip, Thomas Hook, A. G. Ege
Executor(s): Roger Birnie (son), Margaret Birnie (daughter)
Signed with his signature

Bixler, Jeremiah   of Carroll County

February 25, 1850

April 1, 1850

Number 323, Folio 565   April 1, 1850

To my beloved father, Abraham Bixler, my interest in the land I own jointly with my brother, George, which was purchased on April 10, 1843 and containing the tracts "Wises Mill", "Charles and Adams Choice", "Inglers Addition" and "Friendship."

Witnesses: Benjamin Lippy, George Edward Wampler, Henry Sherman
Executor(s): not named
Signed with his signature

Bollinger, Catherine   widow of Joseph Bollinger, late
of Baltimore County
March 8, 1839
May 27, 1839
Number 52, Folio 90   May 27, 1839

To Catherine Bollinger (wife of Christian Miller), ten dollars. To my daughter, Barbara (wife of David Jones), twenty five cents as her full share of my estate. To my grandchildren (the children of my deceased son, George Bollinger), the sum of twenty five cents to be shared among them. To my son, Daniel Bollinger, my house clock. If my daughter, Elizabeth Bollinger, is to living with me at the time of my decease then she is to have the sum of ten dollars. My son, Peter Bollinger, received a cow from me valued at twenty dollars and that shall be considered his share. To my son, Jacob Bollinger, a note for fifty dollars which I hold against my son, Daniel Bollinger. The remainder of my estate is to be sold and the proceeds are to be equally divided among my children, namely: Elizabeth Bollinger, Daniel Bollinger, Jacob Bollinger, Andrew Bollinger, Susanna Bollinger (wife of Jacob Bowman), Sarah Bollinger (wife of George Kerchane) and Molly Bollinger (wife of Jacob Bowman, junior), and Peter Bollinger.

Witnesses: Jacob Warner, Jacob Lammott, Henry Shauck
Executor(s): Daniel Bollinger (son)
Signed by his mark

Bond, Christopher   of Frederick County
November 8, 1841
March 21, 1842
Number 126, Folio 210   March 21, 1842

To my niece, Henrietta Bond of Carroll County, twenty five dollars and my family Bible. To my granddaughters, Sarah Ann Myers and Emaline Myers (children of my deceased daughter Eleanor Myers), one hundred dollars each. My executor should collect any money owed me by Henry Kepp (through the court of Frederick County) and this should go to my son, Peter Bond. My executors should sell my farm in Carroll County on the tract of land called "Lee Castle" which contains one hundred and thirty four acres, and the proceeds from the sell of this land should be equally divided among my sons, namely: Joshua, Larkin, Peter and Charles. The residue of my estate should be equally divided among my four sons, namely: Joshua, Larkin, Peter and Charles.

Witnesses: Basil Hayden, Israel Rinehart, William N. Hayden
Executor(s): Peter Bond (son)
Signed with his signature

Bond, Samuel   of Carroll County
                                                March 2, 1849
                                                April 23, 1849
Number 297, Folio 529   April 23, 1849

To my son, Edward Bond, all the land and plantation in Carroll County that was conveyed to me by the estate of Nicholas Hall Brown (Joseph Shaffer was the trustee for the estate of Nicholas Hall Brown and it was with Joseph Shaffer that I conducted the land transaction) containing about one hundred and forty three acres. To my son, Edward Bond, the sum of two hundred dollars, one broad tread wagon with cover and one bedstead with bedding. To my son, Andrew Jackson Bond, the land in Carroll County that was conveyed to me by John Williams called "Worth But Little" containing about seven acres. To my son, Andrew Jackson Bond, my two negro women named Julia Ann and Eliza Ann.

Witnesses: M. G. Cockey, Nicholas Kelly, Samuel Nichols
Executor(s): Edward Bond (son), Andrew Jackson Bond (son)
Signed with his signature

Bonecker, George William   of Carroll County
                                              May 12, 1841
                                              August 9, 1841
Number 109, Folio 182   August 9, 1841

To my son, William Bonecker, five shillings and no more from my estate. To my wife, Catherine Bonecker, all my personal property of every description for her use during her natural life. After the death of my wife, all my property should go to my daughter, Eliza Haller.

Witnesses: George Jacob, John Ogg, David Beyers
Executor(s): Catherine Bonecker (wife)
Signed with his signature

Boring, Ezekiel (senior)   of Baltimore County
                                              not included
                                              April 23, 1838
Number 28, Folio 46   May 7, 1838

I have already given land to the following children, namely: Ezekiel Boring, Mary Boring, Elizabeth Schaul, and Temperance Shekels. To the heirs of my eldest son, the late Thomas Boring, my land in Baltimore County called "Habitation Rock." I give a tract of land in Frederick County (on the Frederick Road leading from Westminster to Littlestown) to the heirs of my deceased daughter, Sarah Shaffer, and those heirs being Mary Magdelane Shaffer and Ezekiel B. Shaffer. To my wife, Hester Boring, the plantation where I now reside and all my personal property during her lifetime provided that she stays my widow. If my wife should remarry then the balance of my estate should be sold and divided as follows: to my grandson, heir of my deceased son John Boring, five hundred dollars; an equal share of the balance to the heirs of Thomas Boring; an equal share of the balance to the heirs of Elizabeth Shaul; an equal share of the balance to the heirs of Temperance Schekels; an equal share of the balance to the heirs of Sarah Shaffer; an equal share of the balance to the heirs of John Boring.

Renunciation
David Frankforter renounces his right as executor and defers said executorship to Thomas Sator. Witnessed on May 14, 1838 by Jacob Reese.

Witnesses: Jacob Frankforter, Frederick Hamburgh, Jesse Shultz
Executor(s): Thomas Sator, David Frankforter
Signed with his signature

Bosley, Joshua   of Carroll County
                                                          March 29, 1843
                                                            June 29, 1846
Number 230, Folio 423   June 29, 1846

To my son, Thomas Bosley, that tract of land where I now live containing one hundred and nineteen acres lying in Carroll County called "Everything Needful" on condition that he pay six hundred dollars to my two daughters Rachel Jackson (wife of Bendago Jackson) and Kesiah Cattrider (wife of Joshua Cattrider). To my son, Shadrack Bosley, the tract of land where he now resides in Carroll County containing one hundred and six acres on condition that he pay my daughter, Belinda (wife of George Sellers), two hundred dollars. All of my personal property should be equally divided among my daughters, namely: Rachel Jackson, Kesiah Caltrider and Belinda Sellers. To my dearly beloved wife, Ann Bosley, the house where she now resides and use of the garden. To my second son, Joshua Bosley, one dollar and no more. To my eldest son, James Bosley, one dollar and no more.

Witnesses: David Fowble, John Stansbury, Samuel Deahofe
Executor(s): James Bosley (son)
Signed with his signature

Bosley, Shadrack			of Carroll County
						July 1, 1847
						August 30, 1847
Number 257, Folio 469			August 30, 1847

To my beloved wife, Sarepta, all my estate both real and personal during her widowhood. Any profit from my estate should be used to maintain, clothe and educate my children until they become of age. After the death or marriage of my wife, my property should be sold. One third of the proceeds should go to my wife and the balance should be equally divided among my lawful heirs [not named].

Witnesses: Jacob Kerlinger, Jacob Yingling, Heinrich N. Steffy
Executor(s): Adonijah Sater
Signed by his mark

Bower, Esther			of Carroll County
						May 7, 1838
						October 17, 1842
Number 138, Folio 238			October 17, 1842

To my nephew, David Bower, twenty dollars. To my brother, Stephen Bower, all my estate both real and personal.

Witnesses: Joseph Englar, Alexander H. Lenseney, Henry H. Harbaugh
Executor(s): Stephen Bower (brother)
Signed with her signature

Bowser, Isaac			of Carroll County
						May 23, 1836
						March 22, 1841
Number 95, Folio 162			March 22, 1841

To my wife, Delila, all my furniture and one cow during her natural lifetime or widowhood. To my daughter, Harriet, one horse or mare, one cow and twenty dollars. All my other personal effects should be sold and the remaining proceeds should be divided between my wife, my daughter Mary (wife of John Lucabaugle) and my daughter Harriet. My real estate which is in Baltimore County adjoining the lands of Henry Zimmerman and George Fair should go to my wife, Delila, during her natural life or widowhood. My daughter, Harriet, should have the privilege to remain living with her mother. Upon my wife's death or marriage, my personal and real property should be divided equally unto my two said daughters.

Witnesses: Samuel Fair, Aaron Shauck, Henry Shauck
Executor(s): John Lucabaugle (son in law)
Signed by his mark

Brown, Ann   of Baltimore County
                                    August 4, 1836
                                    August 12, 1837
Number 12, Folio 22   September 4, 1837

To my son, Elias Brown, my negroes called Nat, Dick, Poll, Daniel, Abraham, Catharine, Cassandra and Peter. To my daughter in law, Susannah E. Brown, my chest of drawers. To my son, William Brown, my silver and mahogany table. To my granddaughters, the daughters of my son William, my clothes to be shared equally. That the residue of my household furniture should be appraised by Nicholas Dorsey, George W. Warfield and Henry Carter and sold at fair value. The proceeds of which should be put in savings to be given to my granddaughters, daughters of my son William, when they reach the age of sixteen.

Witnesses: N. Dorsey, Abel Servenor, George W. Warfield
Executor(s): Elias Brown (son)
Signed with her signature

Brown, Edward   of Carroll County
                                           April 28, 1843
                                           June 16, 1846
Number 227, Folio 417   June 16, 1846

To my loving brother, Jesse Brown, and sister, Rachel Brown,
all my real and personal property.

Witnesses: John B. Devries, Henry Devries, Christian Devries
Executor(s): Jesse Brown (son)
Signed by his mark

Brown, Jacob   Yeoman of Frederick County
                                           (Pine Run Hundred)
                                           July 28, 1833
                                           September 3, 1838
Number 34, Folio 56   September 3, 1838

To my loving wife, Catherine, one horse, three milk cows, three
hogs, three sheep, two beds with bedding, her spinning wheel
and kitchen furniture. The rest of my goods, stocks, chattels,
merchandises and household furniture should be sold at public
auction to pay for my funeral and debts. My real estate should
be appraised and my sons, if of age, may purchase my lands at
the appraised value. If my sons refuse to buy my real estate
then these lands shall be sold after one year of my death (with
the exception of the Tavernhouse and fifty acres of land
adjacent to David Feesers). To my beloved wife, Catherine, the
Tavernhouse and fifty acres mentioned above for her natural
life as long as she stays my widow. If my wife, Catherine,
should remarry then her properties should be sold and the
proceeds divided among my children, namely: Elizabeth (wife
of John Little), Susan (wife of Jacob Leister), Sarah (wife of
Adams Stonesifert). If my daughter, Sarah, should die then her
share is to go to her own children, namely: Samuel, Joseph,
Polly, Jacob, Matilda, Lucianna, Catharina and Daniel as they
come of age or marriage (whichever comes first). If any of my

other daughters are single at the time of my death, I give them their bed and bedstead, spinning wheel and one hundred dollars at their sixteenth birthday or their wedding day (whichever comes first).

Renunciation
Jacob Leister refuses to act as executor of the estate of Jacob Brown. Witnessed on September 1, 1838 by Michael Scholl (junior) and David B. Earhart.

Witnesses: Michael Scholl (junior), John Streavig, George Koons
Executor(s): Samuel Brown (son), Jacob Leister (son in law)
Signed with her signature

Brown, Jesse   of Carroll County
                                          April 28, 1843
                                          April 2, 1844
Number 172, Folio 305   April 2, 1844

To my loving brother, Evan Brown, and my sister, Rachel Brown, all my estate.

Witnesses: John B. Devries, Henry Devries, Christian Devries
Executor(s): Evan Brown (brother)
Signed by his mark

Brown, Joshua   of Carroll County
                                          April 24, 1849
                                          February 18, 1850
Number 318, Folio 557   February 18, 1850

To my beloved wife, Nancy Brown, during her widowhood the following: two feather beds with bedstead, two cows, stove, corner cupboard, kitchen wares and utensils, iron kettle, iron pot, six sets of silverware, one table, three chairs, linens, bureau, two hogs, two sheep, one horse, side saddle, one washing tub and two buckets and kitchen furniture. After my wife's decease or marriage, this personal property should be sold and the proceeds should be equally divided among my three daughters, namely: Nancy Koutz, Rebecca Brown and Ruth Brown. I also give my wife during her widowhood, the following: the small room in my house where I now reside, privileges of the house and kitchen, one third of the garden, one third of the spring house, yearly amounts of fifteen bushels of good clean wheat, ten bushels of corn, five bushels of rye, two hundred pounds of good pork, one hundred pounds of good beef, a sufficient amount of firewood, all the fruit she desires and pasture for her livestock. To my sons, George and David Brown, my home plantation where I now live which was bequeathed to me by my father (the late George Brown of Frederick County which is now Carroll County) through his will dated December 10, 1811. Also to my two sons, George and David, a tract of land called "Cranbury Meadows" as well as a tract of land called "Peters Plague" on condition that they provide for my wife as previously mentioned. One hundred and fifty dollars to each of my daughters, namely: Rebecca Brown, Ruth Brown and Nancy Koutz. I give two hundred and fifty dollars to be equally divided among my four sons, namely: Jacob Brown, Joshua Brown, Noah Brown and John A. Brown. To my son, David Brown, one horse, cow, plough and furrow, one wagon, harrow and one bed with bedstead. To my daughters, Rebecca Brown and Ruth Brown, an "outfit such as a setting off as is customary for girls in their circumstances." The reminder of my estate is to be sold and the proceeds should be divided as follows: to my daughter, Elizabeth Houck (wife of George Houck), the sum of one hundred dollars; to my daughter, Nancy Koutz, fifty dollars; to my daughter, Rebecca Brown, fifty dollars; to my daughter, Ruth Brown, fifty dollars; the rest should be equally divided among my six sons – Jacob Brown, Joshua Brown, John A. Brown, Noah Brown, George Brown and David Brown.

Renunciation
George Brown refuses to act as executor and requests that
David Brown (the other mentioned executor) be granted letters
testamentary. Witnessed February 18, 1850 by Michael
Sullivan.

Witnesses: David A. Snider, Peter Sellers, Michael Sullivan
Executor(s): George Brown (son), David Brown (son)
Signed with his signature

Brown, Nicholas Hall   of Carroll County
                                          June 5, 1838
                                          July 2, 1838
Number 32, Folio 52   July 2, 1838

The land that was conveyed to me by the estate of Joshua
Brown which is adjacent to the lands of John Sweigart (along
the old public road to the county road leading from Van Bibbers
to Westminster) should be sold to pay my debts. Also the land
known as "Dry Works" near John Roop's dam should be sold to
pay my debts. If I still have debts outstanding, then my house
and lot in town near the lands of Isaac Shriver (adjoining the
town of Westminster) should be sold to cover my remaining
debts. The residue of my estate should go to my "dear and
beloved wife Ruth my Executrix in whom I have full
confidence ... she shall have full power and authority to
manage and direct all my effects." My wife should have control
of my estate for the period of ten years after my death or until
her death (whichever should come first). Then after ten years
from my death (or at the death of my wife), my estate should be
sold and my wife is to have her part (according to the laws of
the land and the orphan's court) and the balance should be
equally distributed among my children, namely: Belinda (wife
of William Barnes), William Stansbury, Nicholas Hall, Neilson,
Ruth, Susan, George, Elizabeth Ann, Andrew Jackson, Charles
Wesley and Charity Brown. If Belinda (wife of William

Barnes) should die, then her portion should be equally divided among her own heirs.

Witnesses: Isaac Shriver, Horatio Price, George Shriver
Executor(s): Ruth Brown (wife)
Signed with his signature

Brown, Peter   of Carroll County
                                                      June 28, 1839
                                                  December 14, 1840
Number 88, Folio 150   December 28, 1840

To my beloved wife, Mary Brown, all my livestock to include two milk cows, two young heifers, three hogs, five sheep and all the household and kitchen furniture during her lifetime or widowhood. To my daughter, Barbery, one bed with bedstead and bedding, one chest and half of the money from my personal estate. To my daughter, Cathron, one bed with bedstead and bedding. To my daughter, Leadey, one bed and bedstead. To my daughter, Sofid, one bedstead and bedding. To my daughter, Sevelley, one bedstead and bedding. Ten dollars to each of my three sons, namely: Henry, Barney and John. To my three sons the money owed to me from my debtors which should be equally divided. Those individuals, who owe debts to me, include: James Walcker, Jacob Mearing, William Halsel and Isaac Raxton.

Renunciation
George Little refuses to act as executor of the estate of Peter Brown. Witnessed on December 28, 1840 by J. Henry Hoppe.

Witnesses: Abraham Koontz, Joseph Keefer
Executor(s): George Little (son in law)
Signed with his signature

Brungard, Mary   of Carroll County
                                          June 14, 1845
                                         March 20, 1848
Number 274, Folio 496   March 20, 1848

To the Amos Brungard, resident of York County in Pennsylvania, the sum of one thousand and eighty dollars as well as a chest of drawers. The said Amos Brungard is the son of Jacob Brungard. To Susanna Brungard, resident of Carroll County, the sum of one thousand and eighty dollars as well as all my bedding, my spinning wheel, clothes and one chest. The said Susanna Brungard is now the wife of William Rhorbach.

Witnesses: Jacob Campbell, David Whiteleather, Joshua F. Kopp
Executor(s): Amos Brungard (of York County, Pennsylvania)
Signed by her mark

Bucher / Bucker, Christian   of Carroll County
                                        February 7, 1844
                                        December 2, 1844
Number 189, Folio 340   December 23, 1844

To my grandson, David Bucher, and to my granddaughter, Mary Bucher, (both being children of my son David) my dwelling plantation in Carroll County. My dwelling plantation contains tracts of land known as "Baxters Choice" and "Hookers Meadow Resurveyed" which are bounded by the lands of Aaron Stocksdale, Catherine Fringer, William James Fowble, John B. Chenoweth, Jacob Fringer, George Algire (along the county road leading from Browns Mill to the Hanover turnpike). My grandchildren, David Bucher and Mary Bucher, may have this land on three conditions: (1) pay my daughter in law, Rachel Bucher (widow of Abraham Bucher) fifty dollars (2) pay my grandson, Noah Bucher (son of Abraham Bucher), fifty dollars (3) allow my daughter in law, Mary Bucher (widow of David Bucher), to remain living in the dwelling house where I now reside throughout her widowhood and keep her (the said Mary Bucher) maintenance as well. The remainder of my estate is to go to my grandson, David Bucher.

Renunciation
Jesse Bucher refuses to act as executor and desires that letters of administrations be granted to David Bucher (grandson of said deceased). Witnessed on January 6, 1845 by John Joseph Baumgardner.

Witnesses: John J. Brown, Joshua F. C. Allgire, John Sweeden
Executor(s): Jesse Bucher (grandson and son of David Bucher)
Signed with his signature

Buckingham, Obadiah   of Carroll County
                                        February 18, 1839
                                            April 22, 1839
Number 51, Folio 88   April 22, 1839

To my dear wife [not named] all my personal property with the exception of my negro woman named Pat who is to be freed four years after my death. To my wife all my real estate (and mill) for her to sell at her own will. The proceeds should be divided equally among: my wife, my children [not named] and my two grandchildren (Lovelace M. Gorsuch and Nathan J. Gorsuch). After my wife's death, my real estate should be sold and equally divided among my children and two grandchildren.

Renunciation
Freeborn Gardner refuse my claim as executor and desire that the executorship be granted to Nicholas and Obadiah Buckingham, the other two named executors. Witnessed on April 22, 1839 by Edward Jordan.

Witnesses: L. Gardner, Thomas Miller, Edward Jordan
Executor(s): Nicholas Buckingham (son), Obadiah Buckingham (son), Freeborn Gardner (son in law)
Signed with his signature

Burgess, Richard H.   of Carroll County
                                              March 28, 1847
                                                May 3, 1847
Number 251, Folio 459   May 3, 1847

To my beloved wife, Henrietta Burgess, my house and lot in Middleburg with all the furniture for her use during her widowhood. After the marriage or death of my wife, this property should be sold and the proceeds are to be equally divided among my four children, namely: Theodocia Virginia Burgess, Emily Jane Burgess, Richard Bonaparte Burgess and Margaret Elizabeth Burgess. To my daughter, Theodocia Burgess, my gold patent lever watch and my mahogany stand. To my daughter, Emily Jane Burgess, my mahogany secretary. To my son, Richard Bonaparte Burgess, my double shot gun. One year after my death, my executor should sell the rest of my property (including the lot in New Windsor currently occupied by G. W. Wilson). The latter could continue to be rented if difficult to sell and the rent profits should go to my wife. If the aforementioned lot is not sold by the time that my daughter, Margaret Elizabeth Burgess, reaches the age of sixteen then it must be sold at that time.

Witnesses: John W. Wilson, Emanuel Warner, William H. Engel
Executor(s): Daniel Engel
Signed with his signature

Carlyle, Ebenezer   of Carroll County
                                               May 13, 1845
                                             August 11, 1845
Number 208, Folio 382   August 11, 1845

To my daughter, Anne Carlyle, my cow and chain, my clock, stove, bedstead and bedding, all my household and kitchen furniture, utensils, brass and iron kettle, churn, tubs and pots. Also to my daughter, Anne Carlyle, a portion of the fifty five acres of land called "Margarets Delight" which was conveyed to me by Michael Fulkerth in 1816 and which includes buildings and the farm where I currently reside. Should my daughter, Anne Carlyle, die without heirs then her portion should be equally divided among my other grandchildren, namely: Esther Foutz, Ebenezer Foutz and Jacob Foutz. To my daughter, Mary Woods, the other portion of "Margarets Delight." Should my daughter, Mary Woods, die without heirs then her portion should be equally divided among my grandchildren previously mentioned. To my daughter, Margaret Caylor, the sum of one hundred dollars. "I give and bequeath to my namesake Ebenezer Fulkerth" the sum of eighty dollars. To my son, David R. Carlyle, my carriage, tools and the balance of my personal and real property (excluding the wood lot which I have recently sold to Abraham Caylor).

Witnesses: Philip Boyle, Abraham Caylor, William Engleman
Executor(s): John Roop (my trusty friend)
Signed with his signature

Cassell, Henry   of Carroll County
                                       March 30, 1841
                                       January 17, 1842
Number 117, Folio 193   January 17, 1842

To my son, Jacob Cassell, the farm where I now reside called "Resurvey on Mill Lot" containing one hundred and six acres. Also to my son, Jacob Cassell, the land called "Look About" which adjoins the land of George Cassell and John Roop and contains about forty acres. I give these lands to my son, Jacob Cassell, on two conditions: (1) he pays my daughter, Catherine Nicodemus, the sum of one hundred dollars and sixty six cents (2) he pays the children of my deceased daughter, Rachel Nicodemus, the sum of one hundred dollars and sixty six cents. To my son, Jacob Cassell, my eight day clock, the stove and pipe in the family room, one plantation wagon, one seed plow, one harrow, two shovel ploughs, the Jack screw, one log chain, and one churn. To my son, Joseph Cassell, both parts of a tract of land called "The Resurvey on Lookabout" deeded to me by George Case and William Durbin (William Durbin at the time was acting executor of Frederick Tawney's estate). My clothes, money, notes, accounts and bonds are to be equally divided among my two sons, Jacob Cassell and Joseph Cassell. My property in Baltimore City should be sold and the proceeds divided equally among my five children, namely: Rachel Nicodemus, Jacob Cassell, Catherine Nicodemus, Isaac Cassell, Joseph Cassell and the heirs of my deceased daughter, Rachel Nicodemus. "I hereby except and set apart for the purpose of a burying ground that part of my land which has been enclosed for that purpose with the addition of ten feet on the west side to be kept in good order and enclosed by the owner of the farm and for the use of the family relations."

Witnesses: David Cassell, Abraham Baile, John Lohr
Executor(s): Joseph Cassell (my son)
Signed with his signature

Chalfant, James   of York Borough, York County,
                                       Pennsylvania
                                               October 13, 1842
                                               December 10, 1842
Number 255, Folio 466   August 6, 1847

My real and personal property should be sold except for that which my beloved wife, Mary Ann Chalfant, may choose too keep for herself and the children. If my wife should remarry, then all my property should be equally divided among my wife and children. I appoint Edward Jessop, of the City of Baltimore, to be the guardian of my minor children.

Witnesses: Joseph W. Jessop, Joel Fisher, Martha Chalfant
Executor(s): Jonathan Jessop (of York County, Pennsylvania) and Edward Jessop (of Baltimore City)
Signed with his signature

Chapman, Ann   of Carroll County

                                        April 24, 1842

                                        March 6, 1848

Number 276, Folio 499   April 3, 1848

To my daughters, Mary Ann Merring and Rebecca Merring, my house and lot in Middleburgh. To Mary Ann Merring, my colored girl called Eliza Jane (on condition she not be sold out of the family). To my daughter, Sara Odel, two hundred dollars which is currently held in the Savings Institution of Baltimore. I also give to my daughter, Sara Odel, my colored boy called Henry. To Mary E. Chapman, one hundred dollars which is currently held in the Savings Institution of Baltimore. To Ann Rebecca Merring, my bed. To Penelope Merring, my bed curtains. To Ann Maria Odel, my chest of drawers. To my three daughters (Mary Ann Merring, Rebecca Merring and Sarah Odel) and to the children of William Chapman, I give all my bed clothes and wearing apparel to be shared equally. The residue of my estate is to be equally divided among my children, namely: William Chapman, Mary Ann Merring, Rebecca Merring and Sarah Odel.

Witnesses: Isaac Dern, J. Adams Fuss, Jess Trone
Executor(s): William Chapman (son), George Merring (son in law)
Signed with her signature

Chapman, James   of Baltimore County

                                        March 3, 1832

                                        April 13, 1846

Number 223, Folio 407   April 13, 1846

To my beloved wife, Rachel Chapman, "my Mansion House" with the plantation where I now reside as well as all my real and personal property. "Whereas I now own three girls and one boy (people of colour) and slaves for life, and it is my will and desire, that they shall all have their freedom, at and after the death of my beloved wife, as aforesaid, therefore I do hereby manumit and set free, my yellow girls and yellow boy (that is to say) De Ann Smith, Kitturah Smith, Lydia Smith and Ephraim Smith, to be free from all manner of bondage and service to any one from and after the death of my wife as aforesaid."

Witnesses: Thomas Jordan, Allen Baker, William Jameson
Executor(s): Rachel Chapman (wife)
Signed with his signature

Cockey, Eurith   of Carroll County
                                        November 1, 1843
                                        April 2, 1844
Number 173, Folio 307   April 2, 1844

My executor should sell my interest in a tract of land in Carroll County called "Urath Bramwells right of dower" which is now held in the possession of the said Urath Bramwell. The proceeds should be shared equally among my daughters [not named] when they reach the age of eighteen.

Witnesses: Thomas E Stocksdale, Thomas Demoss, William Stone
Executor(s): Mordecai G. Cockey (husband)
Signed with her signature

Codd, John   of Carroll County
                                        February 10, 1841
                                        April 5, 1841
Number 96, Folio 163   April 5, 1841

The children of my negro man, Allen Collins, should have my lot of land which adjoins the land of John Petterson and contains about three fourths of an acre.

Witnesses: Nicholas Dorsey, John Frizell, Thomas Picken
Executor(s): not named
Signed by his mark

Conaway, Zachariah   of Carroll County
February 15, 1848
March 6, 1848
Number 272, Folio 492   March 6, 1848

To my beloved wife, Hellen Conaway, one third part of all my real estate, also one horse, one cow and fifty dollars. To my sons, Charles Conaway and Zachariah Conaway, my real estate called "Conaways Venture Improved" and "Beasmans Discovery Corrected" to be shared equally. These tracts of land situated in Carroll County were deeded to me by my late father, Charles Conaway (in his will recorded in Baltimore County). These tracts of land also include the land that was deeded to me by James O. Headdington. To my sons, Charles Conaway and Zachariah Conaway, all my personal property to be shared equally. To my son, Nathan Conaway, three hundred dollars which should be paid by his brothers (Charles and Zachariah). To my granddaughter, Eliza Jane Conaway (daughter of Rachel Busby), one hundred dollars to be paid by my sons (Charles and Zachariah) when Eliza reaches the age of eighteen or at the day of her marriage (whichever comes first). To my daughter, Belinda Jacob, two hundred dollars to be paid by my sons (Charles and Zachariah). To my daughter, Nancy Hill, twelve dollars annually to be paid by my sons (Charles and Zachariah) for the duration of her natural life.

Renunciation
Zachariah Conaway and Nathan Conaway both renounce their claim and refuse to act as executors, asking that letters of testamentary are transferred to Charles Conaway, the other mentioned executor. Witnessed March 6, 1848 by William Whalen.

Witnesses: William Whalen, Abraham Prugh, Joshua Beasman
Executor(s): Charles Conaway (son), Nathan Conaway (son), Zachariah Conaway (son)
Signed with his signature

Conly, Frances   of Carroll County
                                        October 3, 1841
                                    November 22, 1841
Number 115, Folio 190   November 22, 1841

All of my clothes should go to the poor. To Rachel Dell, my corner cupboard with all my queens ware, crockery and glass ware. The residue of my property should be sold. The remaining proceeds (after my debts are paid) should go to the Trustees of the Roman Catholic Church near Westminster for the use of keeping the church in repair.

Witnesses: William Shreev, George Wivel
Executor(s): Jacob Mathias (of Westminster)
Signed by her mark

Conner, Elizabeth   of Baltimore County
                                       October 16, 1833
                                       August 28, 1847
Number 256, Folio 468   August 28, 1847

To my grandson, James Owings, the feather bed with bed furniture that I currently use as well as all the silver plates and spoons. To Arianna Kelly, I give her my negro girl called Mary Ann to hold until the time that Mary Ann shall be freed by the deed of manumission and on condition that Mary Ann not to be sold out of the state. To Elizabeth Owings, my negro girl called Fanny on condition that she not to be sold out of the state. My negro woman called Rebecca and her brother called Samuel shall be set free at my death. To Elizabeth Owings, the balance of my estate. The legacy left to Elizabeth Owings and her heirs should not be encumbered in any way by her husband, Richard Owings.

Witnesses: Otho Shipley, Nicholas Kelly, William P. Barnes
Executor(s): John Elder (of Baltimore County)
Signed by her mark

46

Cookson, Joseph   of Carroll County

April 3, 1845

June 15, 1846

Number 226, Folio 413   June 15, 1846

To my wife, Rachel Cookson, the following: the use of and profits arising from my home farm, free use of the wood lots (the wood lots that was conveyed to me by Silas Hibberd and John Roop in 1837), the use of the horses, wagon and ploughs. All of these privileges for my wife are to continue until my son, Dennis Cookson, turns twenty one years old. I give to my wife, four cows, five hogs, my carriage and harness, my horse, kitchen furniture and feed for maintaining her livestock. When my son, Dennis Cookson, arrives of age, my wife should continue to be maintained in the same manner for the remainder of her widowhood. To my son, John Cookson, my horse called "Barney" and three hundred dollars. To my daughter, Caroline Cookson, two hundred dollars when she arrives of age. To each of my three sons, a silver watch when they arrive at age. To each of my two daughters, a silver tea spoon set, when they arrive at age. When my youngest son shall reach the age of twenty one, I direct that all of my real property should be divided into two equal parts. The south part (which I brought in 1828 from Paul Monroe who was acting as trustee) should go to my son, John Cookson, on condition that John provides a road for the family to access the wood lot. To my son, Dennis Cookson, the north part of my land. In the final distribution of my estate, I ask that each of my three sons should receive five hundred dollars more than my two daughters.

Renunciation
John Weaver renounces his right and claim to the executorship. Witnessed June 15, 1846 by Jesse Weaver.

Witnesses: Philip N. Boyle, Daniel Zollickoffer, Francis Haines
Executor(s): John Weaver (friend), Rachel Cookson (wife)
Signed with his signature

Cookson, Samuel

of Frederick County

May 8, 1833
April 17, 1837

Number 2, Folio 2

April 17, 1837

To my son, Joseph Cookson, the farm and land where we both currently reside. The farm contains the tract of land that was conveyed to me by Barbara Myers and the tract of land that was conveyed to me by Rudolf Switzer (adjoining the lands of Daniel Zollickoffer and William Curey). To my beloved wife [not named], the house where I now reside including all furniture along with the garden and stable "during her natural life and no longer." I also give to my wife all the silver money that I have at my death plus "as much superfine flour for bread and as much pork, bacon and beef as she shall want for her own use, and find her firewood cut and drawed to the door to her satisfaction, and find one cow always in milk and one horse to ride whenever she shall want to ride my executor shall find food for said cow and horse summer and winter and he is to use said house occasionally when she doth not want it all the above my executor is to find her as long as she thinks proper to live in said house and remain my widow and no longer and my executor shall pay my said wife the sum of thirty dollars current mony annually." To my daughter, Mary Haines (wife of William Haines), one thousand dollars.

Witnesses: Joseph Weaver, Samuel Weaver, John Weaver
Executor(s): Joseph Cookson (son)
Signed with his signature

Cornell, Mary

of Frederick County

June 18, 1833
June 19, 1843

Number 156, Folio 270

June 19, 1843

To my sister, Esther (wife of John Paxton), my cloak. To my niece, Ann (wife of Samuel Hess), my clothes and all my furniture. I hold a note against Samuel Hess in the amount of four hundred dollars of which he shall pay ten dollars to each of my siblings, namely: Elizabeth Frame, William Cornell, Jesse Cornell and Esther Paxton. The rest of the money owed to me by Samuel Hess shall go to my niece, Ann (wife of Samuel Hess).

Witnesses: Abraham Null, George Wilt, Samuel Null
Executor(s): Samuel Hess
Signed by her mark

Correll, Elizabeth   of Carroll County
                                        July 31, 1849
                                      October 22, 1849
Number 308, Folio 541   October 22, 1849

To my brother, Joshua Sherfigh, my German Bible and my little hour compass. To Lucinda Luckenbaugh, all my clothes. Any balance remaining should be divided between my brother, Joshua Sherfigh, and Lucinda Luckbaugh.

Witnesses: Philip Boyle, Jesse Hess
Executor(s): John Stoner (senior)
Signed by her mark

Correll, Jacob   of Frederick County
                                       April 10, 1835
                                        April 7, 1841
Number 97, Folio 164   April 7, 1841

To my beloved wife, Elizabeth Correll, all my farm and personal property during her life. To my daughter, Elizabeth Martin (wife of Jacob Martin), two hundred and fifty dollars. To my daughter, Ann Whitmore (wife of David Whitmore), three hundred and twenty five dollars. To my daughter, Magdelane Shoemaker (wife of Abraham Shoemaker), three hundred and fifty dollars. To my three sons John Correll, Jacob Correll and Christian Correll each a tract of land in lieu of the cash that I intended for them.

Witnesses: John Smelser, David Foutz, Cornelious Baust
Executor(s): Jacob You (my friend)
Signed by his mark

Creigh, John   of Baltimore County
                                                          June 27, 1836
                                                          November 16, 1840
Number 85, Folio 147   November 16, 1840

To William James Fowble all my property both personal and real. If William James Fowble does not marry and have heirs, the land should go to the siblings and children of Melcher Fowble (junior). To Julian Fowble (sister of William James Fowble) one hundred dollars when she turns sixteen.

Witnesses: Daniel Steell, Jacob Fringer, John J. Brown
Executor(s): Richard Hooker
Signed with his mark

Criswell, Elijah   of Carroll County
                                                          February 3, 1851
                                                          February 17, 1851
Number 349, Folio 596   February 17, 1851

To my beloved wife, Mary Magdalene Criswell, all my personal property to include one horse, two milk cows, twelve head of sheep, one shot gun (the hogs are her own property in her own right), and all household effects for her to sell in order to pay off my debts.

Witnesses: William Jordan, James Williams, Nathan Williams
Executor(s): Mary M. Criswell (my dear wife)
Signed with his signature

Crouse, Elizabeth   of Carroll County
                                        October 14, 1850
                                        October 28, 1850
Number 338, Folio 584   October 28, 1850

I ask that my executor dispose of my real estate in Taneytown
at public sale. To my daughter, Catherine Crouse, one cow,
bureau, and one bed well furnished. The balance of my
personal property should be sold. To my daughter, Mary Jane
Crouse, thirty dollars. To my son, Frederick Crouse, fifteen
dollars and twenty five cents. To my daughter, Barbary Crouse,
fifty two dollars. To my daughter, Rebecca Crouse, ten dollars.
To my son, Joseph A. Crouse, ten dollars. The balance of my
estate should be equally divided among: the children of my son
John Crouse, the children of my son Isaac Crouse, my daughter
Rebecca Crouse, my son Joseph A. Crouse and my daughter
Catherine Crouse.

Witnesses: John Harman, Joseph Bowers, Jeremiah Shunk
Executor(s): William Hiteshue (brother)
Signed with her signature

Crumbacker, Catherine   of Carroll County
                                        October 23, 1840
                                        February 18, 1850
Number 317, Folio 555   February 18, 1850

To my nephew, William Ecker (resident of Carroll County),
two hundred dollars. To my nephew, Jacob Ecker (son of
John), three hundred dollars, my carriage and harness. Two
hundred dollars to each of my nephews, namely: David W
Ecker, Samuel Ecker and Jonas Ecker. To my niece, Deborah
Danner (wife of Daniel Danner of Frederick County), two
hundred dollars and my blue and white coverlet. To my
nephew, Samuel Ecker, my blue bordered fine calico quilt and
all my German books. To Abraham Caylor and John Hess two
hundred dollars to be used for the needy members of the

Funckard society. I give to my niece, Elizabeth Myers (wife of David Myers of Frederick County), one hundred dollars. The residue of my estate should be equally divided among my nephews and niece, namely: David W. Ecker, Samuel Ecker, William Ecker, Jacob Ecker, Jonas Ecker and Deborah Danner.

Witnesses: Samuel Ecker, Jonas Ecker
Executor(s): William Ecker (nephew)
Signed with her signature

Crumbacker, Margaret/Mary   of Seneca County, Ohio
   January 19, 1843
   December 2, 1845
Number 213, Folio 393   December 2, 1845

All my personal and real estate and money due to me from William Roberts of Carroll County, Maryland should go to my three grandchildren, namely: Mrs. Mary Jane Ogle, Elizabeth Bentley and Thomas Henry Bentley.

Witnesses: Joseph Ogle, John Ogle, L. A. Hall
Executor(s): Thomas Ogle
Signed by her mark

Cunningham, Margaret   of Carroll County
   February 10, 1843
   June 12, 1843
Number 155, Folio 269   June 12, 1843

To Julian Weakley (wife of Charles Weakley) all my personal estate. To Julian Weakley my land called "Bachelor's Chance or Choice" containing fifty acres.

Witnesses: Abraham Wampler, John Shamer, Jacob N. Norman
Executor(s): not named
Signed by her mark

Davidson, Susan   of Carroll County
                                       October 12, 1844
                                       January 27, 1845
Number 194, Folio 353   January 27, 1845

To my step sister, Mary Longbottom, the sum of eight dollars.
To my niece, Mary Elizabeth Davidson, the sum of five dollars.
To Mary Longbottom and Mary Elizabeth Davidson, all of my
clothing to be divided equally. The balance of my estate should
be sold and the proceeds equally divided between my brother,
Jesse Davidson, and my two nephews, Joseph William
Davidson and John Wesley Davidson.

Witnesses: David Roop, J. Davidson
Executor(s): Joseph William Davidson
Signed by her mark

Davis, Elizabeth S.   of Carroll County
                                       August 2, 1845
                                       September 1, 1845
Number 210, Folio 388   September 1, 1845

To my niece, Elizabeth G. D. Warner, the sum of eight hundred
dollars to be paid to her when she arrives at the age of sixteen.
Also to my niece, Elizabeth Warner, my bed with bedstead and
bedding, one bureau, one chest and six silver tea spoons. The
residue of my estate should be equally divided among my four
brothers, namely: Samuel Davis, Henry S. Davis, George H.
Davis and Francis F. Davis.

Witnesses: Henry S. Davis, George H. Davis, Adam C. Warner
Executor(s): Henry S. Davis (brother)
Signed by her mark

Davis, John   of Carroll County
                                            October 16, 1839
                                              March 23, 1840
Number 72, Folio 130   March 23, 1840

To my loving wife, Harriot Davis, the use of all my property both real and personal during her widowhood for the support of herself and my children. After the death or marriage of my wife, all my property should be sold and the proceeds equally divided among my heirs [not named]. I also empower my wife to complete the transaction to sell a tract of land called "Addition to Treadaways Quarter" (lying south of the Stoney Ridge road) to Thomas Marsh.

Witnesses: John E Tevis, Elisha Dorsey, Christian Devries (junior)
Executor(s): Harriot Davis (my loving wife)
Signed by his mark

Davis, Thomas   of Carroll County
                                              May 13, 1840
                                      June 13, 1842 (codicil)
                                           September 1, 1845
Number 209, Folio 384   September 1, 1845

To my daughter, Elizabeth S. Davis, the promissory note that I hold against her. To my son, Samuel Davis, the promissory note that I hold against him. To my son, Henry S. Davis, the promissory note that I hold against. To my son, George H. Davis, the promissory note that I hold against. To my son, Francis F. Davis, the promissory note that I hold against him. All of these notes are dated January 14, 1839. To my granddaughter, Elizabeth G. D. Warner, twelve hundred dollars when she reaches the age of eighteen. To my dear wife, Amelia Davis, twelve hundred and fifty dollars and my mulatto woman called Bet. The residue of my estate should be equally divided among my five children, namely: Elizabeth S. Davis, Samuel Davis, Henry S. Davis, George H. Davis and Francis F. Davis.

Codicil

"Bequest to wife and whereas the property which I now possess hath been chiefly acquired by the joint industry and frugality of my dear wife and myself and thinking some addition to her portion necessary the better to enable her to live with convenience and comfort..." The residue of my estate of every description should go to my said wife for her natural life. This is in addition to the twelve hundred and fifty dollars and mulatto woman called Bet. The property is to go into the hands of my son, Henry S. Davis, for the support and maintenance of his mother. At her death, then the residue of my estate is to be divided among my five named children.

Witnesses: Cornelius Grimes, Gassaway S. Grimes, Gustavus Dorsey, Nathan McNew
Executor(s): Henry S. Davis (my son)
Signed with his signature

Deahofe, John   of Carroll County
                                          March 14, 1844
                                          June 3, 1844
Number 177, Folio 314   June 3, 1844

To Elias Moyers, the plantation where I now reside (on condition that the said Elias Moyers maintains the road from Lance Rorbeaugh's land to the County road and also on condition that he pay my executors the sum of six hundred dollars). My children shall have the following exact amounts listed which excludes the money that I have already given them, to wit: to my son, John H. Deahofe, $148.48; to my daughter, Elizabeth Nacc, $504.03; to my son, Moses Deahofe, $242.12; to my son, Jacob Deahofe, $181.9; to my son, Samuel Deahofe, $585.75; to my daughter, Catherine Doll, $312.16; to my son. Michael Deahofe, $221.94.

Renunciation
Jacob W. Boring refuses to act as executor and desires that the

letters of testamentary be granted to Jacob Deahofe (the other named executor). Witnessed on June 3, 1844 by James Kelly.

Witnesses: Ezekiel Boring, James Kelly, Henry Lippy
Executor(s): Jacob Deahofe (my dear son), Jacob W. Boring
Signed with his signature

Defenbaugh, Catharine   widow of John Defenbaugh,
                                   Carroll County
                                            December 13, 1841
                                                 May 9, 1842
Number 130, Folio 217   May 9, 1842

To my grandson, Noah Meyerly, the sum of twenty five dollars. To my granddaughter, Lydia Meyerly, the sum of twenty five dollars. To my granddaughter, Sarah Meyerly (wife of Joshua Brown), the sum of twenty five dollars. To my granddaughter, Dorothy Meyerly, the sum of twenty five dollars. The residue of my estate should be equally divided between my two daughters, namely: Catherine Gilbert and Susannah Gilbert.

Witnesses: Jacob Mathias, Henry Mourer
Executor(s): Adam Gilbert
Signed by her mark

Dell / Dill, Nicholas   of Frederick County
                                            December 9, 1835
                                            September 9, 1839
Number 60, Folio 108   November 9, 1839

My executors should sell all of my chattel, transfer all my stock in the bank of Westminster and collect all money owed to me. After my funeral charges have been paid and a pair of grave stones has been purchased, the balance of the proceeds should go to my four daughters, namely: Esther (wife of George Roons), Elizabeth (wife of Lewis Mouse), Catherine (wife of

Henry Bechtel) and Hannah (wife of Peter Banker).

Witnesses: Abraham Koontz, David Freser, David Diehl
Executor(s): John Baumgartner, John Koontz
Signed with his signature

Dell, Samuel J.   of Carroll County

October 27, 1848

November 6, 1848

Number 285, Folio 511   November 6, 1848

To my wife, Mary Ann Dell, all my estate of every description.
After the death of my wife, my estate should go to my daughter
and her heirs [not named].

Witnesses: Joshua Yingling, Samuel Durbin, Charles Henneman
Executor(s): Mary Ann Dell (wife)
Signed with his signature

Denning, Mary   of Carroll County

January 28, 1843

December 4, 1843

Number 163, Folio 286   December 4, 1843

To Nancy Kelly, all my clothes. My son, Robert Steel, no
longer has to repay the one hundred dollar note he owes to my
estate. To my son, Joseph Steel, one dollar. To my son,
Thomas Steel, three hundred and fifty dollars. The residue of
my estate should be equally divided among the following
named persons: my son, Robert Steel, and his three children
(Joseph Hays Steel, Mary Steel and Ann Maria Steel); to the
fours sons of my son Joseph Steel (John Thomas Steel, James
Henry Steel, William Robert Steel and Joseph Wesley Steel).

Witnesses: Samuel Evans, Benjamin Gorsuch
Executor(s): John Thomas Steel (grandson)
Signed by her mark

Devilbiss, Susannah   of Carroll County
                                         January 19, 1840
                                         January 27, 1840
Number 68, Folio 125   January 27, 1840

To my niece, Adahzillah Devilbiss (who currently resides with me), the sum of five hundred dollars, my bed, family Bible, table linens and my saddle with bridle. To my sisters, Sarah Lugenbeel and Mary Cover, all my clothes. Five hundred dollars should go to the missionary society of the Methodist Episcopal church for the use of the African mission. The residue of my personal property should be sold. I direct that my brother, Levi Devilbiss, sells to my other brother, Thomas Devilbiss, the tract of land in Frederick County. The residue of real property should be equally divided among my sisters, Catherine Angel (of Ohio) and Mary Cover (of Frederick County) to be used for educating their children.

Witnesses: David W. Naill, Samuel Ecker, Andrew Nicodemus
Executor(s): Levi Devilbiss (brother), Thomas Devilbiss (brother)
Signed with her signature

Diehl, Jacob   of Carroll County
                                    December 15, 1848
                                        January 8, 1849
Number 288, Folio 516   January 8, 1849

That my wife, Elizabeth Diehl, all of the rights and use of my property until my youngest son reaches the age of twenty one. When my youngest son reaches the age of twenty one, then my wife should have a portion of that property enough to maintain her and my three youngest children, however, the profits arising from my property should go to my three younger sons, namely: Samuel, Jacob and Jonas. To my daughter, Mary Diehl Cassell, one thousand five hundred and fifty eight dollars. To my son, John Diehl, five hundred and twenty five dollars as well as one thousand and thirty three dollars the latter coming from property that I own in the state of Ohio. To my son, Henry W. Diehl, one thousand five hundred and fifty eight dollars. To my son, Samuel Diehl, one thousand five hundred and fifty eight dollars. To my son, Jacob Diehl, one thousand five hundred and fifty eight dollars. To my youngest son, Jonas Diehl, one thousand five hundred and fifty eight dollars. The parcels of land that I own in Tuscarawas County, Ohio (one of which was conveyed to me in 1847 by Isaac Slingluff, and the other conveyed to me in 1848 by Christian Deardorff) I authorize my executors to sell. To my wife, Elizabeth Diehl, the sum of one thousand five hundred and fifty eight dollars.

Renunciation
Elizabeth Diehl refuses to act as executor and requests that letters testamentary be granted to John Diehl (the other mentioned executor). Witnessed January 8, 1849 by Philip Boyle.

Witnesses: Jacob Keim, Thomas J. Townsend (Jr.), Philip Boyle
Executor(s): Elizabeth Diehl (wife), John Diehl (son)
Signed with his signature

Dods, Sarah   of Carroll County
                                            May 23, 1848
                                            July 31, 1849
Number 304, Folio 537   July 31, 1849

To my nephew, Alfred Crawford, the sum of two hundred dollars to be paid after the death of my sister, Margaret Dods. To my nephew, John S. Crawford, five hundred dollars to be paid out of the estate of my sister, Margaret. The residue of my estate is to go to my sister, Margaret Dods.

Witnesses: David W. Naill, Philip Weaver, Samuel Hoffman
Executor(s): John S. Crawford (nephew)
Signed with her signature

Dorsey, Eliza C.   of Baltimore County
                                           November 18, 1828
                                           August 30, 1837
Number 13, Folio 23   October 16, 1837

To my husband, Nicholas Dorsey, my land on Middle Island Creek in Tyler County, Virginia. I also give to my husband the residue of my real estate of every description.

Witnesses: Edward Frizzel, Joseph Black, Thomas Beasman
Executor(s): not named
Signed with her signature

Dorsey, Ely C.   of Carroll County
                                           June 20, 1847
                                      September 8, 1847
Number 261, Folio 477   September 8, 1847

To my brother, Otho Dorsey, all my estate of every description.

Witnesses: Archibald Dorsey, Jonathan Dorsey, Nimrod B. Dorsey
Executor(s): not named
Signed with his signature

Dorsey, Mary   of Baltimore County
                                       September 20, 1832
                                    July 2, 1836 (codicil)
                                     November 16, 1846
Number 240, Folio 437   November 16, 1846

To my daughters, Elizabeth Norris and Mary Carr, all my clothes to share equally between them. To my daughter, Elizabeth Norris, the bed and bed linens in the family room. The proceeds arising from my interest in the estate of Col. Henry Gaithers and proceeds arising from the sale of my property in Hampshire County, Virginia, I bequeath as follows: to my son, Henry C. Dorsey, one hundred dollars thirty dollars;

to my son, Nicholas Dorsey, one hundred and thirty dollars; to my daughter, Mary Carr, fifteen dollars. The remainder of the proceeds arising from the estate of Col. Henry Gaithers and the proceeds arising from the sale of my property in Hampshire County, Virginia should be equally divided among my children, namely: Elizabeth Norris, Beal Dorsey, Henry C. Dorsey, Mary Carr and John H. Dorsey. The residue of my estate should go to my son, Nicholas Dorsey.

Codicil
Whereas my granddaughter, Eliza E. Norris, has lived with me for some time and has been kind to me, I give to her the sum of two hundred dollars which should be paid by my executor (my son Nicholas Dorsey) from the proceeds of the land that I have given him. I request that my executor do everything possible in order to prevent having letters testamentary or letters of administrations taken against my estate.

Witnesses: Elisha Bennett, Rezin Bennett, Perry Bennett, Elias Brown, Samuel Bennett
Executor(s): Nicholas Dorsey (son)
Signed with her signature

Dorsey, Mary C.   of Carroll County

March 22, 1844
May 19, 1845
Number 202, Folio 372   May 19, 1845

To my two brothers, Ely C. Dorsey and Otho Dorsey, all my property of every description to be shared equally between them.

Witnesses: Jonathan Dorsey, Archibald Dorsey
Executor(s): not named
Signed by her mark

Durbin, Catherine　　　　　　of Carroll County
　　　　　　　　　　　　　　　　　November 29, 1849
　　　　　　　　　　　　　　　　　December 17, 1849
Number 313, Folio 550　　　　　December 17, 1849

To the Catholic Church in Westminster, twenty dollars. To my nephew, Lewis Fowler, my bureau, cupboard and quilt. To Winfield Keller Fringer, my bed and bedding. To my sister, Comfort Durbin, one blanket. To my sister, Rebecca Fowler, one blanket. My clothes are to be divided among my two sisters, Comfort Durbin and Rebecca Fowler. To my nephew, Lewis Fowler, and Sarah Fringer (wife of Jacob Fringer), the residue of my estate to be shared equally.

Witnesses: Abraham Wampler, John D. Powder
Executor(s): Jacob Fringer
Signed by her mark

Durbin, Charity　　　　　　of Carroll County
　　　　　　　　　　　　　　　　　February 5, 1844
　　　　　　　　　　　　　　　　　February 19, 1844
Number 167, Folio 294　　　　　February 19, 1844

All my estate both real and personal should go to my son, Thomas W. Durbin.

Witnesses: Joshua Smith, Nicholas Durbin, John Smith
Executor(s): Thomas W. Durbin (son)
Signed by her mark

Durbin, Margaret　　　　　　of Carroll County
　　　　　　　　　　　　　　　　　March 18, 1837
　　　　　　　　　　　　　　　　　October 8, 1838
Number 39, Folio 66　　　　　　October 8, 1838

To my niece, Honoria Eck (widow of John Eck), one bed with bedstead and bedding, one table, bureau, wool wheel, one spinning wheel, iron kettle, iron pot, all my earth ware, one cow and two sheep. To Theodore Eck, my desk. To Maria Margaret Eck, one bed with bedstead and bedding and also my red chest. To Lucy Ann Eck, my own bed with bedstead and bedding, one cotton wheel, my spinning wheel and two sheep. To John Thomas Eck (son of Honoria Eck), my stove pipe. My executors should sell the residue of my personal and real property and the proceeds should be divided as follows: to my niece, Honoria Eck (widow of John Eck), a third of the proceeds; to my sister, Ann Hayden (wife of John Hayden), a third (if my sister, Ann Hayden, should die before said distribution then her portion is to go to my niece, Margaret Hayden the daughter of said Ann Hayden); the last third should be equally divided among Theodore Eck, Maria Margaret Eck, Lucy Ann Eck, John Thomas Eck and Margaret Hayden (daughter of my sister Ann).

Witnesses: Jacob Cromer, Jacob Sheffer, Frederick Shuler
Executor(s): John Baumgartner (my trusty friend)
Signed by her mark

Earhart, John   of Carroll County
                                           August 8, 1849
                                         August 20, 1849
Number 306, Folio 539   August 20, 1849

To my beloved wife, Catherine Earhart, all my clothes. My executors should buy a pair of tombstones. All my cash and money owed me (after my debts are paid) should go to my wife. Also to my wife, a horse, three cows, four hogs, two sheep, three bedsteads and bedding, a cupboard, four chests, a cooking stove, table, six chairs, two bureaus, one tub and churn, all my flax and tow linen, two spinning wheels, one cut wheel, one wool wheel, two side saddles and bridles, one tough tray and all my kitchen furniture. To my wife all my land in Carroll County conveyed to me by Adam W. Fieser and his wife Susanna

Fieser which is a piece of a larger tract of land called "Empty Bottle" containing seventy five acres (adjoining the lands of Valentine Earhart, Jacob Getthing, Solomon Arter, Andrew Lohr and William Burgoon). To my wife, Catherine, all my bed clothing, ten bushels of wheat and six bushels of rye. The balance of my personal estate should go to my beloved father, Valentine Earhart, and any claims that he holds against me should be paid out of my estate.

Witnesses: Jacob Geething, Jacob Leister, Edward Leister
Executor(s): David B. Earhart (trusty friend)
Signed by his mark

Earhart, Valentine   of Carroll County
                                      February 15, 1850
                                      February 25, 1850
Number 320, Folio 561   February 25, 1850

To my nephew, Jacob Earhart (son of my deceased brother George Earhart), the sum of one hundred dollars. To David B. Earhart, Jacob B. Earhart and William B. Earhart (all sons of my nephew, Jacob Earhart, the same Joseph Earhart as mentioned previously), each the sum of one hundred dollars. My executors should sell the residue of my personal property and all my real estate. The proceeds (after debts are paid) should be distributed as follows: one third to my daughter in law, Catherine Earhart (widow of my son John Earhart); one half of the remaining portion to my nephew, Jacob Earhart (son of George); one half of the remaining portion to my daughter in law, Catherine Earhart (widow of my son John Earhart).

Witnesses: Jacob Geething, Christian Wisner, Daniel J. Geiman
Executor(s): J. Henry Hoppe
Signed by his mark

Eckenrode, Elizabeth   of Carroll County
                                        September 2, 1850
                                        September 5, 1850
Number 332, Folio 576   September 5, 1850

My husband, John Eckenrode (now deceased), bequeathed to me one thousand dollars and from this I bequeath the following: to the children of my daughter, Mary Therese (wife of John Rinedollar of Carroll County), two hundred and fifty dollars; to the eldest daughter of Mary Therese Rinedollar, one bed; to the children of my daughter, Liddy Elizabeth Harner (wife of Samuel Harner of Carroll County), two hundred and fifty dollars; to the eldest daughter of Liddy Elizabeth Harner, one bed; to the children of my youngest daughter, Catherine Fleischman (wife of John Fleischman of Adams County, Pennsylvania), three hundred and fifty dollars; to the eldest daughter of Catherine Fleischman, one bed; to my sister, Catherine Snauvel (of Taneytown), fifty dollars; the remaining one hundred dollars should be used to purchase my tombstone and pay for the funeral services which should be conducted by Rev. Smith of Baltimore City. The residue of my estate (after all debts paid) should go to the trustees of the Roman Catholic Church of Taneytown.

Witnesses: George Miller, Augustine Arnold, Daniel Snovell, Rev. Anthony Smith
Executor(s): John B. Boyle (of Westminster)
Signed by her mark

Eckenrode, John / Johannes   of Carroll County
                                        February 9, 1845
                                        December 9, 1849
Number 311, Folio 547   December 10, 1849

I direct that I be buried at the Catholic Church in Taneytown. To my wife, Elizabeth, my household kitchen furniture. The residue of my real and personal property should be sold and the proceeds should be distributed as follows: to my wife, Elizabeth, one thousand dollars; to the Roman Catholic Church in Taneytown under the Rev. Nicholas Zockey, one thousand dollars; the residue to be divided equally among my daughters – Lydia (wife of Samuel Harner), Maria (wife of John Reinedollar), Catherine (wife of John Fleshman).

Witnesses: Hugh Shaw, Daniel Snovell, William Fisher
Executor(s): John B. Boyle (friend)
Signed with his signature

Engel, Mary Ann   of Frederick County
                                   September 8, 1832
                                   January 1, 1838
Number 20, Folio 36   January 2, 1838

To my son, Michael, the sum of twenty five dollars. To my son, George, all my goods, chattel and remaining money.

Witnesses: John Baumgartner, George Hawk
Executor(s): George (son)
Signed by her mark

Englar, Daniel   of Carroll County
                                   May 7, 1848
                                   July 2, 1849
Number 303, Folio 536   July 2, 1849

To my nephew and niece, Octavious Augustus Englar and Jane Elizabeth Englar (the children of my deceased brother Jacob), each the sum of thirty seven dollars and fifty cents. To my niece, Sophia Lightner (daughter of my deceased brother John), the sum of twenty five dollars. To Sarah Carl, the sum of twenty five dollars. The residue of my estate should go to the widow and children of my deceased brother, David, and should be shared equally among them, namely: Anna Englar, Abraham,

Phebe, Mary Ann, Catherine and Elizabeth Englar.

Witnesses: William Shepherd, Washington Senesey
Executor(s): Abraham Englar (nephew)
Signed by his mark

Englar, David (senior)   of Carroll County

August 2, 1838

August 26, 1839

Number 58, Folio 105   August 26, 1839

To my beloved wife, Elizabeth Englar, one third of my house
and one third of all the crops produced on the farm where I now
reside and all the firewood that she desires to be provided by
my son, Jonas Englar. To my daughter, Elizabeth Englar, a
dowry of furniture similar to what I gave her sisters. The
residue of my personal property (money excepted), should go to
my wife. To my son, Jonas Englar, the farm where I now
reside being a part of a tract of land called "Mountain Prospect"
and the wood lot that was conveyed to me by Joshua Howards
called "Legh Castle" (on condition that my son Jonas pays my
wife, Elizabeth Englar, six thousand five hundred dollars in
nine annual and equal payments starting two years after my
death). To my son, David Englar, the farm that was conveyed
to me by Christian Ely (on condition that my son pays my
estate seven thousand five hundred dollars in nine equal annual
payments starting one year after my death). Having already
provided my son, Joseph Englar, with the farm where he now
resides I consider him to have his portion in full. Having
already provided my son, Nathan Englar, with the farm where
he now resides I consider him to have his portion in full. To
my eldest daughter, Lydia Roop, two thousand five hundred
dollars less the money that she owes me. To my third son,
Josiah Englar, two thousand five hundred dollars less the
money that he owes me. To my youngest daughter, Elizabeth
Englar, two thousand five hundred dollars less the money that

her mother will provide to her. To my daughter, Hannah Nicodemus, two thousand five hundred dollars less the money that she owes me. The residue of my estate should be equally divided among my seven children: Nathan Englar, Josiah Englar, David Englar, Jonas Englar, Lydia Roop, Hannah Nicodemus and Elizabeth Englar.

Witnesses: D. W. Naill, Philip Englar, Abraham Caylor
Executor(s): Nathan Englar (son), David Englar (son)
Signed with his signature

Englar, Elizabeth   of Carroll County
                                                    December 1, 1847
                                                    November 26, 1849
Number 309, Folio 542   November 26, 1849

To my son, Joseph Englar, my silver tea spoons and my large rocking chair. To my grandson, John David Kinzer, the sum of twenty dollars to be paid when he reaches the age of twenty one. To my daughter, Lydia Roop, my best side saddle. To my daughters, Lydia Roop and Hannah Nicodemus, my clothes to be shared equally between them. To my son, Josiah Englar, my desk and my book case on condition that he pays my estate eight dollars. To my son, Jonas Englar, my eight day clock on condition that he pays my estate fifteen dollars. To my son, Jonas Englar, my single bedstead and two tables without leaves and all my tubs. The residue of my household and other property should be equally divided into six portions and should be divided among my six children, namely: Nathan Englar, Josiah Englar, David Englar, Jonas Englar, Lydia Roop and Hannah Nicodemus.

Witnesses: Simon Coppersmith, David W. Naill
Executor(s): Jonas Englar (son)
Signed with her signature

Englar, Joseph of Carroll County

June 12, 1842

March 10, 1845

Number 197, Folio 361 March 10, 1845

To my wife, Esther Englar, the annual interest of five percent on a principal of five thousand dollars which should be paid to her annually (if the interest is not found to be sufficient then she may take money from the principal). To my wife, a horse with saddle and bridle, a cow with chain, hay and pasture for said cow and horse and as much firewood as she needs which should be cut and hauled to the house for her (my son, Levi Englar, should be trustee for the money set aside for my wife and he should also provide the labor to maintain my wife as described). I also direct that my wife should have the lower bedroom and the room directly above it in the farm where I currently reside along with privileges to the kitchen, cellar, spring house and half of the garden. My wife should have entire use of the following: two bed and bedsteads, case of drawers, corner cupboard and contents, dining table and set of chairs, clock and case, stove, irons, shovel, tongs, two large wash tubs, pots, skillet, brass tea kettle and coffee mill. To my son, Levi Englar, my farm called "Pleasant Spring" also part of "Haines Inheritance" containing together five hundred and forty acres (on condition that he maintains my wife as described previously). To my son, Levi Englar, five hundred dollars or an equal amount of my personal property. The residue of my personal property should be sold and the proceeds should be equally divided between my five daughters and youngest son, namely: Susannah Haines, Deborah McKinstrey, Samuel Englar, Lydia Roop, Mary Englar and Martha Englar. If my daughters, Mary and Martha Englar, remain unmarried then they should be able to continue to live in and have use of my house. "Whereas it may be necessary to give an explanation of the reason why I have given my son Levi Englar as before directed. I therefore state that I did it not only in consideration of his industry and frugality, but in consideration of the

69

services and time he marked for me since he arrived at the age of twenty five years, and for which I have made him no other compensation."

Witnesses: Jacob Snader, Joseph Foutz, Philip Boyle
Executor(s): Levi Englar (son)
Signed with his signature

Evens, John   of Carroll County
                                    December 29, 1840
                                    June 28, 1841
Number 107, Folio 179   June 28, 1841

To my daughter, Susannah, one feather bed with bedstead and bedding, one spinning wheel and a three year old heifer. To my daughter, Catherine, one feather bed with bedstead and bedding and one spinning wheel. To my son, William, fifty cents. To my daughter, Elizabeth Taylor, fifty cents. The residue of my personal property should go to my wife [not named]. All of my real estate should go to my wife. After the death of my wife, my estate both real and personal should be sold and the proceeds should be equally divided among the following named children, namely: Joseph, Lewis, Levy, Susannah and Catherine.

Renunciation
Samuel Taylor, the sole executor of the estate of John Evens, refuses to act as executor and requests that Amos Evens (son of John Evens) be appointed as executor. Witnessed on June 28, 1841 by Stephen Oursler.

Witnesses: Elijah Woolery, Nimrod Woolery, Stephen Oursler
Executor(s): Samuel Taylor (son in law)
Signed by his mark

Everly, Levi   of Carroll County
                                    November 17, 1844
                                    February 17, 1845
Number 195, Folio 355   February 17, 1845

To my wife, Rebecca Everly, two cows, five hundred pounds of bacon, twenty bushels of wheat, twenty bushels of corn, ten bushels of potatoes, two bedsteads with bedding, trunnel bed with bedding, linens, bureau, desk, corner cupboard, ten plates, stove, leaf table, side saddle and riding bridle, crockery, kitchen furniture, my large family Bible, dried fruit, apple butter, buckets, six chairs and a breeding sow. The residue of my personal estate and all my real estate should be sold and the proceeds should be distributed equally between my wife and children [not named].

Witnesses: Abraham Wampler, Jacob Bankert, David Knipple
Executor(s): Rebecca Everly (wife), David Leister (father in law)
Signed with his signature

Ewing, William   of Carroll County
                                    February 8, 1839
                          February 9, 1839 (codicil)
                                  August 12, 1841
Number 184, Folio 328   August 12, 1841

The proceeds from the sale of both my real and personal property should be divided into twenty equal shares and distributed as follows: to my niece, Nancy Watt (wife of Robert Watt of Donnegal County in the Kingdom of Great Britain and Ireland), two shares; to the heirs of my deceased nephew, William Wilson (late of Baltimore County), two shares to be distributed to said heirs as they reach the age of twenty one and I appoint Jane Wilson (widow of William Wilson) as Trustee for said heirs; to my niece, Elizabeth Wilson, two shares; to my niece, Mary Wilson, three shares owing to her "dutiful and affectionate conduct to me"; to my niece, Jane Buchanan (wife of John Buchanan), two shares; to my niece, Isabella Wilson, three shares owing to her "dutiful and affectionate conduct to me"; to my nephew, Robert Wilson, two shares; to my niece, Martha Wilson, two shares; to the children of my niece, Rebecca Dunn (wife of William Dunn of Baltimore), two shares to be divided equally among them at the age of twenty one (Rebecca Dunn may choose a Trustee, but Rebecca and William Dunn are not allowed to be Trustees for their children).

Codicil
That my executors not sell my slaves unless it is on condition that they may not be taken out of the state of Maryland.

Renunciation
Edward Ireland, the surviving executor of the estate of William Ewing, renounces his executorship. Witnessed August 17, 1844 by William Bean and N. Browne.

Witnesses: E. Harrington, N. Browne, George W. Allison
Executor(s): Edward Ireland and Benjamin Bennett
Signed with his signature

Fair, George   of Carroll County
                                           October 21, 1843
                                           October 11, 1847
Number 262, Folio 478   October 11, 1847

To my eldest son, Peter Fair, the land and dwelling house where he now resides for the sum of fifteen dollars an acre. The residue of my estate should be sold and the proceeds equally divided among my children, namely: my son, Peter Fair, one share; the share for my deceased son George Fair (junior) should be equally divided among his children namely, William, Ephraim and Sarayann (Sarayann is now deceased and her share should go to her two children); to my son, Samuel Fair, one share; to my daughter, Eve (widow of Jacob Grogg now wife of Jacob Michels), one share; to my daughter, Margaret (wife of

John Bollinger), one share; to my daughter, Mary (wife of Daniel Marichel), one share; to my youngest daughter, Susan (wife of Daniel Sharrer), one share. To, William Shultzs, Catherine Trone, Elizabeth Peterman and John Shultz, each twenty five dollars which is coming to them from their mother.

Witnesses: John Beecher, Samuel Shue, Joshua Lammott
Executor(s): Henry Fair (nephew)
Signed by his mark

Fanning, William   of Carroll County
March 7, 1840
January 25, 1841
Number 89, Folio 152   February 8, 1841

To my niece, Susan Ann Cook (daughter of my sister Nancy Cook), five hundred dollars to be given to her at age eighteen. My negro man, James Green, should be set free three months after my death "on account of his extraordinary good qualities." To my beloved sister, Nancy Cook, the remainder of my estate.

Witnesses: Amon Richards, Owen F. Buckingham, Benjamin Williams
Executor(s): Nancy Cook (sister)
Signed with his signature

Folkerth, Margaret   of Carroll County
March 2, 1837
September 7, 1840
Number 85, Folio 145   September 7, 1840

To David R. Carlyle, my eight day clock and chest. To Anna and Mary Carlyle, the residue of my estate to share equally.

Witnesses: D. W. Naill, Samuel Winter, Joseph Winter
Executor(s): Ebenezer Carlyle (friend)
Signed by her mark

Foltz, John   of Carroll County

                                    April 8, 1837

                          November 6, 1837

Number 17, Folio 30   November 6, 1837

After the death or marriage of my beloved wife, Ann Mary Foltz, my estate should be sold including my interest in the tracts of land "Hockstadt" and "Gotham" situated in Carroll County. The proceeds should be equally distributed as follows: to my daughter, Sarah (wife of Michael D. G. Pfeiffer); to my daughter, Ann Mary (wife of Michael Wilson); to my grandson, John Foltz (son of my daughter Ann Mary Wilson).

Renunciation
Philip Gore refuses to act as executor. Witnessed on November 6, 1837 by Jacob Gitt.

Witnesses: Jacob Gitt, George Weaver (of H), James Marshall
Executor(s): Philip Gore, John Foltz (grandson)
Signed with his signature

Forney, John   of Carroll County

                        December 18, 1843

                            April 24, 1848

Number 280, Folio 505   April 24, 1848

To my grandson, John Shorb, fifty dollars. To my wife, Christiana, one bedstead, bedding and cow. To my son, Jacob Forney, a house and lot on the tract of land "Terra Rubia." The residue of my estate should be equally divided among my wife and children, namely: Catherine Shorb, Jacob Forney, Abraham Forney, Susan Sluss, David Forney and Christiana Ohler.

Witnesses: Isaac Dern, George Angel, John A. Koons, Christian Schlimmer
Executor(s): David Forney (son), John Sluss (son in law)
Signed by his mark

Forrest / Forest, Jonathan   of Carroll County

April 8, 1841
October 30, 1843
Number 161, Folio 282   October 30, 1843

To my daughter, Sarah Forest, my plantation where I now reside which contains about sixty nine acres as well as sufficient firewood for her life provided she remains unmarried. If my daughter, Sarah Forest, marries then the said plantation should be sold. My daughter, Sarah Forest, should be given four hundred dollars from the proceeds of the sale of my plantation with the residue being equally divided among my five children, namely: Jonathan, Charity, Susan, Milly and Jacob. To my daughter, Sarah Forest, all my hollow ware castings, stove, pots, kettles, walnut table, kitchen table, all my wooden ware, cupboard and two thirds of the contents of the cupboard, two flour barrels, my family Bible, one feather bed and bedstead with linens, six silver tea spoons, china tea ware, cow, four hogs, half the grain growing in my fields and six chairs. To my daughter, Charity Whittle, my large family Testament with notes. My daughter, Charity Whittle, should be able to keep her home with my daughter, Sarah Forest. To my two sons, Jonathan Forest and Nelson Forest, all my clothes and books. The balance of my personal estate (including my pewter ware) should be sold and the proceeds should be divided equally among my five children, namely: Jonathan, Charity, Susan, Milly and Nelson. To my grandson, John Whittle, the sixteen acres that I have already sold to him. To Maria (formerly my colored girl), the bedstead and clothes she now uses and it is my desire that Maria shall keep her home with my daughter, Sarah Forest.

Witnesses: Joseph Englar, Joseph Smith, John Smith
Executor(s): Jonathan Forest (son)
Signed with his signature

Foutz, Solomon

Number 47, Folio 81

of Frederick County
February 7, 1838
February 11, 1839
February 11, 1839

To my son in law, John Stoner, the part of a tract of land called "Meadows Branch." The said tract is the same part that I sold to my son, David Foutz, and the said tract adjoins both the land of Jacob Yon and the mill surveyed by Peter Swinehart. I also give to my son in law, John Stoner, one hundred dollars. To my son, Joseph Foutz, the fifteen acres that lies west of aforementioned property "Meadows Branch". To my son, Joseph Foutz, one hundred dollars. To my daughter, Elizabeth Foutz, one horse and a stove. All my books are to be equally divided among: Joseph Foultz, David Foutz, John Stoner (son in law) and Elizabeth Foutz. The residue of my personal property should be sold and divided among: Joseph Foultz, David Foutz, John Stoner (son in law) and Elizabeth Foutz.

Witnesses: Abraham Myers, John Fleegle, Philip Boyle
Executor(s): David Foutz (son), John Stoner (son in law)
Signed with his signature

Fowler, Richard

Number 343, Folio 589

of Carroll County
November 20, 1850
December 30, 1850
December 30, 1850

To my brother, George Fowler, the parcel of land where he now resides which I have already conveyed to him. To my nephews, Benjamin Fowler, John Fowler, Edward Fowler, Lewis Fowler, Henry Fowler, Dominick Fowler and Andrew Francis Fowler (all of the sons by my brother Edward Fowler), the tract of land which adjoins the land where I currently reside, to my said nephews to share equally. The aforementioned land also adjoins the lands of George Brown, Jacob Powder and my brother, Edward Fowler. To my brother, Edward Fowler, all that land that was conveyed to me by John Fetterling which contains about nine acres. The balance of my real and personal estate should go to my nephew, Benjamin Fowler (son of Edward Fowler), on condition that he pays my debts and pays fifty dollars to my nephews, John and Joseph Fowler (sons of my brother George Fowler).

Witnesses: Abraham Wampler, Jacob Myerly, Jesse Manning
Executor(s): Benjamin Fowler (nephew)
Signed with his signature

Frank, Johannah / Johanna   of Carroll County
October 10, 1839
November 18, 1839
Number 65, Folio 120   November 18, 1839

To my daughter, Elizabeth Martain, five dollars. To my daughter, Sarah Ebaugh, five dollars. To my daughter, Mary Shaffer, five dollars. To my daughter, Rachel Shamer, five dollars. To my daughter, Susanna Ruby, five dollars. The residue of my property both real and personal should go to my son Henry Frank.

Witnesses: Isaac Green, George W. Derr, George Richards
Executor(s): Henry Frank (son)
Signed by her mark

Frankforter, J. Adam   of Carroll County
December 20, 1837
January 1, 1838
Number 19, Folio 34   January 1, 1838

My son, David Frankforter, should maintain my property for five years after my death and pay all my debts from profits arising from the tan yard and from the sale of any of my personal property (the latter as necessary). My son, Jacob

Frankforter, may continue to live on the land that he now occupies for five years after my death. To my wife, Elizabeth, my best bed. I desire that my son, David Frankforter, should furnish my wife with all necessities that she may require during her life. After five years after my death, my estate should be sold. My son, David Frankforter, should have five hundred dollars for his service to me. The residue of the proceeds from my estate should be divided equally between my children, namely: David Frankforter, Jacob Frankforter and Catherine (and Catherine's heirs).

Witnesses: Jacob Gitt, Henry N. Brinckman, Jacob W. Boring
Executor(s): David Frankforter (son)
Signed by his mark

Franklin, Charles   of Carroll County
                                  October 5, 1839
                                   August 3, 1840
Number 81, Folio 142   August 3, 1840

To my son, Joshua Franklin, the tract of land where I now reside called "Hails Range" containing two hundred and twenty acres. To my son, Rezin Franklin, the tract of land where he now resides which is on the south side of the Liberty Road and also adjoins the lands of Elijah Porter, James Gosnell, Zachariah Barnes and Zadock Barnes. The residue of my real and personal property should be sold and distributed as follows: to my daughters, Amelia Picket, Elizabeth Witt, Anna Barnes, one thousand dollars to share equally; to all my living children, Joshua Franklin, James Franklin, Rezin Franklin, Charles W. Franklin, Amelia Pickett, Elizabeth Witt and Anne Barnes, the balance to share equally.

Witnesses: Nathan H. Owings, Benjamin Lindsay, David Lindsay
Executor(s): Joshua Franklin and Rezin Franklin (my trusty and well beloved sons)
Signed with his signature

Freed, Laurantz   of Baltimore County
December 4, 1836
April 17, 1837
Number 5, Folio 7   April 17, 1837

All my real and personal property should remain in the hands of my wife, Elizabeth, during her natural life. After the death of my wife, my executor should sell my property and the proceeds equally distributed to my children, namely: daughter, Mary (wife of Thomas Bollency); son, Jacob; daughter, Elizabeth (wife of Henry Minter); daughter, Catherine; daughter, Rachael.

Witnesses: Jacob Gitt, Peter Gettier, John Kively
Executor(s): Peter Sawble (potter)
Signed by his mark

Fringer, Nicholas   of Frederick County
August 1835 (day not legible)
July 27, 1840
Number 80, Folio 141   July 27, 1840

To my dearly beloved wife, Margaret Fringer, my house and lot in Taneytown for her widowhood. After my wife's death or marriage, the said lot and house be sold and the proceeds should be equally divided among my children [not named]. To my wife, Margaret, the interest of sixteen hundred dollars to be paid annually. After my wife's death or marriage the said money should be equally divided among my children. To my wife, Margaret, one cow, two hogs, three chairs, two bedsteads and bedding, table, clock, corner cupboard, stove, kitchen furniture, large copper kettle and thirty dollars. To my son, Nicholas Fringer, fifty dollars. The residue of my estate should be sold and the proceeds equally divided among my children.

Witnesses: Abraham Lightenwalter, Israel Hiteshue, Joseph Shunk
Executor(s): George Fringer (son), Jacob Fringer (son)
Signed with his signature

Frizell, Nimrod | of Carroll County
November 25, 1842
December 19, 1842
Number 142, Folio 243 | December 19, 1842

To my wife, Ann Frizell, all my personal and real estate during her widowhood. After my wife's death or marriage, my estate should be sold and the proceeds equally divided among the following: my son, William Frizell; my daughter, Ann Eliza Frizell; my daughter, Ellen Frizell; my son, John Frizell; my daughter, Hannah Frizell; one share should go to my grandchildren, Alfred Frees and Mary Ann Frees (children of my deceased daughter Mary).

Witnesses: Joshua Smith, Jacob Fisher, John Baumgartner
Executor(s): William Frizell (son), Ann Frizell (wife)
Signed with his signature

Frock, Michael | of Carroll County
May 10, 1838
August 22, 1842
Number 134, Folio 224 | August 22, 1842

To my sons, William Frock and Jacob Frock, all my clothes. To my wife, Catherine, two cows, two hogs, two beds with bedsteads and bedding, stove, table, six chairs, clock, chest, corner cupboard, large German Bible, spinning wheel, copper kettle, two iron pots, two tin buckets, one wooden bucket, two tubs and any other kitchen furniture that she may require. To my son, William Frock, my tract of land in Carroll County where both myself and my son, William Frock, now resides. This land called "Patience Care" was conveyed to me by John Baker on April, 15, 1805 and is recorded in the Liber books of Frederick County. To my son, William Frock, my tract of land called "The Fifth Part of the Resurvey on Lookabout" conveyed to my by Frederick Taney on December 14, 1807 and is recorded in the Liber books of Frederick County. To my son,

William Frock, the tract of land called "The Resurvey on Lookabout" conveyed to me by John Mikesell (senior) in April 1814 which is recorded in the Liber books of Frederick County. The aforementioned lands are to go to my son, William Frock, on condition of the following: that he supports and maintains my wife, Catherine; that he allows my tenant, James Hines, to remain and the rent profit should go to my wife; that he should pay the following to my children and grandchildren, namely: to my son, Jacob Frock, eight hundred and ten dollars; to my daughter, Elisabeth (wife of Adam Humbert), eight hundred and ten dollars; to my daughter, Susannah (wife of John Humbert), eight hundred and ten dollars; to my granddaughter, Susannah Frock (daughter of my deceased son Michael Frock), two hundred and seventy dollars; to my granddaughter, Rebecca Frock (daughter of my deceased son Michael Frock), two hundred and seventy dollars; to my grandson, Henry Frock (son of my deceased son Michael Frock), two hundred and seventy dollars. I bequeath to my son, William Frock, for the term of one year my tracts of land in Carroll County called "Tiger's Delight", "Mollys Delight", "Patience Care" and "James Fancy" containing all together one hundred and fifty four acres conveyed to me by David B. Earhart and Jacob Yingling (executor of John Yingling deceased) dated July 24, 1837 and recorded in Carroll County. I ask that my executors sell the above mentioned lands after one year of my death and that the proceeds should be distributed as follows: to my grandchildren, Susannah Frock, Rebecca Frock and Henry Frock (children of my deceased son Michael Frock), eighty dollars each; the balance of the proceeds are to be equally divided among my children, William Frock, Jacob Frock, Elisabeth Humbert and Susannah Humbert. All my personal property should be sold and divided equally among my previously named children.

Witnesses: Johannes Flickinger (senior), John Weiner, John Flickinger (junior)
Executor(s): William Frock (son), Jacob Frock (son)
Signed with his signature

Fuss, Mary

of Frederick County

February 6, 1836

June 8, 1840

Number 77, Folio 137

June 8, 1840

To my daughter, Anne (wife of Abraham Buffington), all my personal estate.

Witnesses: Thomas Jones, Elias Grimes, Jacob Zumbrun
Executor(s): Abraham Buffington (son in law)
Signed by her mark

Galt, Mary

of Carroll County

January 6, 1844

September 23, 1844

Number 187, Folio 335

September 23, 1844

My clothes should be shared equally among my daughters: Mary Jones (wife of William Jones), Susan Shaw (wife of William Shaw) and Rebecca Shunk (wife of Benjamin Shunk). My negro slave, Ann Eliza, should be freed after May 17, 1855. To my sons, Samuel Galt and Sterling Galt, one hundred dollars each. The rest of my property should be shared equally among my children: James Galt, Samuel Galt, Moses Galt, Sterling Galt, Susan Shaw, Mary Jones and Rebecca Shunk.

Witnesses: Joseph Eck, Adam Lichtenwalter
Executor(s): Samuel Galt (son)
Signed by her mark

Garber, Catherine

of Carroll County

September 5, 1840

January 3, 1848

Number 267, Folio 485

January 3, 1848

To my two granddaughters now living with me, Eliza Halberstad and Lydia Halberstad, three beds with furniture, two chests and bureau with contents and as much kitchen furniture as they require, to be shared equally. The residue of my estate should be sold and the proceeds should be equally divided between my grandchildren, namely: Eli Halbertstad, Eliza Halberstad and Lydia Halberstad.

Witnesses: Abraham Caylor, Jesse Woods, John Hess
Executor(s): Jacob You (my trusty friend)
Signed by her mark

Garber, John   of Carroll County
                                          April 13, 1838
                                    October 14, 1839
Number 63, Folio 117   October 14, 1839

To my wife, Catherine Garber, one hundred dollars, two cows, three beds and furniture, one bureau, one corner cupboard with contents, two chests with contents, one table, six chairs, and all the grain growing. To my wife, Catherine, full use of the house where she now resides including the wagon, mare, hogs, sheep, beehives, clock, stove and pipe, cookstove, two copper kettles, all furniture not mentioned above, the windmill in the barn, shovel, hoe and mattock for use during her widowhood. I give all my clothes to my sons, Solomon Garber and Michael Garber. If my wife should marry, then my real and personal property should be sold and the proceeds should be distributed as follows: to Eliza Holberstar, one hundred and fifty dollars; to Eli Holberstar, one hundred and fifty dollars; to Lydia Holberstar, one hundred and fifty dollars; and the balance to be divided equally among my children (Solomon Garber, Michael Garber, Mary Oyster (wife of John Oyster), Susanna Smith, Rebecca Orendorf and Sarah Martin).

Witnesses: John Roberts, Henry H. Harbaugh, Charles Hitesheu
Executor(s): Solomon Garber (my son of Frederick County)
Signed with his signature

Garrettson, Aquila of Baltimore County
October 31, 1836
September 5, 1837
Number 15, Folio 25 September 11, 1837

To my housekeeper, Ann Smith, a support during her natural life of not less than one hundred dollars annually, two beehives, all my clothes and all the household and kitchen furniture. To Mary Greenfield (daughter of Jacob Greenfield of Harford County), one hundred and fifty dollars. To Bennett Billingslea, one dollar. To Elizabeth Freeborn Billingslea, "the interest of one thousand dollars to be paid her by her four sons by her first husband Richard Garrettson who shares my estate at their mothers request, to be paid her annually." I hereby grant and reserve a piece of ground sufficient for six graves which is currently marked with four stakes between the chestnut tree near the barn. I direct that I should be buried there and that my executors maintain this gravesite out of the proceeds of my estate. The residue of my real and personal property as well as all my reading books are to be equally divided among: Thomas Henry Garrettson, James Aquila Garrettson, Richard Freeborn Garretson and William Edward Garrettson (sons of my sister's daughter by her first husband, Richard Garrettson) when they reach the age of twenty one years. If none of the sons of Richard Garrettson should survive to the age of twenty one, then the proceeds are to go to the children of Bennett M. Billingslea (second husband of Elizabeth, my niece).

Renunciation
Richard Jacobs refuses to act as executor and defers to George Jacobs, the other mentioned executor. Witnessed September 11, 1837 by John J. Baumgartner.

Witnesses: George Bramwell, Mordecai G. Cockey, John Malehorn
Executor(s): George Jacobs, Richard Jacobs
Signed with his signature

84

Geiman, Christian   of Carroll County
                                         September 14, 1845
                                         December 15, 1845
Number 214, Folio 395   December 15, 1845

The real estate and property where I now reside should be
equally divided among my children after taking out what has
already been given them, namely: John Geiman, Mary Royer,
Elizabeth Miller, Jacob Geiman, Samuel Geiman, Joseph
Geiman and Abraham Geiman. My personal property should be
equally divided among my five sons previously mentioned.

Witnesses: Daniel J. Geiman, David Roop, George Petry
Executor(s): Joseph Geiman (son), Abraham Geiman (son)
Signed with his signature

Geiman, David   of Carroll County
                                         June 7, 1837
                                         August 9, 1837
Number 11, Folio 20   August 9, 1837

My wife [not named] should live rent free with either my son
Daniel or David, her choice. To my eldest son, Daniel, a
portion of my plantation where I know live called "Windfall."
"Windfall" was conveyed to me by Whiteleather and this land
lies between the properties of the Sullivans and Shafers. To my
second son, David, the other portion of the plantation where I
now reside. This portion is the land that was conveyed to me
by Jacob Rusel. The division of the land between Daniel and
David begins at the stone on the County Road agreeable with
the survey that Jacob Leiman created continuing to the spring
and schoolhouse on a line of the tract of land called "Pleasant
Meadow" and then on to the land of Jacob Shafer). To my son,
David, the land conveyed to me by Peter Zensz and the land
conveyed to me by John Ritter. To my daughter, Rebecka Roop
(wife of David Roop), the land conveyed to me by Jacob
Myerly, also a piece of land conveyed to me by David Myerly

and a tract of land conveyed to me by Jacob Rusel. The residue of my estate should be equally divided among my three children.

Witnesses: David Leister (of Jacob), George Croul, David Myerly
Executor(s): Daniel J. Geiman (son), David Geiman (son), Rebecka Roop (daughter and the wife of David Roop)
Signed with his signature

Gillis, John   of Carroll County
                                         December 9, 1837
                                         January 13, 1838
Number 21, Folio 37   Not proven

To my brother, Joseph H. Gillis, and to my sister, Jerusa Gillis, two thirds of my interest in the estate of our deceased father in consideration for their kindness and attention towards me. To my sister, Milly Bonham (wife of Richard Bonham), and to my sister, Susannah Wilson (wife of Amon Wilson), the remaining one third interest in my father's estate. To my brother, Joseph H. Gillis, my watch and clothes. The balance of my estate should be equally divided among my siblings provided that the dower provided for my dear mother from my deceased father's estate is sufficient to provide her with comfort.

Witnesses: Augustus Riggs, William Curken, James L. Riggs
Executor(s): Joseph H. Gillis (brother)
Signed with his signature

Gist, Joshua   of Carroll County
                                         November 1, 1837
                                         November 21, 1839
Number 66, Folio 122   November 21, 1839

To my daughter, Harriet Gist, my plantation and house on a part of land called "Long Farm" which adjoins the land that I sold to

William Winchester. I reserve a piece of land for the Gist family for a burying ground. To my daughter, Federal Ann Bonaparte Gist, all the residue of my plantation containing a portion of "Long Farm", "Neighbours Friendship" and a tract called "Fellsdale" which was conveyed to me by Basil Dorsey Stephenson. The residue of my real estate in the state of Maryland is to go to my son, Joshua C. Gist. I also give to my son, Joshua C. Gist, my secretary desk. My real estate in Kentucky which adjoins the lands of John Bates should be equally divided among: my grandson, Henry Clay Gist; my son, Joshua C. Gist; my son, George W. Gist; my son, Thomas Gist; my granddaughter, Mary S. Gist; my granddaughter, Sarah H. Owings. My real estate in Kentucky on the banks of Lick Creek should be equally divided among: my grandson, States Gist; my grandson, Aubrey G. Jones; my grandson, Harvey Jones; my grandson, Edwin Jones; my grandson, Mordecai Gist; my grandson, George W. Gist; my grandson, Richard Gist. To my daughter in law (wife of my son, Thomas Gist), a judgment I hold against Westminster, Taneytown and the Emmitsburg turnpike road company. To my grandson, Mordecai Gist (son of my daughter Rachel Gist), one hundred dollars for "his services and attention to my business." To my son, George W. Gist, all my clothes. I desire that my granddaughter, Mary S. Gist, be allowed to live with her mother, Harriet Gist, on my home plantation free of charge. That my negro man, Richard, should remain on my home plantation and serve my daughter, Harriet, for the term of nor more than three years after my death at which point he should be set free. The residue of my personal estate should be shared equally between my two daughters, Harriet Gist and Federal Ann Bonaparte Gist.

Witnesses: John Cockey, Robert Lyon, H. H. Montell
Executor(s): Joshua C. Gist (son), Samuel D. Lecompte, James Raymond
Signed with his signature

Gorsuch, Ann   of Carroll County
                                                October 7, 1850
                                                October 21, 1850
Number 337, Folio 582   October 21, 1850

To my son, Perrygrine, the profits from the sale of my colored girl, Harriett (who should be sold for a term until she reaches the age of thirty five). To my children, John Washington and Eliza Ann, all my furniture to share equally. To my daughter, Eliza Ann, all my clothes. The residue of my personal property consists of five negroes, namely: Georg, Polly, Honour (who should be sold for the term of only one year after my death), Clorosa and Manerva (the latter two girls should be sold for a term until they reach the age of thirty five). The proceeds should be divided as follows: to my son, Lovelace, one-sixth; to the children of my daughter Sarah Stocksdale (Julian Virginia, Fletcher Gorsuch, Lucretia Naoma and George Washington), one-sixth divided equally; to my son, Nathan, one-sixth; to my son, Thomas Jefferson, one-sixth; to my son, John Washington, one-sixth; to my daughter, Eliza Ann, one-sixth.

Witnesses: William Gorsuch, Samuel J. Jordan, Abraham Lamott
Executor(s): John W. Gorsuch (son)
Signed by her mark

Gosnell, Comfort   of Carroll County
                                                July 31, 1851
                                                August 11, 1851
Number 389, Folio 611   August 11, 1851

To Elizabeth Dise (a girl that I raised), fifty dollars, a heifer she calls her own and all my household furniture. To my sister, Sarah Gosnell, the balance of my estate.

Witnesses: Aquila Pickett, Samuel Choate, William W. Pickett
Executor(s): Joshua C. Gist
Signed by her mark

Gosnell, Peter   of Carroll County
                                        November 10, 1839
                                        July 29, 1844
Number 182, Folio 324   July 29, 1844

To my dearly beloved wife, Sarah Gosnell, one bed and bedstead, cow and side saddle with bridle. My colored girl, Rachel, and my colored boy, Reuben, should have the privilege of choosing their master and they shall not be sold out of the state of Maryland. I appoint my son, Samuel Gosnell, as guardian for my son, William Gosnell. The remainder of my personal property and real estate (except my wood lot and tract of land called "Berrys Place") should be sold and the proceeds distributed equally among: the heirs of my deceased son Joseph Gosnell, my son William Gosnell, my son David Gosnell, my son Amos Gosnell, my son Samuel Gosnell, my son Herod Gosnell, my son John Gosnell, my son Rooney Gosnell, my son Nimrod Gosnell, my daughter Sarah Davis, my daughter Susanna Price and my daughter Mary Evans.

Witnesses: Alexander Gillis, Thomas Hood, Peter Gosnell
Executor(s): David W. Naill
Signed by his mark

Gosnell, Sarah   of Carroll County
                                        November 28, 1848
                                        September 15, 1851
Number 363, Folio 617   September 15, 1851

To Elizabeth Dicks, fifty dollars. The residue of my estate should go to my sister, Comfort Gosnell. After the death of my sister, Comfort Gosnell, my estate should go to my friend, Joshua C. Gist.

Witnesses: Reuben Conaway, Abraham Zile, John H. Criswell
Executor(s): Joshua C. Gist (friend)
Signed with her signature

Gosnell, William   of Carroll County
                                      October 30, 1838
                                      August 5, 1839
Number 54, Folio 96   August 5, 1839

To my two sons, William S. Gosnell and Charles A. Gosnell, four hundred dollars upon arriving at legal age. All my colored people should be set free as described and not be sold out of the state of Maryland. My colored woman, Mariah, should be freed two years after my death and only be sold with her baby daughter, Hannah (born on January 23, 1837) and the said Hannah should be freed at the age of twenty one. My colored boy, Lewis, (born on March 11, 1823) should be freed at the age of twenty five. My colored girl, Lydia, (born on December 25, 1824) should be freed at the age of twenty one. My colored boy, John, (born on October 5, 1830) should be freed at the age of twenty five. My colored boy, Enoch, shall be sold for the balance of time that he has left in service and then shall be set free. I give my colored girl, Lydia, to my dearly beloved wife, Matilda Gosnell. All my real estate should go to my wife until the time that my youngest child comes of age. Once my youngest child is of age, my estate should be sold. One third of the proceeds should go to my wife and the residue equally divided among my children, namely: William S. Gosnell, Charles A. Gosnell, Harriett Gosnell and Eurith Gosnell.

Witnesses: John Lantz, Joseph Weaver, Samuel Weaver
Executor(s): John Weaver (friend)
Signed with his signature

Grammer, Henry   of Baltimore County
                                      October 12, 1825
                                    February 8, 1841
Number 90, Folio 153   February 15, 1841

To my daughters, Ann Mary Grammer and Rachel Grammer, as much out of my estate as I have already given to my daughter,

Mary Chatherine Epaugh. My beloved wife, Rachel Grammer, may take all of the rest of my personal and real estate (where I now reside in Baltimore County on the north side of the road leading from Westminster to Manchester) that she desires for her use during her widowhood. After the death or marriage of my wife, my estate should be sold and the proceeds equally distributed among my seven children: Andrew Grammer, Simon Jonas Grammer, Ann Mary Grammer, Mary Catherine Epaugh, Rachel Grammer, Dorratha Grammer and Rebecca Grammer.

Witnesses: John Reese, Samuel Shaffer, Michael Sullivan
Executor(s): Henry Epaugh (son in law)
Signed with his signature

Greenwood, John   of Carroll County
                                    May 20, 1850
                                    August 12, 1850
Number 330, Folio 573   August 12, 1850

To my dearly beloved wife, Barbary Greenwood, one third of my personal property and one third of the rent or interest from my home farm. To my son, Daniel Greenwood, the land where he now resides called "The Resurvey on part of Poplar Spring" which adjoins the land of James C. Atlee and Noah Worman and contains fifteen acres at a rate of fifty five dollars per acre. To my son, John W. Greenwood, the land where he now resides called "Mount Pleasant" adjoining the lands of Daniel Raines at a rate of ten dollars an acre. My colored man, Harry, should not be sold out of the state. My son, Joseph Greenwood, owes my estate only one thousand dollars instead of the larger amount that he owes me. I have already given to my son in law, John Swartzbaugh and his wife, what I have intended to for them. The residue of my estate should be sold. Twenty five dollars each to my grandchildren (upon lawful age), namely: John Swartzbaugh, Uriah Swartzbaugh, Milton Swartzbaugh, Julia Swartzbaugh, Barbary Swartzbaugh and Rosannah

Swartbaugh. To my daughters, Catherine Greenwood, Barbary Greenwood and Magdalena Greenwood, each six hundred dollars. To my daughter, Rosannah Bart, five hundred dollars. To William Henry Greenwood, one hundred dollars. The residue should be equally divided among my sons, Joseph Greenwood, Daniel Greenwood and John W. Greenwood.

Witnesses: Noah Worman, Josiah Greenwood, David W. Naill
Executor(s): Daniel Greenwood (son), John W. Greenwood (son)
Signed with his signature

Greenwood, Ludwick   of Carroll County
                                        June 2, 1844
                              September 23, 1844
Number 188, Folio 337   September 23, 1844

To my son, Josiah Greenwood, two hundred and sixty five dollars. To my son, Uriah Greenwood, two hundred and fifty dollars. To my son, Jeremiah Greenwood, one hundred and fifty dollars. To my son, Isaiah Greenwood, one hundred dollars. My son, Uriah, may exchange his horse for a different horse from my stock. The remainder of my personal estate should be sold. My family should remain on my property until my youngest child becomes of age. To my dearly beloved wife, Catherine, one third of my personal estate and one third of the rents arising from my real estate. After my youngest child comes of age, my real estate be sold and after my wife's third has been taken out the proceeds should be equally distributed among my children, namely: to my son, Josiah Greenwood; to my son, Uriah Greenwood; to my son, Jeremiah Greenwood; to my son, Isaiah Greenwood; to my son, David Henry Greenwood; to my daughter, Margaret Greenwood; to my daughter, Elizabeth Greenwood.

Witnesses: Israel Norris, Jacob Landes, David W. Naill
Executor(s): Joshia Greenwood (son), Uriah Greenwood (son)
Signed with his signature

Greenwood, Philip   of Carroll County
                                                    May 9, 1850
                                                    May 27, 1850
Number 326, Folio 568   May 27, 1850

To my father, John Greenwood (senior), three of my horses
(called Short, Fox and Sam), two of my colts (called Figure and
Light), two cows, one heifer, two young bulls, all my hogs, all
my superfine flour and the interest in my crop currently in the
ground. To my mother, Barbary Greenwood, one cow, all of
my sheep, the interest in my beehives and my small trunk. To
John W. Greenwood, my three year old colt and one cow. To
William H. Greenwood, two of my horses (called Dragon and
Charly), one cow, one heifer, two silver watches and my
shotgun. To Eliza Jane Greenwood, one heifer. To my sister,
Barbary, one large trunk.

Witnesses: Samuel Ecker, George Harris, William H. Greenwood
Executor(s): John W. Greenwood
Signed with his signature

Grimes, Margaret   of Carroll County
                                                    November 23, 1839
                                                    February 8, 1840
Number 69, Folio 126   February 17, 1840

To Elenora Dixon (wife of George Dixon), the sum of five
dollars. The remainder of my estate should be sold and the
proceeds should be equally divided among the children of
Elenora Dixon [not named].

Witnesses: George Nichols, Caleb Dority, Abram England
Executor(s): Eleanora Dixon (wife of George Dixon)
Signed with her signature

Groff, Francis   of Carroll County

                                   February 4, 1846

                                   September 6, 1847

Number 260, Folio 473   September 6, 1847

To my beloved wife, Catherine Groff, all my personal property with the exception of my negro girl, Elizabeth Horn, as she should be freed after my wife's death. My executors should purchase two tombstones for myself and my wife. If my wife should not survive me, then my personal estate should go to George K. Bishop of Berks County, Pennsylvania. If both my wife and George K. Bishop should not survive me, then my personal property should be equally divided among: John M. F. Bishop, Susan Cassady (wife of Thomas Cassady), Mary Bishop and Angelina Bickley (wife of Franklin Bickley) of Bucks County, Pennsylvania. All my real property should go to my wife, Catherine Groff, for her natural life and after her death my real estate should be sold and the proceeds distributed as follows: to my negro woman, Elizabeth Horn, two hundred dollars; to Joseph Hahn, two hundred dollars as compensation for the work and labor he has done for me; to Abraham Erb (son of my deceased sister Barbara Erb), five hundred dollars; to the children of my deceased sister Mary Shriver (wife of Isaac Shriver), five hundred dollars to share equally; to George K. Bishop, one fourth of the residue; to the children of my deceased sister Elizabeth Troxell (wife of John Troxell), one eight of the residue to share equally; to the children of my deceased brother John Groff, one eighth of the residue to share equally; to the children of my deceased brother Jacob Groff, one eighth of the residue to share equally; to the children of my deceased sister Christina (wife of Peter Fleck), one eighth of the residue to share equally; to Francis Henry Bates, one sixteenth of the residue; to the children of Matilda Good (who was the wife of Isaac Cooper), one sixteenth of the residue to share equally; to Jacob Erb and Peter Erb (the children of my deceased sister Barbara Erb who is the wife of Peter Erb), one sixteenth of the residue to share equally; to George K. Bishop, one sixteenth of the residue. Lastly, my two minor children should be "continued in the hands of my executor until they shall come of lawful age."

Witnesses: Isaac Biehl, Isaac Hesson, Jacob Crawford, Peter Hesson
Executor(s): David B. Earhart (friend)
Signed by his mark

Haeffner, Maria Apollonia   of Taneytown, Carroll County

March 18, 1841

May 12, 1841

Number 103, Folio 171   May 12, 1841

To Clarissa Swope (of Taneytown), three hundred dollars, my bed clothes, bedding and bureau. To Henry Swope (senior), two hundred dollars. To Frederick J. C. Naylor and Augustus Jethro Naylor (sons of Mary and James Naylor), to share jointly my shares of stock in the Bank of Westminster. To my brother, Benjamin Haeffner, for his lifetime the interest accruing on my certificate of deposit at the Frederick County Savings Institution and after his death this certificate of deposit should go to his children. The residue of my property is to go to the Evangelical Lutheran Seminary in Gettysburg, Pennsylvania.

Witnesses: Philip Hann, James McKillip, Daniel F. Levofee
Executor(s): William Rudisel
Signed with her signature

Hahn, Jacob   of Carroll County

June 4, 1838

June 14, 1841

Number 106, Folio 176   June 14, 1841

To my wife, Mary, two beds and bedsteads, one bureau, the large tin plate stove, one table, four chairs, two iron pots, one frying pan, one copper tea kettle, one iron kettle, the corner cupboard, all the queens ware, white earthen ware, silverware, turning churn, two tubs, one cow, two hogs, fifteen bushels wheat, fifteen bushels corn, five bushels rye and five bushels potatoes. The residue of my personal estate should be sold and the proceeds should go to my wife, Mary, and if there is any left then it should go to children and grandchildren herein named. My son, Samuel Hahn, should annually give one third of the proceeds of the rent arising from my land and one third of the produce arising from my land to my wife, Mary, during her widowhood. My son, Samuel Hahn, should provide accommodations (the two rooms in my dwelling house, privilege of the kitchen as well as use of the cellar, spring house, bake oven, garden and stable) and maintenance (hay and pasture for cattle, cut firewood) for my wife, Mary, during her widowhood. After the death or marriage of my wife, all my real estate should be sold and the proceeds should be divided as follows: to my son, Samuel, one share; to my son, Abraham, one share; to my daughter, Elizabeth, one share; to my daughter, Sally, one share; to the children of my deceased daughter Rachel (my three grandchildren - Mary Ann Mearing, Jacob Mearing, Lidia Mearing) one share to be divided equally among them; to the children of my deceased daughter Polly (my granddaughters - Eliza Hann and Rachel Hann), one share to be equally divided among them; to my son, Samuel Hahn, one share which should be solely used for the benefit of my daughter Catherine (wife of Isaac Hahn). I leave nothing further for Daniel Cover (husband of my daughter Susannah), as he is indebted to me. I leave nothing further for my son, Joseph Hahn, as he is already indebted to me.

Witnesses: Josiah Baumgartner, Jacob Lynn, Andrew Hahn
Executor(s): Samuel Hahn (son)
Signed by his mark

Haines, Daniel   of Carroll County

                                         March 4, 1844

                                        March 16, 1846

Number 220, Folio 404   March 16, 1846

To my daughter, Susan Ann Williams (wife of Levin Williams), all my estate both real and personal "to and for her separate use."

Witnesses: Aquilla G. Barnes, Amos Williams, Abraham Lamott
Executor(s): Levin Williams (son in law)
Signed by his mark

Haines, Esther   of Carroll County

                                         January 29, 1848

                                        October 10, 1851

Number 366, Folio 619   October 13, 1851

To my son, Reuben Haines, all the estate bequeathed to him by the will of my husband (William Haines). I discharge my sons, Ephraim and Nathan Haines, from any claims that I may hold against them. To my sons, Stephen, John and Reuben, all my money that may be due to them by the will of my husband and I hereby discharge them of any debts that I might hold against them. To my sons, Ephraim, Stephen, Reuben, John and Nathan Haines, the sum of thirty dollars each. To my daughter, Sarah Biggs (wife of William Biggs), "for her sole separate and exclusive use and free from the marital rights" the interest on two hundred dollars to be paid to her annually and after the death of my daughter, Sarah Biggs, this money should be equally divided among her children. To my daughter, Sarah Biggs, one half of my clothes and one half of my furniture. To my daughter, Ruth Plummer, one half of my clothes and the remaining half of my household furniture. To my daughter, Ruth Plummer, for her use and free from the marital rights of her husband, Abner Plummer, I give the rest and residue of my estate.

Renunciation
Abner M. Plummer refuses to act as executor. Witnessed on October 13, 1851 by George W. Manro.

Witnesses: William Engleman, Joel Haines, Levi Cayler
Executor(s): Abner Plummer (son in law)
Signed with her signature

Haines, Mary   of Carroll County

                                       February 12, 1845

                                       March 17, 1845

Number 198, Folio 365   March 17, 1845

All my personal property to be shared equally among my four children, namely: Abraham Haines, Catherine Shuey, Mary Baile and Lydia Bigham. Provided that they put a "common tomb stone to my grave and also to my deceased husband grave tomb stone... to put tomb stone to my son Joel Haines Grave."

Witnesses: Richard Smith
Executor(s): not named
Signed by her mark

Haines, William   of Carroll County

                                       July 10, 1844

                                       July 15, 1844

Number 179, Folio 319   July 15, 1844

All my personal property should be sold and the proceeds distributed as follows after my wife's (Dorothy Haines) third: to my son, John Thomas Haines; to my son, Hashabiah Haines; to my son, Jacob Haines; to my son, Francis Haines.

Witnesses: John Yingling, George Utz, Michael Sullivan
Executor(s): Francis Haines (father)
Signed with his signature

Hammond, Rachel widow of Frederick County
November 12, 1829
August 17, 1846
Number 235, Folio 430 August 17, 1846

The interest arising from the land that I hold in Liberty Town of which the principal amount is two thousand dollars (Abraham Jones is in obligation to me for this note), should go on an annual basis to my sister, Eleanor Roberts. To my "little relative, Rachel Ramall, who now resides in my family", the sum of one hundred and twenty dollars, a bed with bedding and my walnut drawers (when she reaches the age of eighteen). To my little granddaughter, Ann Eliza Roberts, the bond of obligation I hold against Carroll Hammond which is to be invested in some savings bank or institution and should remain accruing interest until she arrives at the age of eighteen. All the money owed to me on various claims should be collected and from those monies, sixty dollars should go to my executor. The balance of my monies should be equally divided between the two orphan sons of Nick Hammond (when they arrive at the age of twenty one). My negro man, Phil, should be paid wages for his labor effective May 15, 1840. After my death he shall be able to purchase his freedom by paying my executors fifty dollars. Twenty five dollars should be equally divided among the following individuals: Lavinia Bayplot, the daughter of Sarah William (Mrs. Elizabeth Jhill) and the blind daughter of Norris Meredith. All of these three ladies are currently pensioners of this neighborhood. The sum of twenty dollars should go to the trustees of the New Methodist Meeting House in Union Town. The residue of my estate should go to my son in law, William Roberts.

Witnesses: Moses Shaw, John Roberts, Edward J. Collins, A. McIlhanny
Executor(s): William Roberts (son in law)
Signed with her signature

Harman, John   of Carroll County
                                     December 6, 1839
                                     March 16, 1840
Number 71, Folio 128   March 16, 1840

To my beloved wife, Elizabeth Harman, part of my land in Carroll County containing the buildings and orchard where I currently reside which adjoins the land of Cornelius Few and Magdalena Rinehard and which was deeded to me by George Kemp. To my wife, Elizabeth Harman, a cow, a heifer, three shoats, three sheep, two beds with bedsteads and bedding, eight day clock, corner cupboard, stove, dining table, four chairs, chest, bench, two spinning wheels, Dutch oven, all my German books, all my clothes, axe, weaving looms, linens and ten dollars worth of kitchen furniture. My executors should sell all my lands and personal property not bequeathed to my wife and the proceeds should be distributed as follows: to my wife, Elizabeth Harman, one third of the proceeds; to the children of my son, John Harman, one eleventh of the balance after my wife's thirds; to the children of my son, Jacob Harman, one eleventh; to the children of my daughter, Eve (wife of John Heldebridle), one eleventh; to the children of my son, Daniel Harman, one eleventh; to the children of my daughter, Christina (wife of George Stary), one eleventh; to the children of my daughter, Susannah (wife of John Shriner), one eleventh; to the children of my deceased daughter, Rebecca (wife of Peter Haifleigh), one eleventh; to the children of my daughter, Ann Mary (wife of Peter Rhudulph), one eleventh; to the children of my daughter, Catherine (wife of George Kemp), one eleventh; to the children of my daughter, Rachel (wife of Henry Sell), one eleventh; to the children of my daughter, Elizabeth (wife of Samuel Young), one eleventh.

Witnesses: Peter Banker, Stephen Keys, James C. Few
Executor(s): John Henry Hoppe
Signed with his signature

100

Harner, Christian   of Carroll County

April 7, 1837

July 5, 1841

Number 108, Folio 180   July 5, 1841

To my beloved wife, Dorathy Harner, one cow, one bed, one spinning wheel, kitchen furniture and any other household articles. The residue of my personal property and the land in Carroll County called "Owings Chance" containing seventy two acres should be sold. One third of the proceeds should go to my wife, and the residue should be equally divided among my children, namely: Frederick Harner, Jacob Harner, Michael Harner, Andrew Harner, Elizabeth Jakes and Mary Heck. To my son, Andrew Harner, an additional fifty dollars. My son, John Harner (living in Wayne County, Ohio), has already received his share.

Witnesses: Peter Mark, Frederick Riever, Nicholas Fringer (jr)
Executor(s): John Jones
Signed with his signature

Harrison, Nicholas   of Carroll County

December 1, 1842

January 23, 1843

Number 144, Folio 247   January 23, 1843

To my dear wife, Mary Ann Harrison, all my real and personal property during her widowhood. After the death or marriage of my wife, my estate should be equally divided among my children [not named]. All my servants should be manumitted at the age of thirty. My servant, Caroline Johnson (about the age of three months), should be freed at the age of thirty years such that my heirs have no claim over her after she turns thirty.

Witnesses: John Stansbury, Samuel Deahofe, Amon Price
Executor(s): Mary Ann Harrison (wife)
Signed with his signature

Hartley, James   of Carroll County

January 22, 1850

February 16, 1850

Number 319, Folio 560   February 18, 1850

To my dear wife, Martha Hartley, my house and lot where I now dwell which was deeded to me by Nancy Pickett (dated January 10, 1845) and contains three quarters of an acre. After the decease of my wife, this lot and house should go to my daughter, Mary Ann Catherine Hartley. To my daughter, Mary Ann Catherine Hartley, my lot adjoining my said dwelling which was deeded to me "by Thomas Pickett of Ezekiel Gearing" dated October 18, 1849. The residue of my estate should go to my daughter, Mary Ann Catherine Hartley.

Witnesses: Andrew P. Barnes, Rezin Franklin, Thomas Hood
Executor(s): Mary Ann Catherine Hartley (daughter)
Signed by his mark

Hatton, Lydia   of Frederick County

August 1, 1836

April 17, 1837

Number 6, Folio 9   April 17, 1837

To my son, Joel Farquhar, my eight acre lot lying near Union Bridge post office in Frederick County and my four acre lot near the borough of York in Pennsylvania on condition that he pay my debts. To my daughter, Deborah Farquhar, my house and lot on which Jesse Landes now resides including all buildings. To my daughter, Deborah, all my personal property on condition that she pay my two grandchildren, Elizabeth and Deborah Hughes, one hundred dollars each as they come of the age of eighteen.

Witnesses: William Shepherd, Thomas Shepherd, Joshua Moore
Executor(s): Joel Farquhar (son)
Signed with her signature

Hebbard, William B.   of Carroll County
                                              January 15, 1839
                                              April 15, 1839
Number 49, Folio 85   May 13, 1839

To my beloved wife, Susan, all the property from her father's estate and after her death this should go to my son, John Marshall. The residue of my estate should be equally shared among my five children, namely: Mary Ridgely Patterson, William A. Hebbard, Ann Robinson Hebbard, Moses B. Hebbard and Lydia Hebbard.

Witnesses: Isaac Dern, Peter Weyant, James Smith
Executor(s): Susan F. Hebbard (wife), E. E. Hall
Signed with his signature

Henderson, John   Colored man of Carroll County
                                            January 2, 1843
                                              April 3, 1843
Number 150, Folio 257   April 3, 1843

"I will...that my wife Lydia take charge of all my children...to raise [until] they arrive at...age." To my wife, Lydia, my colored boy called Henry, and he should be freed after the death of my wife. The rest of my estate should go to my wife.

Witnesses: R. A. Kirkwood, E. L. Crawford, Henry Cover
Executor(s): Lydia Henderson (wife)
Signed by his mark

Henestoffle, Anna   of Carroll County
                                              April 10, 1839
                                             August 9, 1841
Number 110, Folio 182   August 16, 1841

All my real and personal property should be sold and the proceeds should be distributed as follows: to my daughter,

Polly Null (wife of Henry Null), two hundred dollars; to my daughter, Anna (wife of Thomas Downey), one hundred dollars; John Henestoffle, one share of the residue; to my daughter, Polly Null, one share; to my son, Henry Henestoffle, one share; to my daughter, Anna Downey, one share; to my son, Ulrick Henestoffle, one share; to my son, Samuel Henestoffle, one share.

Witnesses: Jacob Gitt, Frederick Hamburgh, Henry Saltzgiver
Executor(s): Frederick Ritter
Signed by her mark

Herner, Michael   of Carroll County
                                                      April 18, 1840
                                                      April 15, 1841
Number 99, Folio 166   April 25, 1841

My wife, Susannah, may choose as much of my household and kitchen furniture as she deems necessary and the residue of my personal estate should be sold. The proceeds from my personal estate should be distributed as follows: to my sons (John, Jacob and Michael), three hundred dollars each; to my daughter, Polly (wife of John Straley), three hundred dollars; to my daughters (Elizabeth, Susanna, Catherine, Lydia and Magdalena), three hundred dollars each; to my grandchildren (Catherine, Elizabeth, John, Jacob and Rebecca – children of my deceased son Peter), one hundred dollars to be shared equally; to my grandson, Amanuel Herner (son of Jacob), one hundred dollars. The balance of my estate should be sold and put at interest for the use of my wife, Susannah. My wife, Susannah, will have the privilege of residing with my son Michael and all my children will share the responsibility of maintaining her. After the death of my wife, my estate should be equally divided among my children, namely: John, Jacob, Michael, Polly, Elizabeth, Susannah, Catherine, Lydia and Magdalena.

Renunciation
John Herner and Jacob Herner both refuse to act as executor
and all right should be granted to Michael Herner. Witnessed
April 26, 181 by Jacob Bowers.

Witnesses: Jacob Bowers, Samuel Rinedollar, Joseph Fink
Executor(s): John Herner (son), Jacob Herner (son), Michael
Herner (son)
Signed by his mark

Herner, Susannah   of Carroll County
                                             September 10, 1842
                                                   May 3, 1847
Number 250, Folio 458   May 3, 1847

To my grandchildren (meaning the children of my son Peter),
the sum of one dollar each. The residue of my estate should be
equally divided among the rest of my children, namely: John
Herner, Mary (wife of John Shaley), Elizabeth (now widow
Crafts), Susannah Werhime, Lydia (wife of Samuel Hahn),
Jacob Herner, Michael Herner, Magdalena (wife of Daniel
Hessone), Catherine (wife of John Sample).

Witnesses: Joseph Fink, Jacob Snider
Executor(s): Michael Herner (son)
Signed by her mark

Hess, Charles   of Frederick County
                                                   May 6, 1835
                                             September 2, 1839
Number 59, Folio 107   September 2, 1839

My personal property (after debts paid) should go absolutely to
my wife, Magdalena. My real estate should go to my wife,
Magdalena, for her natural life. After my wife's decease, my
estate should be sold and the proceeds distributed as follows: to

my grandson, David Menzer, ten dollars; to my son, Daniel, one sixth of the residue; to my daughter, Elizabeth (wife of John Linn), one sixth; to my son, Henry, one sixth; to my, Samuel, one sixth; to my son, John, one sixth; to my daughter, Sarah (wife of Samuel Rever), one sixth. To my sons (Daniel, Henry, Samuel and John Hess), all my clothes to be divided equally.

Witnesses: Abraham Null, William Cornell, Samuel Null
Executor(s): Henry Hess (son)
Signed with his signature

Hesson, Baltzer   of Frederick County
                                                   January 1, 1834
                                                      June 30, 1838
Number 31, Folio 50   July 9, 1838

My clothes should be equally divided among my sons, namely: Peter, Daniel and Jacob. My books are to be equally divided among my children, namely: Peter, Daniel, Jacob, Margaret, Barbara and Louis. The proceeds from the sale of my personal property should be divided as follows: to my son, Abraham, one hundred dollars; to my son, John, one hundred dollars; the residue to my children, Peter, Daniel, Jacob, Margaret, Barbara and Louis. The land where I now reside which contains about one hundred and forty two acres in Frederick County called "Lehmans Range" and "The Resurvey on Lehmans Choice" should go to my children (Jacob, Margaret, Barbara and Louis) for one year after my death and after one year this land should be sold. The money arising from the sale of my real estate is to be equally divided among my children, namely: Peter, Daniel, Jacob, Margaret, Barbara and Louis.

Witnesses: Sterling Galt, Josiah Baumgartner, Francis J. Baumgartner
Executor(s): Peter Hesson (son), John Baumgartner
Signed by his mark

Hesson, Elizabeth

Number 378, Folio 639

of Carroll County
March 15, 1837
February 16, 1852
February 16, 1852

To my sister, Margaret Hesson, my tract of land which contains one hundred and five acres and being part of a tract of land called "Ohio" situated in Carroll County which was conveyed to me by Peter and Veronica Hull (dated April 13, 1802 and recorded in Frederick County). The residue of my estate including both my real and personal property with all money and bonds should go to my sister, Margaret Hesson, in consideration for the faithful and affectionate manner in which she has attended to me. I do ask that my sister, Margaret Hesson, purchase a set of gravestones for me and have them erected at my grave. I ask that my sister, Margaret Hesson, give to my nephew, Benjamin Hesson (Benjamin is the son of my deceased brother John Hesson), the sum of one hundred dollars.

Witnesses: Joseph Wivel, Jacob Baumgartner, Francis J. Baumgartner
Executor(s): Margaret Hesson (sister)
Signed by her mark

Hill, Hannah

Number 102, Folio 170

of Frederick County
April 27, 1835
May 10, 1841
May 28, 1841

All my real and personal property should go to my sister, Lydia Hill, and after her death all my estate should go to "my near friend and kindsman" Samuel Lina.

Witnesses: William W. Patterson, Abraham Null, Jacob Cornell
Executor(s): Lydia Hill (sister), Samuel Lina (friend)
Signed by her mark

Hinds, Patrick   of Carroll County
                                       February 22, 1837
                                       October 8, 1838
Number 36, Folio 60   October 8, 1838

My executors should sell both my personal and real property
and after paying my debts, they should purchase a tomb stone
as equal in quality as that of my wife, Easters. All the
remaining proceeds should go to the Trustees of the Catholic
Church at Taney town.

Witnesses: Joseph Wivell, Francis Baumgartner, James Wivell
Executor(s): John Adelsperger (trusty friend of Carroll County)
Signed with his signature

Hiteshew, Mary   of Frederick County
                                       May 25, 1829
                                       May 1, 1843
Number 152, Folio 263   May 1, 1843

To my daughter, Elizabeth Shriver (wife of Nathaniel Shriver),
all my money and interest arising from the notes that I currently
hold. To my grandchildren (being the children of my daughter
Elizabeth Shriver), after the death of their mother (my
daughter) my grandchildren should have the principal of the
money and also all my goods and chattel to be divided equally
among them.

Renunciation
Evan McKinstry refuses to act as executor and desires that the
role of executrix be granted to the youngest daughter of Mary
Hitechue (daughter of the deceased). Witnessed on April 18,
1843 by Nicholas Norris and George Yandis.

Witnesses: George Yandis, Evan McKinstry, Michael Shank
Executor(s): Evan McKinstry (my trusty friend)
Signed by her mark

Hoffman, Jacob   of Carroll County
                                                      April 21, 1837
                                                          May 1, 1837
Number 7, Folio 10   May 1, 1837

To my dearly beloved wife, Fredericka Hoffman, all my real and personal property for her natural life.

Witnesses: Samuel Evans, Richard F. Williams, David W. Naill
Executor(s): Fredericka Hoffman (wife)
Signed with his signature

Hoffocker, John   of Carroll County
                                                  August 17, 1840
                                                  October 14, 1850
Number 334, Folio 579   October 14, 1850

My property should be sold and the proceeds should be divided into eight equal portions, namely: to my son, John Hoffocker, one share; to my son, George Hoffocker; to my son, Samuel Hoffocker; to my daughter, Julian (wife of John Bowman); to my son, Jacob Hoffocker; to my son, David Hoffocker; to my son, Henry M. Hoffocker; to my executors, one share, to be kept in trust for my daughter, Catherine (wife of John Hare).

Witnesses: Jacob Kerlinger, John C. Rice, George Shuman
Executor(s): Jacob Hoffocker (son)
Signed by his mark

Hollingsworth, John   of Carroll County
                                              November 13, 1840
                                                      June 14, 1841
Number 105, Folio 175   June 14, 1841

To my dearly beloved wife, Mary Ann R. Hollingsworth, fifteen hundred dollars, my colored boy called Horace (to serve until January 1, 1850 and then freed) and my colored girl called

Hester (to serve until January 1, 1855 and then freed). The residue of my estate of every kind (including my land in Kentucky), should go to my wife for her widowhood provided that she maintain and educate my children.

Witnesses: Jesse Hollingsworth, E. E. Hall, John Sumwalt
Executor(s): Mary Ann R. Hollingsworth (wife)
Signed with his signature

Hood, James (of John)   of Carroll County
February 23, 1839
March 24, 1839 (codicil)
May 29, 1839
Number 53, Folio 92   May 29, 1839

My land called "Bagdad" adjoining Piney Run should go to my son William. If my son William should not have heirs then the land, at his death, should go to the children of my daughter Mary Worthington. To my son, William, three thousand dollars to be placed into the hands of my son in law, John F. Worthington, with the annual interest going to my son until his marriage at which point he shall have the principal. All my negroes should be equally divided among my daughter, Mary Worthington, and my son, William. To my wife, Sarah, one third of my property as well as my house and furniture during her natural life. The residue of my property should go to my daughter, Mary Worthington.

Codicil
Since the writing of my will, I no longer think that my son, William, will be fit to manage the property that I intended for his use. "...still with the fondness of a father hoping for the best, I was disposed to place it in such manner as to encourage him to do right. From recent circumstances I have been compelled to withdraw all hope that he will ever be able to manage the property and I now place the whole, real, personal and mixed in the hands of my son in law John F. Worthington,

who is directed to furnish William with a decent support...But in case William by a course of steady rational and correct conduct establishes the fact that he is capable of properly estimating and managing property then and in that case this my codicil shall cease..."

Renunciation
Mary Govans Worthington, daughter of James Hood (of John), having been appointed executrix along with my husband, John Folly Worthington, of Baltimore County renounces her right as executrix. Witnessed June 8, 1839 by Sarah L. Hood.

Witnesses: Gustavus Warfield, Thomas Hood, Zadock M. Waters, Henry W. Hood
Executor(s): John F. Worthington (son in law), Mary Worthington (daughter)
Signed with his signature

Hooker, Mary   of Carroll County
                                                        June 15, 1838
                                                        June 18, 1838
Number 30, Folio 49   June 25, 1838

To my granddaughter, Mary Ann Hooker, one side saddle, spinning wheel, large chest, all my clothes, one high bedstead feather bed and bedding, one other small feather bed, cow and calf which she calls her own and one hundred dollars (given to me by Jonathan Parrish in his will intended which was for her). To my son, Lloyd Hooker, the remaining legacy left to me by the will and estate of Jonathan Parrish. To my son, Lloyd Hooker, two feather beds bedsteads and bedding, two cows, a yearling, all my hogs and the residue of my personal property.

Witnesses: William Jameson, John Robertson, William Stansbury
Executor(s): Lloyd Hooker (son)
Signed by her mark

Horton, William   of Carroll County
                                                          June 26, 1850
                                                      February 3, 1851
Number 348, Folio 595   February 3, 1851

To my son, Isaac Horton, all my property "both real and personal after paying the following donations." To my daughter, Sarah Owens, one cent. To my son, Thomas Horton, one cent. To my daughter, Clarricy Sadler, one cent. To my youngest daughter, Mary Poole (wife of Aaron Pole), one cent. To my daughter, Mary Lowman, one cent. My son, Isaac, should take care of his mother and my dear wife, Nelly Horton.

Witnesses: Beale Buckingham, William H. Haines
Executor(s): Isaac Horton (son), Stephen Penn (of Stewart)
Signed by his mark

Houck, George   of Manchester, Carroll County
                                                    November 30, 1840
                                                    December 14, 1840
Number 87, Folio 150   December 14, 1840

To my loving wife, Catherine, all my personal and real estate for her natural life. After my wife's death, my estate should be equally divided among my living children [not named].

Witnesses: Ezekiel Boring, Joseph Gardner
Executor(s): William Houck (son)
Signed with his signature

Howard, Elizabeth Ann   of Carroll County
                                                          May 8, 1837
                                                         July 11, 1837
Number 9, Folio 13   July 25, 1837

To my sister, Jemima Howard, my gold watch, six silver tea spoons, sugar tongs, mahogany bureau, mahogany table, one pair brass Andirons, one bedstead and bedding, side saddle and bridle, half of my table linens and towels bequeathed to me by our mother, my clothes and the residue of my estate.

Witnesses: Samuel Greenhult, Asbury O. Warfield, D. W. Naill
Executor(s): Jesse L. Warfield
Signed with her signature

Hyder, John   of Uniontown, Carroll County
                                    June 1, 1840
                                    March 12, 1847 (codicil)
                                    March 27, 1848
Number 275, Folio 497   March 27, 1848

To my wife, Catherine Hyder, my dwelling house and lot "for many years past occupied by us situate in Uniontown." To my wife, Catherine Hyder, the wood lot of about seven to eight acres that was conveyed to me by William Roberts. To my wife, Catherine Hyder, "all my moveable property, live stock, household goods and furniture of every kind and description" excluding the house that at the time of my death has been claimed by my children. To my wife, Catherine Hyder, fifty shares of stock in the Bank of Westminster. Any residual cash or bonds should be given in equal shares to my seven children, namely: Adeline Delaplane Euclid, Caroline, Sophia, Elizabeth, Mary Carmack, Ann Lucinda and John Franklin. To my daughter, Caroline (wife of Charles Hiteshaw), one hundred and fifty dollars more than her share.

Codicil
"...the portion or share which I willed to my daughter Adeline Delaplane, to her personally that is to pay the same over to her only and to no other person and that her own receipts for same or this order shall be good and valid notwithstanding her covertures, and in the event she should depart this life before my estate is settled, then and in such case I hereby will and bequeath her portion to the rest of my children..."

Renunciation

Catherine Hyder, widow of John Hyder, renounces her right and claim to the executorship and desiring that the role be fully granted to Jacob Hyder of Frederick County. Witnessed on March 17, 1848 by Tobias Cover.

Witnesses: Daniel Sullivan, John M. Ferguson, John W. Swartbaugh
Executor(s): Catherine Hyder (wife), Jacob Hyder (brother)
Signed with his signature

Hyle, Joseph   of Carroll County
                                    March 30, 1851
                                    May 26, 1851
Number 355, Folio 606   May 26, 1851

To my wife, Elizabeth Hyle, all my goods, chattel, personal and mixed property of every description.

Witnesses: J. Henry Hoppe, John Beggs, L. Lamborn
Executor(s): Elizabeth Hyle (wife)
Signed by his mark

Jones, Jacob   of Carroll County
                                    June 2, 1846
                                    September 7, 1846
Number 237, Folio 434   September 7, 1846

To my beloved wife, Elizabeth G. Jones, all my estate.

Witnesses: M. G. Cockey, William Horner, Henry H. Roberts
Executor(s): Elizabeth G. Jones (wife)
Signed with his signature

Kautz, George

Miller of Carroll County
(formerly Baltimore)
August 22, 1839
June 29, 1840

Number 79, Folio 139

June 29, 1840

To my nephew, Joshua Kautz (son of my deceased brother Michael Kautz), one hundred dollars upon arriving at the age of twenty one. To my niece, Rachel Kautz (daughter of my brother Henry Kautz), one hundred dollars as well as all the clothes and jewelry of my late wife, Rachel. My executor should purchase "a set of good and decent tombstones and have them erected at my grave." All my personal effects should be sold and the proceeds equally divided between my mother, Elizabeth Kautz (widow), and my brother, Henry Kautz.

Witnesses: George Warner, John Streavig, Henry Shauck
Executor(s): Henry Kautz (brother)
Signed with his signature

Kautz, Henry

of Carroll County
July 14, 1845
August 11, 1845

Number 207, Folio 380

August 11, 1845

After one year of my death, my executors should sell all my real estate in Carroll County and in the state of Indiana. The proceeds of my real estate should be divided as follows: to my beloved wife, Lydia, one third provided that she remains my widow; the balance to be equally divided among my children [not named].

Witnesses: Jacob Kerlinger, Jacob N. Harman, John Streavig
Executor(s): George Warner (father in law)
Signed with his signature

Keefer, Henry   of Carroll County
                                      August 29, 1848
                                    September 4, 1848
Number 284, Folio 510   September 4, 1848

The farm where I am currently residing should be sold. My beloved wife, Catherine, should have as much of my personal property as she desires. The residue of my personal estate should be sold. To my beloved wife, Catherine, twelve hundred dollars in lieu of her dower. The residue of the proceeds from my estate should be equally divided among my children [not named].

Witnesses: George Mearing, Henry B. Cromer, John Delphey
Executor(s): John B. Boyle (friend)
Signed with his signature

Keefer, Joseph   of York County, Pennsylvania
                                          April 3, 1848
                                   October 15, 1849
Number 361, Folio 613   October 15, 1849

To my son, Steavon Keefer (of Hanover, York County, Pennsylvania), sixty dollars and the land lying in Carroll County on the turnpike from Gettysburg to Baltimore near the Silver Run church. To my son, Steavon Keefer, seventy five dollars and the land in Frederick City, Maryland called "Searches Farm" on the turnpike road adjoining the Tavern Stand. To my son, Harvey Keefer, sixty five dollars for maintaining and lodging me.

Witnesses: David Bixler, Joseph Althoff
Executor(s): Stephen Keefer (son)
Signed with his signature

Keim, Jacob

of Carroll County

December 17, 1847

March 26, 1849

Number 295, Folio 526

March 26, 1849

After my funeral charges are paid and my wife's portion taken out, I devise the following: to my dearly beloved wife, Barbara Keim, as much of my personal property in the way of household and kitchen furniture that she desires and the privilege of residing in the house until the time of sale. Also that Jacob Muses remains on my home as a tenant until the time of sale and that he is to provide all things to continue the comfortable support of my wife. To my wife, the interest of one thousand dollars during her life and if she is wanting then she should have as much of the principal as necessary. The whole of my real estate should be sold between the April and July after my decease. The proceeds of my estate should be equally divided between my daughters (Hannah Myers, Elizabeth Diehl, Sarah Shuse) and my grandson (Jacob Shuse).

Witnesses: Peter Engel, David Engel (of J), David W. Naill
Executor(s): Jacob Diehl (son in law), Lewis Shuse (son in law)
Signed with his signature

Keys / Keyes, Elizabeth

of Carroll County

October 10, 1838

October 29, 1838

Number 43, Folio 76

October 29, 1838

To my brother, David Keys, and his son, Samuel Keys, all my land in Carroll county called "Honours delight" containing twenty five acres to be shared equally. The remainder of my estate should go to my brother, David Keyes.

Witnesses: Samuel Moffet, Micagy Stansbury, Michael Lynch
Executor(s): Abraham Stonsyffer
Signed with her signature

Kiler, Simon   of Carroll County
                                           March 30, 1839
                                           October 7, 1839
Number 62, Folio 115   October 7, 1839

To George Kiler, the sum of ten dollars. To Hester Chilcote, the sum of one hundred dollars. To Elizabeth Banks, the sum of one hundred dollars. One hundred dollars should be divided equally among the heirs of John Kiler (senior), namely: John Kiler, Mary Kiler and Andrew Kiler. To the Trustees of Winter's Church, the sum of twenty dollars to be used in keeping the church yard in good repair. To Elizabeth Crawford, the interest arising from the twelve shares of stock that I hold in the Bank of Westminster. After the death of Elizabeth Crawford, the stock in the bank of Westminster should be equally divided among the heirs of David Kiler and Isaac Kiler, namely: Susanna Kiler (daughter of Isaac); Andrew, Mary, Isaac and Jacob Kiler (all the heirs of David Kiler). To Elizabeth Crawford, the sum of seven hundred and fifty dollars. To Elizabeth Rebecca West, the sum of sixty dollars when she arrives at the age of twenty one years. To Isaac Kiler, my small farm known by the name of "Raredane Place" which contains about fifteen acres. To Isaac Kiler, the sum of one hundred dollars. To Jacob Kiler, the sum of two hundred dollars. To David Kiler, the plantation on which he is currently residing called "Stevensons Place" which contains about eighty acres and also my land called "Dells Place" which contains about forty acres. To David Kiler, the sum of one hundred and seventy dollars. The residue of my personal and real estate should be sold and the proceeds should be equally divided between David Kiler and Elizabeth Crawford.

Witnesses: Abraham Baile, Henry Haines, Jacob Nicodemus
Executor(s): David Kiler (nephew)
Signed by his mark

King, Adam   of Carroll County
                                                    December 21, 1844
                                                    June 20, 1845
Number 193, Folio 350   June 20, 1845

To my dear wife, Elizabeth, the farm where I reside called "Red Hills" to be held in trust as long as she lives and she should have all profits arising from said land. To my wife, three hundred dollars, cow, twenty bushels wheat, fifteen bushels corn, three hundred pounds of pork, twenty yards carpeting, six chairs, rocking chair, bureau, table, stove, bedstead with bed and bedding, and all the kitchen furniture she desires. The farm that was conveyed to me by the Administrations of Detrick Bishop and where my son, Jacob, now dwells should be sold. As my son, John, owes me four hundred dollars and my son, Jacob, owes me four hundred dollars and my son in law, George Reifsnider, owes me two hundred dollars, I give and bequeath to my daughter, Mary Ann Feeser, four hundred dollars and my daughter, Catherine Reifnsider, two hundred dollars in order to make them equal. The balance of my estate should be equally divided among my four children, namely: John, Jacob, Catherine and Mary. After the death of my wife, Elizabeth, I desire that my sons, John and Jacob, purchase the farm where I currently reside for four thousand dollars. If my sons agree to purchase my farm, then I ask that they pay my daughters, Mary Ann and Catherine, two hundred dollars each for five years. If my sons do not purchase my farm, then I give my daughters the same opportunity with the same condition.

Renunciation
George Reifsnider refuses to act as executor.   Witnessed January 20, 1845 by Jacob Feeser.

Witnesses: John Swope, Joseph Topper, John Keenig
Executor(s): John King (son), Jacob King (son), George Reifsnider (son in law), James Feeser (son in law)
Signed by his mark

Knippel, Christopher   of Carroll County
October 20, 1843
June 29, 1846
Number 231, Folio 425   July 6, 1846

To Barbara Knipple (widow of my son George), the use of my lands for a term of five years after my death. If Barbara should die or remarry or after the term of five years (whichever takes place first), then my executors should sell my real estate. To Barbara Knipple (widow of my son George), eighty four dollars. All my personal property should be sold. The proceeds from my estate should be equally divided into seven shares: to my son, John Knipple, one share; to my son, David Knipple, one share; to my daughter Rachel (wife of George Mathias), one share; to my grandson, John Knipple (of my deceased son George Knipple), one share; one share to the children of my daughter, Polly (now deceased but was the wife of David Becker), to share equally; to my granddaughter, Elizabeth Knipple (wife of William Null and a daughter of my son George now deceased), one share; to my granddaughter, Polly Knipple (now wife of Peter Lightner and the daughter of Barbara Knipple), one share.

Witnesses: Peter Krideler, Jacob Stagner, Peter Stegner
Executor(s): John Henry hopper (friend)
Signed with his signature

Knock, Basil   of Carroll County
April 8, 1845
July 14, 1845
Number 205, Folio 377   July 14, 1845

To my daughter, Elizabeth Wheeler, one dollar which in addition to what I have already given her is considered her full share. To my son, Thomas Knock, one dollar. To my daughter, Mary Duvall, one dollar. To my grandson, Basil Shipley (son of my deceased daughter Julia Ann Shipley), one red heifer, my feather bed and bedding. The sum of five dollars should be equally divided among my grandchildren (all children of my daughter Julia Ann Shipley who is now deceased) when they reach legal age, namely: Lewis Henry Shipley, George Shipley, Rachel Ruth Shipley, Hannah Shipley and Mary Ann Shipley. The residue of my estate should be equally divided between my daughter, Honor Knock, and my son, Ezekiel Knock.

Witnesses: Charles W. Hood, W. W. Warfield, Wesly Day
Executor(s): Ezekiel Knock (son)
Signed by his mark

Koons, Abraham   of Carroll County
                                                    May 12, 1845
                                              December 22, 1851
Number 371, Folio 628   December 22, 1851

To David Martin (my step or half brother of Middleburg), my house and lot where I now dwell in Middleburg, Carroll County. To Thomas Franklin Martin (son of David Martin), my silver watch, bed with bedstead and bedding, and all my other personal property of every description.

Witnesses: James Todd, Hanson T. Clabaugh, Emanuel Warner
Executor(s): Upton Scott
Signed by his mark

Koons, Benjamin   of Carroll County
                                                    April 21, 1851
                                                     May 26, 1851
Number 354, Folio 605   May 26, 1851

To my wife, Eliza Koons, three beds with bedsteads and bedding, one bureau, six split bottom chairs, one cow, two hogs and as much kitchen furniture as she desires (the latter should not exceed the value of twelve dollars). My real estate (including the farm where I currently reside which is situated in Carroll County and contains ninety eight acres) and the residue of my personal estate should be sold. The proceeds of my estate should go to my wife, Eliza Koons.

Witnesses: John Frock, Cyrus K. Mumma, Abraham Hays
Executor(s): Benjamin Shunk
Signed by his mark

Koons, Christiana /   of Carroll County
Christena
                                     May 4, 1844
                                     July 29, 1844
Number 181, Folio 322   July 29, 1844

To my sisters, Phebe Kizer and Catherine Keefer, all my clothes to be shared equally. The rest of my personal property (including my bureau, bed and bed clothes) should be share equally among my brothers and sisters, namely: Benjamin Koons, Samuel Koons, Conrad Koons, Phebe Kizer and Catherine Keefer.

Witnesses: Isaac Dern, James Todd, William A. Warner
Executor(s): Henry Keefer (brother in law)
Signed with her signature

Koons, Jacob   of Carroll County
                                     December 27, 1845
                                     January 12, 1846
Number 215, Folio 397   January 12, 1846

One year after my death, my farm where I now reside should be sold. To my beloved wife, Catherine, sixteen hundred and sixty six dollars which is her right of dower. To my beloved wife, Catherine, one cow and as much of the household and kitchen furniture as she desires. To my son, Ephraim, my two horses called Ball and Fox, my wagon and my field trough. To my daughter, Rebecca, fifty dollars. To my daughters, Sarah and Mary Jane, the sum of twenty five dollars each. Also each of my daughters, Rebecca, Sarah and Mary Jane, should have one cow. My lot and house and my lot now occupied by David Hull should be sold. The residue of my estate should be equally divided among my children, namely: David, Jacob, John, Ephraim, Ann Catherine (wife of David Martin), Rebecca, Sarah and Mary Jane (Ephraim, Rebecca, Sarah and Mary Jane have received more than their siblings as I have already advanced considerable amounts of money to my older sons).

Witnesses: Abraham Buffenton, John White, John B. Boyle
Executor(s): David Koons (son)
Signed with his signature

Koons, Joseph   of Carroll County
                                          January 19, 1846
                                          February 23, 1846
Number 219, Folio 402   February 23, 1846

To my beloved wife, Rebecca Koons, all my lands for the term of twelve years after my death, plus four cows, two heifers, seven hogs, two set of horse gears, carriage, wagon, plough, double shovel plough, harrow, one cutter, stove, all my beds and bed clothes, and all the household and kitchen furniture that she desires and one hundred and twenty bushels of wheat. The residue of my personal property should be sold and the balance to be put at interest for the duration of twelve years. After twelve years after my decease, I desire that my lands by sold and that the proceeds of my estate be equally divided among my beloved wife, Rebecca, and my children, namely: Joel, Julian, George, Eli, Ellen, Edwin, John and Martha.

Witnesses: John White, David Hull, Isaac Dern
Executor(s): Peter Koons (brother)
Signed with his signature

Kopp, Joseph   of Carroll County
                                                April 13, 1849
                                                February 2, 1852
Number 375, Folio 634   February 2, 1852

To my beloved wife, Elizabeth, one bed and bedstead, four
sheets, two coverlets, two quilts, one bureau, one table, six
chairs, carpeting for one room, curtains for one bed, one pot,
one pan, shovel and tongs, one coffee pot, one tea pot, one set
of plates, one set of cups and saucers, six tea spoons, six table
spoons, six knives and forks, two table clothes, one ten plate
stove and pipe, one clock and case, one looking glass, two tin
buckets, one axe, one spade, one rake, one hoe, one coffee mill,
one copper kettle and all the venetian blinds in the house. To
my wife, Elizabeth, the interest on two thousand dollars to be
paid to her on a semi-annual basis provided that she stays my
widow. After my wife's death or marriage, all the personal
property and money that my wife has should be equally divided
among my children. My executors should divide my land in
Carroll County into such lots as to be the most advantageous
for profits. The residue of my personal and real property
should be sold and equally divided among my children, namely:
Catherine (wife of Andrew Kerick), Elizabeth (wife of George
Lippy), the heirs of my beloved son John Kopp, Mary Ann
(wife of Peter Merkle), the heirs of my beloved son Joshua F.
Kopp, Margaret (wife of Samuel B. Fuhrman) and Martha (wife
of Daniel Myers). I loaned my son, John Kopp, two hundred
dollars on March 28, 1835 and as such, that amount should be
deducted from the share going to his heirs (a father's share).
As Sarah Kopp (widow of my deceased son Joshua F. Kopp)
purchased at the sale of her deceased husband both furniture
and personal property amounting to ninety four dollars and
twenty seven cents of which I hold a note as security (dated
January 22, 1847 to Joseph M. Parke who was the administrator
of Joshua F. Kopp's estate), that the said Sarah Kopp should be
released from this debt and the amount should be equally taken
out of the share for the heirs of Joshua F. Kopp. Whereas my

son, Joshua F. Koppe, was (in his lifetime) largely indebted to me and that I do not believe the final settlement of his estate was able to pay the debts I hold against him. As such, I fully settle and absolve this debt and this amount should be equally deducted from the shares of the heirs of my son, Joshua F. Koppe. If any of the children of Joshua F. Koppe files a claim against my estate, then they should receive five dollars in lieu of their share. My wife, Elizabeth, should possess all of my real and personal property until it is sold and she should receive sufficient funds from my estate to maintain such property until it is sold.

Witnesses: Joseph Gardner, John N. Steffey, James Kelly
Executor(s): Jacob Campbell, David C. Frankforter (both my worthy friends)
Signed with his signature

Kroft, Peter   of Carroll County
                                                  August 7, 1847
                                               February 21, 1848
Number 270, Folio 489   February 21, 1848

To my beloved wife, Nancy, the land and dwelling where I currently reside (which was conveyed to me by Godfrey Kneller, the heirs of the late Conrad Kerlinger and Joshua T. Kopp) which adjoins the land of Levi Maxfield, Martin Kroh and William Crumrine. To my wife, Nancy, the seven acres conveyed to me by Godfrey Kneller which adjoins David Sullivan's lot and was once part of the estate of the late Ezekiel Boring. To my wife, Nancy, two hundred and fifty dollars. My leasehold properties in the City of Baltimore and in the town of Manchester should be sold and the proceeds should be put into bonds with the annual interest going to my wife, Nancy. After the death of my wife, I give one thousand dollars to my sisters, Margaret (wife of George Gettier) and Susan (wife of John Lilly), to share equally. To my wife, Nancy, one cow, two hogs, one yankee clock, one sideboard, bureau and wardrobe, two stoves, two tables, two beds with bedsteads and bedding, two looking glasses, six chairs, one washing stand, set silver table spoons, silverware, Britannia ware, as many picture frames and pictures as she may wish, copper kettle, brass kettle, all the carpeting and kitchen furniture as she desires, all the poultry, meat, bacon, lard, flour, and all the grain and vegetables growing. The residue of my personal property should be sold and the proceeds should be equally divided among my two sisters Margaret and Susan.

Witnesses: James Kelly, David C. Frankforter, Levi Maxfield
Executor(s): William Crumrine (friend), John Shultz (friend)
Signed with his signature

Krumrine, John   of Carroll County
                                                  October 4, 1837
                                                  November 27, 1837
Number 18, Folio 32   November 27, 1837

All my clothes should be equally divided among my six sons, namely: John, Peter, George, Henry, Jacob and Daniel Krumrine. The residue of my goods and chattel should be sold and the proceeds by distributed as follows: to my son, George Krumrine, fifty dollars and no more of my estate; to my son, John Krumrine, fifty dollars; to my son, Peter Krumrine, fifty dollars; to my son, Henry Krumrine, fifty dollars; to my son, Jacob Krumrine, fifty dollars; to my son, Daniel Krumrine, fifty dollars; to my daughter, Catherine (widow of Peter Mikesell), fifty dollars but if she should bring a claim against my estate for housekeeping then her share should be equally divided among my other children. The balance of my estate should be divided in ten equal shares to the following: to my son, John Krumrine; to my son, Peter Krumrine; to my son, Henry Krumrine; to my son, Jacob Krumrine; to my son, Daniel Krumrine; to my daughter, Mary (wife of George Reead); my daughter, Christina (widow of John Eadinger); to my daughter, Catherine (widow of Peter Mikesell); to my daughter, Susanna (wife of Anthona Wealk); to my daughter, Elizabeth (wife of Samuel Boulinger).

Witnesses: Jacob Baumgartner, Jonathan Sterner, Philip Wentz, David B. Earhart
Executor(s): Henry Krumine (son), George Reead (son in law)
Signed by his mark

Kuhn, John   of Westminster, Carroll County
                                                    April 21, 1845
                                                    March 16, 1846
Number 221, Folio 405   March 16, 1846

To my son, David, and to my daughter, Mary, my house with contents and lot in Westminster where I currently reside for a term not to extend beyond December 1, 1853. After December 1, 1853 my house with contents and lot should be sold and the proceeds from both my real and personal property should be equally divided among my four children, namely: John, David, Samuel and Mary.

Witnesses: William King, William Crouse, David Zepp
Executor(s): John Kuhn (son)
Signed with his signature

Kump, Frederick   of Frederick County
                                                    April 6, 1836
                                                    October 23, 1843
Number 160, Folio 278   October 23, 1843

My personal property should go to my wife, Elizabeth Kump, for her widowhood and after her death or marriage it should be distributed among my children, namely: Peter Kump, Jacob Kump, John Kump, David Kump, Henry Kump, Elizabeth

Kump, Lidda Kump and Rebecca Kump. My real estate should go to my sons, Peter and Jacob Kump. If my sons, Peter and Jacob, do not desire to keep this land then it should be sold after the death or marriage of my wife and the proceeds should be equally divided among my children, namely: Peter Kump, Jacob Kump, John Kump, David Kump, Henry Kump, Elizabeth Kump, Lidda Kump and Rebecca Kump.

Witnesses: Daniel Bowersox, Adam Stonesifer, David B. Earhart, George Humbert
Executor(s): Peter Kump (son)
Signed by his mark
Signed with his signature

Lambert, John   of Frederick County
                                        May 9, 1829
                                        March 26, 1838
Number 26, Folio 43   March 26, 1838

To my only son, John Lambert, my plantation where I currently reside called "Black Oak Hill" containing about two hundred acres provided that he pays the following legacies, namely: to my eldest daughter, Elizabeth Lambert, one hundred and fifty dollars to be paid after one year of my death and a home in the house while she remains single; to my daughter, Charlotte (wife of Peter Geiger), one hundred and fifty dollars after two years after my death; to my daughter, Eleanor (wife of Joshua Metcalf), one hundred and fifty dollars after three years; to my daughter, Polly (wife of Joshua Hide), one hundred and fifty dollars after four years after my death. My personal property should be sold and the proceeds should be equally divided among my four named daughters.

Witnesses: John Smelser, David Smelser, Jacob Gorsuch
Executor(s): John Lambert (son)
Signed with his signature

Lammott, Henry of Carroll County
November 20, 1844
March 3, 1845
Number 196, Folio 358 March 3, 1845

To my daughter, Rachel Knole, my lands called "Kentucky" and "We Found the Beginning" in Carroll County containing about one hundred and twenty acres. To my son, Samuel Lammott, my clothes, watch, house clock and horses. The residue of my property should be sold and the proceeds equally divided among my children, namely: Catherine Hoover, John Lammott, Elisabeth Burly, Samuel Lammott, Sarah Z. Buchon, Jacob Lammott and Julia Ann Wells. One half of the share for my daughter, Elisabeth Burly, should be equally divided among her three children from her first husband. If any of my children brings a claim against my estate, then they should be disinherited.

Witnesses: William T. Hammond, Henry W. Ports, Jacob S. Murray
Executor(s): Samuel Lammott (son)
Signed with his signature

Lammott, Jacob of Carroll County
December 5, 1848
November 4, 1850
Number 339, Folio 585 November 4, 1850

To my wife, Anna Maria Lammott, my plantation where I currently reside lying in Carroll County being made up of several tracts of land known as "Too Late, "Little Rock", "Fox Range", "Lammotts Delight", "Rome", "Lammotts Middle of the World", "Plymouth", "Stoney Hills" and "Miners Course" which contains all together about two hundred and six acres for her widowhood as well as all my personal property to be used for the maintenance and education of my children. The tract of land conveyed to me by George Everhart (acting as the trustee of Daniel Bollinger) should be sold and the proceeds equally divided among my children as they become of age, namely: Jacob, Catherine, Priscilla, Joseph, Benjamin and Daniel Lammott. If my wife remarries, she shall have (in lieu of the above mentioned legacy) the following: two cows, bed and bedstead, bureau, table, six chairs and kitchen furniture. At the death or marriage of my wife, the residue of my estate should be sold and equally divided among my named children.

Renunciation
Ann Maria Lammott, widow of testator, renounces her executorships and assigns Daniel L. Hoover and Jacob S. Lammott. Witnessed November 11, 1850 by Joshua Lammott.

Witnesses: John Werner, Jacob Bowman, Moses Lammott
Executor(s): Anna Maria Lammott (wife), Jacob Lammott (son)
Signed with his signature

Lampert / Lamperd, Mary   widow of Carroll County
                                             October 25, 1838
                                          November 19, 1838
Number 44, Folio 76   November 19, 1838

To my dearly beloved friend, Ludwick Long, the whole of my estate on condition that he raise my three sons until they reach the age of eighteen at the discretion of the Orphan's Court.

Renunciation
"I Ludwick Long do hereby relinquish and renounce my Estate, right title and Interest of in and to all and every Legacy and bequest made to me or intended...excepting and reserving my right to the Executorship..." Witnessed on November 19, 1838 by Jacob Tener.

Witnesses: James H. Gorsuch, Henry Long, Jacob Trine
Executor(s): Ludwick Long (my truly friend)
Signed by her mark

Lane, Elizabeth   of Carroll County
                                                March 20, 1844
                                             September 2, 1844
Number 185, Folio 331   September 2, 1844

My land lying on the falls near Finksburg which was conveyed
to me by Edward Stocksdale (Edward of John Stocksdale) and
Edward's wife Hellen Stocksdale on April 4, 1832 which
contains about eighty acres should go to my nephew, Solomon
Stocksdale, and my niece, Nelly Haines. I expressly desire and
declare that Nelly Haines' husband, Edward Haines, should
have no title or interest whatsoever to said property either with
or without Nelly's consent. To my niece, Nelly Haines, I give
her all my personal property barring all and any claims or
interference by her husband.

Witnesses: Abraham Lamott, Jacob Caple, William Parrish
Executor(s): Solomon Stocksdale (nephew)
Signed by her mark

Lane, Micajah   of Carroll County
                                             December 31, 1840
                                             February 22, 1841
Number 91, Folio 154   February 22, 1841

To George Bramwell and Charlotte Bennett (Charlotte is the
wife of Charles W. Bennett), the sum of thirty dollars each. My
wife, Elizabeth Lane, shall have the use of all my personal
property during her natural life. After the death of my wife, my
personal property should be sold and the proceeds should go to
Mary Bennett (the daughter of Charles W. Bennett) and
Charlotte Bennett (the wife of Charles W. Bennett).

Witnesses: George Bramwell, Mordecai G. Cockey, Israel Leister
Executor(s): George Bramwell
Signed with his signature

Lawrence, John   of Carroll County
                                       December 2, 1848
                                       January 29, 1849
Number 290, Folio 520   January 29, 1849

All my real and personal property should be sold and the
proceeds should be equally divided among my children,
namely: Henry Lawrence, Isaiah Lawrence and Dennis
Alexander Lawrence.

Witnesses: John W. Wright, William H. Long
Executor(s): Daniel Engel
Signed by his mark

Lawson, Moses   of Carroll County
                                       August 30, 1841
                                       February 2, 1846
Number 218, Folio 401   February 2, 1846

All my real and personal property should be sold and my
beloved wife, Elizabeth, should have a sufficient amount of the
proceeds from my estate to maintain her during her natural life.
After the death of my wife, the residue should be equally
divided among my children, namely: Thomas Lawson, Moses
R. Lawson, Sarah Lawson and Ruth Lawson. My sons, Jacob
and John Lawson, are exempted from inheritance as I have
already given them their shares during my lifetime. My son,
Edward Lawson, is excluded from any inheritance from my
estate as he has "not assisted me in realising any part of my
Estate."

Witnesses: Joseph Gardner, David C. Frankforter, Jacob Kerlinger
Executor(s): Moses R. Lawson (son)
Signed with his signature

Lee, Thomas   of Carroll County
                                     1851 [only year given]
                                     December 1, 1851
Number 368, Folio 622   December 1, 1851

To my wife, Honor Lee, all my personal and real property
during her natural life. After the death of my wife, I give to my
son, Robert Lee, the farm on which I currently reside. After the
death of my wife, all my personal property should go equally to
my eight children, namely: Thomas L. Lee, Robert Lee, Maria
Lee, Maranda Lee, Caroline Adams, Honor Vansant, Charlotte
E. Lee and Elisabeth Lee.

Witnesses: Elias Brown, Jesse Hollingsworth, Nathan Browne
Executor(s): Robert Lee (son)
Signed with his signature

Legore, Jacob   of Carroll County
                                     October 2, 1850
                                     December 16, 1850
Number 341, Folio 588   December 16, 1850

To my wife, Rachel Legore, all my property in Carroll County
called "Durbins Mistake" containing ten acres to her for her
natural life. To my wife, four beds and bedsteads, one bureau
and contents, all my carpeting, mantle clock, cooking stove,
corner cupboard and contents, one small tin plate stove and
pipe, two tables, twelve chairs, two chests and contents, one
copper kettle, two iron kettles, one spinning wheel, one wool
wheel, one cow and four hogs which should all be for her use
during her natural life. The residue of my personal and real
property should be sold and the proceeds should go to my wife,
Rachel. After the death of my wife, all my land and remaining
personal property should be sold and the proceeds equally
divided among my children, namely: Eliza Legore, Susan Hahn
(wife of Joseph E. Hahn), John Legore, Ezra Legore, Juliann
Davidson (wife of James Davidson), Rebecca Halverstadt (wife

of Eli Halverstadt), William H. Legore, Ellen Yingling (wife of William H. Yingling), Rachel Legore, Jacob Legore, Jesse U. Legore and Jesse Albert Hann (son of my deceased daughter Maria).

Witnesses: Benjamin Shunk, Jacob Erb, Christopher Erb
Executor(s): Joseph E. Hahn (son in law)
Signed with his signature

Leister, Conrad   of Carroll County
                                      March 2, 1844
                                    March 11, 1844
Number 170, Folio 300   March 11, 1844

To my wife, Magdalena Leister, two cows, one heifer, two hogs, one mare, two bedsteads with bed and bedding, one ten plate stove and pipe, one seven plate stove and pipe, two tables, four chairs, one clock and case, one chest, one bureau, my bed clothing, all my flax and tow linens, all flax, one kitchen cupboard, three tubs, one churn and stand, one spinning wheel, side saddle and bridle, one copper kettle, three iron pots, any kitchen or household furniture as she deems necessary, all my hay and straw, three cow chains, two hay forks, one dung fork, one dung hook, one plough, one winnowing mill, one set of horse gears, all the boards and shingles on the place, all my wheat, rye, corn, oats and potatoes and all my crop growing in the ground. To my wife, Magdalena Leister, all my land situate in Carroll County on the water of Silver Run being part of several tracts of land called "Ohio", "Spillmans Discovery", "Christians Discovery" and "Barbados" for her life. The residue of my personal property should be sold and after a pair of tombstones have been purchased and erected at the graves for myself and my wife, the proceeds should be distributed as follows: to my wife, Magdalena Lesiter, one hundred and fifty dollars; to Elizabeth Tayman, ten dollars; to Eliza Collans (wife of Mathias Collans), ten dollars; to my son, Jacob Leister, one fourth of the residue; to my daughter, Catherine (wife of Jacob Sell), one fourth of the residue; to my daughter, Elizabeth (wife of Jacob Feeser), one forth of the residue; to the children of my deceased son John Leister (Joseph, Levi, John, William and Maria Leister), one fourth of the residue with an additional fifty dollars to be equally divided among them given to them at the age of twenty one. After the death of my wife my personal and real estate belonging to her at the time of her death should be sold and the proceeds should be distributed in four equal shares as follows: to my son Jacob Leister, to my daughter Catherine Sell, to my daughter Elizabeth Fesser and to the children of my deceased son John Leister.

Witnesses: Daniel Yeiser (senior), Daniel Leess, Peter Kump
Executor(s): Jacob Leister (son), David B. Earhart (trusty friend)
Signed with his signature

Leister, Daniel   of Carroll County
                                                July 12, 1846
                                                August 24, 1846
Number 236, Folio 433   August 24, 1846

To my daughter, Rachel Mitten (wife of Miles Mitten), five hundred and fifty dollars to be paid annually in fifty dollar increments. To my daughter, Hannah Rees (wife of Andrew Reese), five hundred and fifty dollars to be paid annually in fifty dollar increments. As I have advanced money to my daughter, Mary Yingling (now deceased), her heirs are excluded from any claim on interest in my estate. The residue of my real and personal property after debts and legacies should go to my son, Henry Leister.

Witnesses: Michael Sullivan, Joshua Plowman, John Trine
Executor(s): Henry Leister (son)
Signed with his signature

Levely / Lovely, Sophia   of Carroll County

September 11, 1845

September 29, 1845

Number 211, Folio 389   September 29, 1845

To Sabina Catherine Weiher (a young woman that lives with me), fifty dollars, one bed with bedstead, bed furniture and one bureau. The residue of my real and personal estate should be divided among my three sisters, namely: Susan B. Cotton, Catherine Little and Elizabeth Hall.

Witnesses: Nicholas Dorsey, Joshua Lee, Joshua Lee (junior)
Executor(s): Catherine Little (sister)
Signed with her signature

Linaweaver, George   of Carroll County

March 23, 1844

May 6, 1844

Number 176, Folio 312   May 6, 1844

To my beloved wife, Ruth Linaweaver, one bed and bedstead, two iron pots, three chairs, all the queens ware and spoons. My executors should sell the remainder of my personal and real property and from the proceeds my wife should have one third. The residue should be divided into six equal parts and distributed as follows: one share to the children of my deceased son Peter Linaweaver (George, Sarah, Cecelia, Peter and Noah) which should be divided equally among them; one share to my daughter Sophia (wife of Henry Reagel); one share to my daughter Emily; one share to my son John; one share to my daughter Seranda; one share to my son Lewis Henry.

Witnesses: Jacob Kerlinger, John Shultz, Michael Gettier
Executor(s): Henry Reagal (son in law)
Signed by his mark and signature

Linderman, John   of Carroll County

January 6, 1844

January 22, 1844

Number 165, Folio 290   January 29, 1844

All my real estate should go to my daughters, Rebecca and Liza Linderman, for their natural life. After the death of my daughters, my real estate should go to my son, John Linderman. My personal estate should go to my beloved wife, Elizabeth Linderman.

Renunciation

"I Jacob Miksell of Carroll County...do refuse to act as executor...and do therefore renounce all my right title and claims...may be granted to Jacob L. Yost who is a relation of said deceased." Witnessed February 3, 1844 by Adam Fridinger.

Witnesses: Jacob Sterner, Jacob Lippy, James Grace
Executor(s): Jacob Mikesell
Signed by his mark

Logue, Richard   of Carroll County

May 30, 1840

August 7, 1840

Number 82, Folio 144   September 7, 1840

To my beloved wife, Mary Logue, my land called "Caladonia" which adjoins the land of George Blizzard to have for her natural life. After the death of my wife, my land should be sold and the proceeds should be equally divided among my children [not named].

Witnesses: Jesse Manning, George Blizzard, Elijah Criswell
Executor(s): Joshua Logue (son), William Logue (son)
Signed by his mark

Loveall, Luther   of Baltimore County

July 5, 1813

November 7, 1842

Number 139, Folio 239   November 7, 1842

My property that in Baltimore County should go to my beloved wife, Rebecca Loveall, during her life. To my beloved son, Enoch Loveall, all my property in Baltimore County after the death of my wife. To my daughter, Rachel Sence, fifty dollars to be paid by my son, Enoch, after one year of my wife's death. To my daughter, Nancy Weekely, sixty dollars to be paid by my son, Enoch, two years after my wife's death. To my daughter, Rachel Sence, fifty dollars to be paid by my son, Enoch, three years after my wife's death. To my daughter, Sarah James, one dollar. The land that I own in Harrison County, Virginia on Finks Fork which was conveyed to me by James Arnold, should be equally divided among my children, namely: Solomon Loveall, Stephen Loveall and my daughter Charity.

Witnesses: George Ebaugh, Jacob Trine, Conrod Terug
Executor(s): Enoch Loveall (son)
Signed with his signature

Loveall, Susannah   of Baltimore County

November 21, 1820

December 24, 1838

Number 45, Folio 78   January 14, 1839

To my daughter, Catherine Loveall, one bed with bedstead, bedding and furniture. The residue of my property should be sold and the proceeds equally divided among my children, namely: John Evens, William Carter and Catherine Loveall.

Witnesses: George Ebaugh, Henry Ebaugh (of George), John Rinehart
Executor(s): John Evens (son)
Signed by her mark

Lucas, Margaret   of Carroll County
                                        August 28, 1841
                                        September 9, 1841
Number 115, Folio 188   September 9, 1841

To my sister, Mary Harpes, one cow and my negro boy called
George to serve her for a term of three years after my death.
One hundred dollars to Perrygreen Lucas (son of my brother
Robert Lucas), to be kept by Amon Shipley until Perrygreen
arrives at lawful age. To Margaret Ann Shipley (daughter of
Amon Shipley), five dollars. My real estate should be equally
divided among my brothers, Bassel Lucas and Robert Lucas.

Witnesses: James Parish, Amon Shipley, Lovelace Gardner
Executor(s): Bassil Lucas (brother), Robert Lucas (brother)
Signed by her mark

Magee, Aquila   of Carroll County
                                        February 3, 1852
                                        February 9, 1852
Number 376, Folio 637   February 9, 1852

To my eldest son, Augustus, all my property where he currently
resides which was conveyed to me by Joseph and William
Stansbury (except that part which has been since divided off by
James Blizzard). I give to my beloved wife, Mary Magee, all
my personal property and after her death it should be equally
divided between Margaret Blizzard and my six remaining
children [not named]. My land should not be sold until my
youngest child has arrived at the age of twenty one, after which
time it should be sold and equally divided amongst my heirs
herein mentioned. I appoint John H. Chew as guardian of my
minor children, namely: Margaretta, Mary Ann and Thomas.

Witnesses: John H. Chew, Kinzy Taylor, Lewis Lamborn
Executor(s): John H. Chew
Signed with his signature

Manche / Menche, John   of Baltimore County
                              January 30, 1836
                              October 9, 1837
Number 16, Folio 29   October 9, 1837

My land in Baltimore County containing two hundred and forty acres should be sold and the proceeds should be distributed as follows: to my beloved wife, Anna Mary, twelve hundred dollars; to my son, David, two hundred dollars; to my son, Samuel, two hundred dollars; the remainder should be equally divided among my five children (Jacob, David, Samuel, Daniel and Catherine). To my wife, Anna Mary, two milk cows, four sheep, four hogs, two beds and bedsteads, one stove, one bureau, one table, one iron kettle, one copper kettle, as much kitchen furniture as she desires, all my books and all the flour and meal in the house at my death. The residue of my personal estate should be sold and the proceeds should be equally divided among my five named children.

Renunciation
Jacob Manche and Samuel Manche refuse to act as administrators. Witnessed on October 7, 1837 by Jacob Kerlinger.

Witnesses: Peter Sawble, Michael Gettier, Jacob Kerlinger
Executor(s): Jacob Menche (son), David Menche (son), Samuel Menche (son)
Signed with his signature

Manche, Julian   of Carroll County
                              December 21, 1841
                              January 24, 1842
Number 118, Folio 195   January 24, 1842

To Joseph Sauble, son of Peter Sauble (Peter Sauble who is now deceased), fifty dollars. To George Sauble (son of Peter Sauble now deceased), thirty dollars. To Amos Sauble (son of

Peter Sauble now deceased), twenty dollars. To John Harbst, the residue of my estate.

Witnesses: James Marshall, Michael Gettier, Jacob Kerlinger
Executor(s): Jacob Ditzler
Signed by her mark

Manning, Richard   of Carroll County
                                         February 13, 1838
                                         February 19, 1838
Number 24, Folio 41   February 19, 1838

To my beloved wife, Nancy Manning, all of my personal and real estate.

Witnesses: William Jameson, David Tawney, Peter Flater
Executor(s): Nancy Manning (wife)
Signed by his mark

Manning, Thomas   of Carroll County
                                         February 27, 1849
                                              March 27, 1849
Number 296, Folio 527   March 27, 1849

The Nuncupative will of Thomas Manning (taken at the Mouls Hotel in Westminster)

After all the money owed to me is received and my debts paid, the residue of my estate should go to my youngest sister, Martha. If the money coming to me is not sufficient to pay my debts and funeral expense then my clothing should be sold (witnessed that he gave all of his tailoring including his Mexican uniform, spear and body belt to his business partner, Mr. Charles Henneman). He requested that if not sold that his clothing should go to his brother in law, Mr. Thomas Crogen, of Baltimore if possible.

Josiah T. H. Bringman testified that he did not believe that the estate of said Thomas Manning would be greater than the amount of two hundred dollars (being the same Thomas Manning that died on the evening of February 28, 1849).

Witnesses: Henry Monaghan, Mrs. Lydia Moul
Executor(s): not named
Signed [given orally]

Manro, Catherine   of Carroll County
                                                April 2, 1837
                                        February 26, 1838
Number 25, Folio 42   February 26, 1838

To my daughter, Hellena Harden, one bureau, one dining table and my family Bible. To my son, Squire Manro, one feather bed and bedding. To my son, Nathan Manro, a sufficient amount of money to purchase head and footstones for the graves of my late husband and my late son John Manro. To my son, David Manro, one bed and bedding. To my granddaughter, Catherine Harden, one feather bed. To my son, Thomas Manro, the residue of my estate with the exception of my negro man called Charles as he should have his freedom after my death.

Witnesses: Joshua C. Gist, Joseph Harden, Jacob Hiltabridel
Executor(s): Nathan Manro (son)
Signed with her signature

Marker, Susannah   of Carroll County
                                        February 1, 1849
                                            March 12, 1849
Number 293, Folio 523   March 12, 1849

To Rachel Wentz, my corner cupboard. To Susannah Wentz, my bed and sufficient bedding, two iron pots, frying pan and iron kettle. To Rebecca Byers (wife of Peter Byers), my high post bedstead and sufficient bedding. To Susannah Myers (wife of John Myers), my flax heckles. The residue of my bedding and clothes should be equally divided among Rachel Wentz and Rebecca Myers. I ask that my executors place a head and footstone at my grave. To John Marker, one hundred dollars. To Valentine Wentz, fifty dollars. To Susannah Wentz, ten dollars. To Susanna Myers (wife of John Myers), five dollars. To Rebecca Royer (wife of Emanuel Royer), ten dollars. To Sarah Warner (daughter of John Warner), five dollars. To Margaret Hahn (widow of Jacob Hahn), ten dollars. To Savilla Young (daughter of Jacob Young), five dollars. To Nancy Fisher, twenty dollars. The residue of my estate should be equally divided among John Marker, Valentine Wentz and Peter Byers.

Witnesses: Benjamin Shunk, David Wantz
Executor(s): John Marker
Signed by her mark

Mathias, Rachel   of Carroll County
                                             November 30, 1850
                                             February 3, 1851
Number 347, Folio 594   February 3, 1851

To my daughters, Maria and Eliza Mathias, each one chest painted red including contents of quilts, coverlets, sheets and linens. The residue of my estate should be sold and the proceeds divided as follows: my son, Elias H. Mathias, is to have as much of my estate as to make him equal with his other siblings; to my daughter, Maria, one share; to my daughter, Eliza, one share: to my son, Elias, one share. My estate should be put at interest until my children arrive at legal age.

Witnesses: Perry Matthias, J. Henry Hoppe
Executor(s): David Knipple (brother)
Signed by her mark

Matthias, George   of Carroll County
                                            December 1, 1841
                                                April 4, 1842
Number 128, Folio 213   April 4, 1842

To my daughter, Rachel Matthias, a chest, bed and bedstead, bureau, six Windsor chairs, large iron kettle, case of drawers, one pair of flat irons, looking glass, one small bake tray and one hundred and fifty dollars. To my son, George Matthias, my broad triad wagon, wagon body and cover, horse stretcher with chains and one hundred and fifty dollars in lieu of his labor done for me. The residue of my personal and real property including my home and wood lot adjoining George Bixler should be sold and the proceeds distributed in equal shares as follows: to my son, David Matthias, a share; to my son, Jacob Mathias, a share; to my son, George Mathias (junior), a share; to my daughter, Catherine (wife of Peter Brian), a share; to my daughter, Sally (wife of John Sawyer), a share; to my daughter in law, Polly (widow of my son John Matthias) and her two children (Perry Matthias and Eliza who is now wife of Emanuel Spangler), a share; to my daughter, Rachel Mathias, a share; to my daughter, Elizabeth (wife of Henry Baumgartner now divorced by an act of the General Assembly of Maryland in 1836), a share; to the children of my daughter Elizabeth Baumgartner (Samuel, Joshua, Lewis and Amanda), five dollars each as they come of lawful age.

Witnesses: Jacob Wine, Peter Panebaker, J. Henry Hoppe
Executor(s): Jacob Mathias (son)
Signed with his signature

Matthias, George W.   of Carroll County
                                                May 23, 1846
                                                June 22, 1846
Number 228, Folio 418   June 22, 1846

My executor should repair (with the cost coming out of my

estate) the building known as the Old House in a sufficient enough manner for my wife, Rachel, to occupy. My wife is to have the privilege of using the kitchen in the brick house, half of the garden, spring house and drying house. I give to my beloved wife, Rachel, two bedsteads and bedding, four chairs, one table, one corner cupboard, one chest, one clothing cupboard cooking stove, as much kitchen furniture as she desires, three cows, three sheep, three hogs, my stock of poultry, spinning wheel and cut reel. After her death, the personal property belonging to her should be sold and the proceeds should be equally divided among my children from oldest to youngest. To my eldest son, Samuel Mathias, the farm where I currently reside known as the home farm which was previously owned by George Matthias (senior) and was conveyed to me by Jacob Mathias (executor of George Mathias the senior now deceased). The wood lot and land conveyed to me by George Everhart (which is divided by a shale line created between the chestnut pole near the land of Abraham Bixler's fence and David Shaffer's fulling mill) containing two hundred and fifty acres, should go to my son Samuel Mathias for the sum of five thousand dollars to be paid out over twelve years without interest. From said lands my son, Samuel, should give my wife the following: fifty bushels of corn, ten bushels of oats and twenty bushels of wheat for each year of her life. My son, Samuel, should keep the cattle and livestock for my wife, grow flax on one eighth of an acre for my wife and provide my wife with one eighth of an acre for growing potatoes. The lot containing forty two acres conveyed to me by J. Henry Hoppe (as executor of Henry Mathias) to my son Samuel for the rate of twenty dollars per acre. To my son, Samuel, my colored woman called Sally for the sum of two hundred and fifty dollars. If my son does not wish to purchase this land and properties then they should be sold. To my son, Samuel, three horses with their gears, two cows, three sheep, any wagon he chooses out of the three that I own, one plough, one harrow, one shovel plough, one stretcher, one double tree, two single trees, two breast chains, two pair of short traces and one three pronged fork. To my sister, Rachel Matthias, the privilege of having one room upstairs in the room that she currently occupies. The crops growing at the time of my death, I order my son, Samuel, to reap and thrash and convert to cash with the proceeds going to pay my debts and I give to my son, Samuel, all my hay and straw as payment for his effort. The residue of my personal property (including my colored girl called Caroline) and any real estate that my son, Samuel, does not wish to purchase should be sold and the proceeds should be divided with one third going to my wife and the residue to be equally divided among my seven children [not named].

Witnesses: Phillip H. L. Myers, John Weaver, Henry Warehime
Executor(s): Samuel Mathias (son)
Signed with his signature

Matthias, Rachel   of Carroll County
                                                        April 4, 1847
                                                        May 24, 1847
Number 252, Folio 461   May 24, 1847

To Samuel Mathias, my corner cupboard. To Priscilla Mathias and Catherine Mathias (daughters of my deceased brother George Mathias), twenty five dollars. To Samuel Mathias, twenty five dollars for services rendered to me during my illness. To Perry Mathias (son of my deceased brother John), ten dollars. To Eliza Mathias (daughter of my deceased brother George), ten dollars. "All my wearing apparel, to be equally divided among my Brothers and Sisters in seven equal shares as follows. To wit, To Jacob, David, Elizabeth, Sally, Catherine, to the children of my deceased Brother John, Perry and Eliza, to the children of my deceased brother George, Samuel, Mary Ann, Priscilla, Catherine, Maria, Eliza and Elias." The residue of my estate should be sold and divided among seven equal shares and distributed to my brother and sisters and the children of my deceased brothers as follows: Jacob Mathias, David Mathias, Sally (wife of John Lawyer), Catherine (wife of Peter Brian), Elizabeth Baumgartner (divorced of Henry Baumgartner), Perry Mathias, Eliza (wife of Emanuel Spangler), one full share to the children of my deceased brother John, one equal share to the children of my deceased brother George (Samuel, Mary Ann wife of David Bachman, Priscilla, Catherine, Maria, Eliza and Elias). I ask that my executors purchase a tombstone and erect it at my grave.

Witnesses: Henry Warehime, John Weaver, J. Henry Hoppe
Executor(s): Samuel Matthias
Signed with her signature

McAlister, John   of Taney Town, Carroll County
                                                                    February 27, 1841
                                                                         April 4, 1848
Number 277, Folio 501   April 4, 1848

To my loving wife [not named] and to my son, James, all my household and kitchen furniture. To my wife, three cows, two sheep, the use of the bay horse and carriage, the interest of two hundred dollars during her life which is to be paid out of the farm where I currently reside which adjoins the lands of the Koons heirs, David Mearing and the heirs of John Creglow and contains one hundred and forty acres. To my wife, one third of the income from my two farms. To my son, James, my farm where I currently reside and the small farm on which George Flegle now resides for the sum of twelve dollars per acre. If my son, James, does not purchase the latter then it should be sold and the proceeds should be divided equally among my children, namely: John W. Alexander, Margaret and Elizabeth. The balance of my estate should go to my son, James.

Witnesses: John Jones, George Fliegle, Samuel Bowers
Executor(s): Samuel McAlister (son)
Signed with his signature

McHanney, Solomon   of Baltimore County
                                              October 30, 1831
                                              June 5, 1837
Number 8, Folio 11   June 5, 1837

To my beloved wife, Juliana McHanney, my house and lot in Hampstead where I currently reside, the two lots in Manchester, the farm containing one hundred and twenty acres in Baltimore County near Wampler's Paper Mill and all my personal property. If my wife remarries, then my real and personal property should be sold and after her third, the residue should be divided equally among my children [not named].

Witnesses: John Fowble (of Jacob), Joshua Lifton, Andrew C. Fowble
Executor(s): Juliana McHanney (wife)
Signed with his signature

McMasters, Sarah   of Harford County
                                              October 8, 1845
                                         January 31, 1848
Number 268, Folio 487   January 31, 1848

To my niece, Eleanor Netts, fifty dollars. To my niece, Sarah Orrick, one hundred dollars and all my clothes. To Caroline Fasnacht (daughter of my niece Sarah Orrick), fifty dollars. To my niece, Mary Ann Hicks, fifty dollars. To Mary Ann Kean (daughter of John and Martha Kean), one hundred dollars and my bed, bedstead and bedding excluding my white counterpane which should go to Caroline Fasnacht. To Sarah Jane Kean (daughter of John and Martha Kean), one hundred dollars. To John Henry Kean (son of John and Martha Kean), one hundred dollars. To my niece, Sarah Orrick, the rest of my property.

Witnesses: James B. Alderson, Jesse B. Robinson, Edward Guyton
Executor(s): John Kean (friend)
Signed by her mark

Merkel, John

Number 273, Folio 494

of Manheim Township, York
County, Pennsylvania
March 19, 1847
March 20, 1848
March 20, 1848

To John Merkle (third son of my brother Henry), my large
family chest and five dollars. To John Merkle (eldest son of
my brother Michael), my new rifle. My clothes should be
equally divided among my brothers: Adam, Jacob and Michael
Merkle. The rest of my estate should go to my wife, Catherine.

Witnesses: Anthony Schmidt, Jacob Bricker
Executor(s): Catherine Merkle (wife)
Signed with his signature

Miller, David

Number 246, Folio 452

of Carroll County
January 3, 1847
March 1, 1847
March 1, 1847

To my dear wife, two hundred and forty dollars. To my wife,
twelve pounds worm seed oil, two head of cattle, bed and
bedstead, stove, bureau and six chairs.

Witnesses: George W. Gorsuch, John W. Gorsuch, William
Buckingam
Executor(s): Mr. Thomas Miller, Amelia Miller (wife)
Signed with his signature

Miller, Michael

Number 192, Folio 346

of Carroll County
December 23, 1844
January 20, 1845
January 20, 1845

To my beloved wife, Anna Maria, one bed with bedstead. To
my son, Jacob Miller, my two wagons, three horses and gear,

two cows, all the grain in the granary, barn and in the ground. The residue of my personal property should be sold. The plantation where I currently reside (situate in Carroll County which contains one hundred and fifty acres and was conveyed to me by John Lemmon), should go to my son, Jacob Miller, provided that he provides my wife, Anna Mary, with "sufficient meat drink and clothing, such as a woman may require and to supply her with a physician when she may require, and to supply her with all the comfort in life she may reasonably want." After the death of my wife, my son Jacob "shall decently bury her in a manner and form agreeing with the principals of a Christian." The residue of my personal estate should be divided equally (I ask that my executors make the legacies for the following people equal to one another and equal to my other legatees as I have already advanced some of them money in my lifetime) among the following children, namely: Jacob Bricker (married to my daughter Christiana), Henry Hoffocker (married to my daughter Elisabeth), the heirs of my son John Miller (now deceased), George Borns (married to my daughter Lydia). The following individuals should not participate in any of the proceeds from my estate as they have already received real estate from me, namely: my son Henry Miller, my son in law John Wilhelm (married to my daughter Catherine) and my son in law Peter Cramer (married to my daughter Mary).

Renunciation
Jacob Bricker refuses to act as executor and requests that the role should be granted fully to Jacob Miller, the other named executor in the will of Michael Miller. Witnessed January 20, 1845 by Jacob Kerlinger.

Witnesses: Thomas Sater, George Schuman
Executor(s): Jacob Miller (son), Jacob Bricker (son in law)
Signed by his mark

Mintzer, Michael   of Carroll County
                                              April 17, 1848
                                           January 15, 1849
Number 289, Folio 518   January 15, 1849

All my personal property and the farm where I currently reside
called "Resurvey on Mackeys Choice" containing two hundred
acres should be sold. The proceeds from my estate should be
distributed as follows: to my children that have already been
advanced money and left home (Polly, George, Simon and
Rachel), one hundred dollars; to my children still at home
(Amos, Catherine and Sarah), one hundred and fifty dollars.
Whereas I have loaned money to my son George and my son in
law, Jacob Frock (husband of my daughter Rachel), these
amounts should be deducted from their shares. The residue of
my estate should be equally divided among my named children.

Witnesses: Samuel Diffendal, George Mearing, Joseph Gernand
Executor(s): John B. Boyle (friend)
Signed with his signature

Mintzer, Sarah   of Carroll County
                                          February 3, 1850
                                            March 18, 1850
Number 322, Folio 564   March 18, 1850

To my brother, Amos Mintzer, one hundred dollars and my
cow. To my sister, Catherine Mintzer, one hundred dollars, one
feather bed and all my bedding provided that she give, Sarah
Frock, some of the bedding. To my sister, Mary Diffendall, the
bed and bedding that I currently use. The balance of my estate
should be equally divided among my siblings, namely: Amos,
Simon, George, Mary, Catherine and Rachel.

Witnesses: George Mearing, Joseph Gernand
Executor(s): Amos Mintzer (brother)
Signed by her mark

Mock, Magdalene   of Taneytown, Carroll County
February 22, 1852
March 1, 1852
Number 380, Folio 642   March 1, 1852

All of my estate should be sold. To Jacob Gouger, the interest of four hundred dollars which should be placed in the hands of Samuel Crouse and said Jacob Grouger should have access to the principal only in necessity or for the purchase of a house. To Jacob Grouger, three hundred dollars. To my niece, Susanna Bishop, one hundred dollars. To my niece, Mary Bishop, one hundred dollars. To my niece, Sarah Bishop, one hundred dollars. To Providence Hawn, one hundred dollars.

Witnesses: Philip Hann, Philip W. Hann, Joseph Shaner
Executor(s): Samuel Crouse
Signed by her mark

Motter, George   of Carroll County
March 13, 1850
April 15, 1850
Number 325, Folio 566   April 15, 1850

My clothes should be equally divided between my sons, namely: William, John and Washington Motter. To my daughter, Elizabeth (wife of John Zeimmer), one bed, bedstead and bedding, two chests, chair and all my bed clothing. To my son, Jacob Molter, ten dollars provided that he returns to the collect the money within ten years after my death. The residue of my estate should be sold and the proceeds equally divided as follows: to my son, William Motter; to my son, John Motter; to my son, Washington Motter; to my daughter, Elizabeth (wife of John Zeimmer); to my daughter, Sarah (wife of John Leese).

Witnesses: Isaac Biehl, Jacob Crawford, David B. Earhart
Executor(s): William Motter (son), John Motter (son)
Signed by his mark

Murray, Jabez   of Carroll County
                                                       May 3, 1845
                                                October 25, 1847
Number 263, Folio 479   October 25, 1847

To my beloved wife, Sarah Murray, all my real and personal
property for her life with the exception of reserving a room in
my home for my daughter, Elizabeth Murray. After the death
of my wife, my estate should be divided among my five
children, namely: Elizabeth, Joshua, Kesiah, Sarah and Maria.

Witnesses: Amon Richards, Stephen Oursler, Elias Brothers
Executor(s): Joshua Murray (son)
Signed with his signature

Murray, Thomas B.   of Carroll County
                                                      March 7, 1850
                                                     June 10, 1850
Number 328, Folio 570   June 10, 1850

To my wife, Catherine Ann, the farm where I currently reside in
Carroll County known by the name of "Merrymans Meadow"
containing fifty acres, also my land called "Sportsman Hall" in
Carroll County containing thirty acres, also my land called
"Stophels Choice" containing two acres, also the land that was
conveyed to me by John W. Murray in Carroll County
containing fifteen acres, and the residue of my personal
property during her widowhood. If my wife should remarry
then she should have no more than one third of my estate.
After the death or marriage of my wife, the residue should be
equally divided among my legal heirs [not named].

Witnesses: Caleb Bishop, Daniel Null, Joseph Ebaugh
Executor(s): Catherine Ann Murray (my dear wife)
Signed with his signature

Myers, Elizabeth   of Carroll County

June 1, 1846

January 5, 1852

Number 372, Folio 629   January 5, 1852

To David Myers of Carroll County, the dwelling house where I currently reside, table, two chairs, butter churn, tubs, barrels, wood axe, four flour bags, three baskets, spinning wheel, cut reel, fire shovel and fire tong. To Eliza Myers (daughter of Isaac Myers of Carroll County), twenty five dollars and three of my best suits. To David Myers, the residue of my estate.

Witnesses: George Bowers, Jacob Reinecker, Christian Yingling (of Jacob)
Executor(s): David Myers
Signed by her mark

Myers, Samuel W.   of Carroll County

March 17, 1843

May 15, 1843

Number 153, Folio 265   May 15, 1843

To my beloved wife, Anna, all my real and personal property provided she remains my widow. If my wife remarries, then I request that my executors take charge of all my property and give to my wife the following: one cow, one bed with bedstead and bedding, six chairs and all the kitchen furniture that she desires. If my wife remains a widow, then after her death I ask that my executors sell all my personal and real property and the proceeds should be divided among my children in equal shares, namely: my son Phillip, my daughter Maria Ellenora Rissiah, my son Samuel, my daughters Susan Catherine and Mary Ann, my son John Thomas (from the oldest to youngest).

Witnesses: George Matthias, Jacob Stonesifer, John Weaver
Executor(s): Phillip Myers (my eldest son)
Signed with his signature

Nace, Peter (the elder)   of Baltimore County
                                     November 13, 1827
                                        April 17, 1837
Number 4, Folio 5   April 17, 1837

To my beloved wife, Tellatha Nace, all my estate during her natural lifetime. After my wife's death, I ask that my executors sell my estate and then convey to my son, George Nace, "one hundred dollars of the United States". The residue of my estate should be divided into ten equal parts (less any notes due to me) to the following: to my daughter, Mary Backman (wife of Henry Backman); to my daughter, Catherine Shade (widow of John Shade); to my daughter, Elizabeth Vaughn (wife of Christopher Vaughn); to my son, John Nace; to my Jacob Nace; to my daughter Ruth Lineweaver (wife of George Lineweaver); to my son, George Nace; to my daughter, Sarah Matter (wife of George Matter); to my son, Peter Nace; to my daughter, Margaret Gittier (wife of Jacob Gittier).

Witnesses: J. Adams Frankfoler, David Houck, Christian Kelbaugh, Jr.
Executor(s): Peter Nace (son)
Signed with his signature

Neff, Conrad   of Belmont County, Ohio
(copy of will)   February 22, 1843
                                        August 2, 1847
Number 254, Folio 464   August 2, 1847

To my wife, Elizabeth Neff, all that part of my home that lays east of Kings run for her support during her life and that she should have all the cattle and furniture and all that she deems fit for her living and that her sister, Sarah Feely, should live out of the same provided that she stays single. After my wife's death, my estate shall be sold and from the proceeds each of my daughters should receive five hundred dollars, namely: Susan, Polly, Ann and that they should all be equally given an "outfit as nigh equal to Hannah." To my sons who are now unmarried, "I will and bequeath an outfit as nigh equal to the outfit which the married ones have received." The balance of my property (land excepted) should be equally divided between my nine sons and four daughters, namely: Henry, Thomas, John, George, Peter, Conrad, William, Benjamin, Jacob, Hannah, Susan, Polly and Ann. To my son, Henry Neff, one hundred seventeen acres (northwest quarter section 28, southwest quarter section 29, township 4, range 3, see plat No. 3). To my son, Thomas Neff, eighty four acres (see plat No. 4). To my son, John Neff, one hundred fourteen acres (see plat No. 2). To my son, George Neff, one hundred twenty nine acres (part of the southwest quarter of section 29, township 4, and range 3). To my son, Peter Neff, eighty two acres (east half of the north quarter of section 29, township 4, range 3). To my son, Conrad Neff, eighty one acres (east half of the southeast quarter of section 23, township 4, range 3) and one hundred dollars. To my son, Benjamin Neff, forty acres (half of the northwest quarter of section 22, township 4, range 3 and also the east half of the southeast quarter of section 28, range 3) and four hundred dollars. To my sons, William and Jacob Neff, the north half of the ridge where John Roder lived.

Witnesses: William C. Kirker, Joseph W. Mulvaney
Executor(s): John Neff (son), Peter Neff (son)
Signed with his signature

Neff, George   of Belmont County, Ohio
(copy of will)   June 24, 1837
                                            March 30, 1846
Number 222, Folio 406   March 30, 1846

To my beloved wife, Margaret, the part of my farm where she currently resides which lies south of the creek to be for her use during her natural lifetime. To my wife all my household goods, kitchen furniture, one horse and two cows. To my son,

George, all my land that lies north of the creek, one horse, harness and bridle, plough and milk cow. To my son, Peter, all my land south of the creek after the decease of my wife, one horse, bridle, harness, plough and cow. To my daughters, Hannah and Elizabeth, one thousand dollars each. The residue of my estate to my beloved wife, Margaret, and should be divided equally among my children at her decease, namely: Jacob, Andrew, Henry, George, Peter, Hannah and Elizabeth.

Witnesses: Thomas DeBertrand, William Workman
Executor(s): not named (Andrew & George Neff appointed)
Signed with his signature

Neff, Hannah   of Carroll County
                                          December 17, 1838
                                          October 18, 1839
Number 64, Folio 119   October 21, 1839

To my sister, Susan Neff, my estate. After the death of my sister, my estate should be sold and proceeds divided according to the law (excluding George Trumbo and William Durbin).

Witnesses: Nathaniel H. Thayer, Levi Shreeve, Jacob Reese
Executor(s): John Nicodemus
Signed with her signature

Neff, Susanna   of Carroll County
                                          December 26, 1839
                                          February 26, 1840
Number 70, Folio 127   February 26, 1840

My property should be sold and proceeds divided according to the law (William Durbin should not benefit from my estate).

Witnesses: John Baugh, Philip Nicodemus, Jacob Nicodemus
Executor(s): John Nicodemus (nephew)
Signed by her mark

Null, Abraham   of Carroll County
                                      December 7, 1842
                                      March 4, 1850
Number 321, Folio 562   March 4, 1850

To my dear beloved wife, Catherine Null, all my personal property that she deems necessary and the residue should be sold and the proceeds divided between my wife, Catherine Null, and my son, Samuel Null. To my wife, Catherine Null, the plantation where I currently reside containing one hundred and fifty acres during her natural lifetime. After the death of my wife, my plantation should go to my son, Samuel Null. To my son, Samuel Null, all my real estate in Carroll County and in Frederick County except for the plantation that I have bequeathed to my wife.

Witnesses: William Cornell, Henry Hess, John Hess, John Cownover, William Cornell
Executor(s): Samuel Null (son), Jacob Zumbrun
Signed with his signature

Ogg, Mary   of Carroll County
                                      May 27, 1840
                                      June 22, 1840
Number 78, Folio 139   June 22, 1840

To my father, George Ogg, nine pounds of wool and the sum of fifteen dollars. To Mary Ogg (daughter of George Ogg), the sum of ten dollars. The rest of my estate should be equally divided between the following: to my brother, John Ogg; to my brother, George Ogg; to John Robert Shipley (the son of Lloyd Shipley) when John Robert reaches the age of twenty one.

Witnesses: Lovelace Gardner, Elias Jordan
Executor(s): John Ogg (brother)
Signed with her signature

Ogg, Sarah   of Baltimore County
                                                  January 18, 1833
                                                  August 13, 1839
Number 55, Folio 98   August 26, 1839

To my daughter, Rachel Williams, fifty acres of "Beasman's
Discovery" which adjoins the lands of my grandson, James O.
Headington, and the lands of my father, Joseph Beasman. To
my grandson, James O. Headington, all the land northeast of
my land which adjoins my father's land. The south part of my
land should go to my daughter, Hellen Conaway provided that
she first pays her debts. To my daughter, Rachel W., a bed and
bedstead, one cherry tree table, stove, six plates, cow and calf
(this should all be taken out of the property that was conveyed
to me by John Williams). To my grandson, James O.
Headington, my gray mare called Bynet, my high bedstead and
bed, "one red painted bedstead under bed and furniture and the
feather beds which his father left in my care for him, one silver
watch and large bible, and sonnet mare named Sade, and one
black boy named Isaac untill he shall arive at the age of forty
five then and at that age if the permit he shall be free." All my
remaining property should go to my brother, William Beasman.

Witnesses: Moses Barnes, Jesse Putterson, Garretson Barnes
Executor(s): James O. Headington (grandson)
Signed with her signature

Ogg, Silvester   of Carroll County
                                                  May 21, 1846
                                                  June 1, 1846
Number 225, Folio 411   June 1, 1846

My executors should sell my portion of a tract of land
purchased by both myself and my brother, Nicholas Ogg, called
"Bashan" which contains three hundred and twelve acres and
was surveyed by Abraham Wampler with my half being one
hundred and fifty four acres. The proceeds from the sale of my

land should be divided as follows: to my brother, Moses Ogg, fifty dollars and the residue should be equally divided among my siblings (George Ogg, John Ogg, Moses Ogg, Nicholas Ogg, Sarah Shockney). To my nephew, Silvester Ogg, all my clothes. To Laban Ogg (son of Nicholas Ogg) one saddle and calf. To my niece, Amanda Ogg, one bed with bedding. To my brother, Nicholas Ogg, one cow and four bushels of wheat. The balance of my personal property should be equally divided among my three brothers: George Ogg, John Ogg and Nicholas Ogg.

Renunciation
Whereas the estate is small, one executor should be sufficient. George Ogg renounces his right as executor. Written on May 30, 1846.

Witnesses: Stephen Oursler, Rachel Blizzard, Elisha Buckingham
Executor(s): George Ogg (brother), Nicholas Ogg (brother)
Signed with his signature

Olinger, Peter   of Carroll County
                                       December 11, 1847
                                       December 27, 1847
Number 266, Folio 484   December 27, 1847

To my beloved wife, Catharine, during her widowhood three brown horses, one colt, four milk cows, six hogs, four sheep, five shoats, wagon, bed and cover, stove and pipe, one corner cupboard, one furrow plough, two shovel ploughs, one harrow, three bed and bedsteads, one table, all the kitchen furniture, one chest, one case of drawers, one clock, iron kettle, iron pots, dutch oven, kitchen cupboard, six chairs, wheat and oats and corn for the livestock, linens, one beef cow, two benches, chains, two saddles, one side saddle, spinning wheel, gears, milk pots, hay carriage, hay forks, all the geese. To my son, Henry Eli Olinger, my grain cradle and scythe. To my son,

Emanuel Olinger, scythe and two sheep. To my daughter, Sarah Ann, one heifer. The residue of my estate should be sold and the proceeds divided equally among my heirs.

Witnesses: Jacob Kerlinger, James Sellers, Jacob Menchy
Executor(s): Jacob Ditzler (friend)
Signed by his mark

Orndoff, Peter of Germany township, Adams County, Pennsylvania

March 13, 1828
October 10, 1842

Number 137, Folio 234 October 10, 1842

To my beloved wife, Rosina, during her widowhood the following: two cows, two beds, bureau, chest, wheat, rye and bacon. The remainder of my personal property and my plantation in Germany township, Adams County, Pennsylvania containing one hundred and twenty eight acres should be sold. To my son, George, one hundred dollars. To my daughter in law, Appolonia (wife of David), fifty dollars. The remainder of the proceeds should be equally divided among my sons (John, Peter, Jacob, Joseph, George and David), my daughters (Mary, Susan, Anne and Ruth) and my granddaughter, Rachel (child of my deceased daughter Elizabeth). To my wife, Rosina, my plantation where my son, Joseph, now lives in Frederick County, Maryland being part of "Resurvey on Brothers Agreement" and "Ross's Range." After the death or marriage of my wife, the property in Frederick County should be sold and the proceeds equally divided among my sons (John, Peter, Jacob, Joseph, George and David), my daughters (Mary, Susan, Anne and Ruth) and my granddaughter, Rachel (child of my deceased daughter Elizabeth).

Witnesses: John Brown, Frederick Bittinger
Executor(s): Joseph Orendorff (son), John Baumgartner (friend)
Signed by his mark

Orndorff, Peter

of Carroll County
November 12, 1846
February 8, 1847

Number 242, Folio 444

February 8, 1847

To my beloved wife, Elizabeth Orndorff, all of my property both real and personal. To my son, Henry Orndorff, one dollar which combined with the money previously paid to him by me during my lifetime should be considered his full share.

Witnesses: Lewis Peters, Jacob Peters, Samuel Baumgardner
Executor(s): not named
Signed with his signature

Panabaker, Peter

of Carroll County
August 30, 1846
February 22, 1847

Number 244, Folio 448

February 22, 1847

To my beloved wife, Mary Panabaker, two cows, two beds with bedding, bureau, chest, corner cupboard, the dishes, kitchen dresser, stove, table, four chairs, clock and case, six sets of silverware, linens, kitchen furniture and one hundred dollars. After the death of my wife, these goods should be sold and the proceeds equally divided among my children and that my grandson, William Greenbury Reagle, shall have the portion of his mother (my deceased daughter Mary Reagle). To my wife, during her widowhood, the use and privilege of two rooms and kitchen in my house as well as use of the garden, spring house and cellar. My wife should be provided annually with eighteen bushels good wheat, ten bushels Indian corn, six bushels oats, hundred pounds of good pork, fifty pounds of beef, sufficient amounts of potatoes, fruit and firewood plus one eighth of my land to sow. To my son, David Panabaker, the plantation where I currently reside in Carroll County which contains tracts called "Winchesters Lot", "United Friendship", "Wills Care Enlarged" the latter conveyed to me by George Everhart (the elder) and one other lot conveyed to me by John Schafer (my father in law). My son, David Panabaker, should provide and maintain his mother as described previously. To my son, David Panabaker, six acres of a wood lot, and tracts of land in Carroll County named "Friendship", "Valley of Jehosephat", "Chance", "Prospect", "Spitters Enclosure" and "Pleasant Hill" all being contiguous and conveyed to me by Margaret Barnes. My son, David Panabaker, should pay: my son, William Panabaker, one hundred dollars after six months of my death; my daughter, Rachel (wife of Samuel Bower), two hundred and fifty dollars after three years; my daughter, Sally (wife of Joseph Hoover), two hundred and fifty dollars after four years; my daughter, Christiana Sophia (wife of John Foltz), two hundred and fifty dollars after five years; my son, John Panabaker, two hundred and fifty dollars after six years; my daughter, Cevilla Panabaker, two hundred and fifty dollars after seven years; my son, Edwin Henry, two hundred and fifty dollars after eight years; to my grandson, William Greebury Reagle, five hundred dollars after sixteen years. To my son, David Panabaker, my wagon, horse, cow, trashing machine, log chain, bed with bedding, my desk and one harrow. To my sons, John Panabaker and Edwin H. Panabaker, the tract of land in Carroll County called "Stoney Valley Enlarged" which was conveyed to me by Margaret Allbaugh as well as the remaining land conveyed to me by Margaret Barnes (not given to my son David) to share equally. To my daughter, Cevilla Panabaker, one French bedstead and bedding, table and six chairs, bureau and fifty dollars intended for her outfit. My negro woman called Let should be freed on the day of my death. To my son, David Panabaker, my negro boy called Levi until Levi reaches the age of twenty seven at which time he should be set free. The residue of my estate should be sold and equally divided among my children and grandson herein named.

Witnesses: Michael Sullivan, Henry Warehime, Samuel Matthias
Executor(s): David Panabaker (son)
Signed with his signature

Parrish, John   of Carroll County
                                              April 3, 1840
                                      November 6, 1843
Number 162, Folio 284   November 13, 1843

All my estate in Carroll County should go to my dear wife, Providence Parrish, during her natural life. After the death of my wife, I bequeath the following. To my eldest daughter, Henrietta Williams, the tract of land called "Flag Meadows", and after the death of my daughter, Henrietta Williams, the land should go to her son, Robert Williams, along with five acres of a parcel of land where Joseph Haynes now resides. All my land called "Deerpark" to my daughter, Mary Haynes (the wife of Joseph Haines), and after the death of my daughter, Mary Haynes, the land should go to her two daughters, Mary Jane and Ann Rebecca. All my personal property should be sold and equally divided between: my two grandchildren, Reuben and Mary Ellen Shockney (children of Rebecca Shockney wife of Charles Shockney) of the State of Indiana.

Witnesses: William Ogg (of George), Amos Williams, Elijah Wooden
Executor(s): Jacob Holmes (my loving friend)
Signed by his mark

Parrish, Johnathan   of Baltimore County
                                         November 19, 1835
                                        September 4, 1837
Number 14, Folio 27   September 11, 1837

The proceeds from sale of my farm where I currently reside should be divided equally among the following: Mary Hooker, Elisabeth Manning, Rachel Manning (daughter of Jesse Manning (of A)), Urith Barnes (wife of Garretson Barnes), Joseph Willis, Levan Williams, Green Williams, Elias Williams, Amos Williams, Johnathan Greenbury Hooker (son of Amos Hooker) and Elizabeth Pedicord (wife of Humphrey

Pedicord). The proceeds from the sale of my land in the neighborhood of Reisterstown called "Qauled Stocksdale neighborhood" and "Pourters Delight" should be divided equally among the following: Cary Garner, Hellen Parrish, Keturah Wheeler, Arch Pourter and Rachel Cook. To Mary Hooker, the sum of one hundred dollars. To Elizabeth Manning (daughter of Jesse Manning (of A)), the sum of fifty dollars. To Rachel Manning, the sum of fifty dollars. To Urith Barnes (wife of Garrison Barnes), the sum of one hundred dollars. To Joseph Willis, the sum of fifty dollars. To Greenbury Williams, the sum of fifty dollars. To Levan Williams, the sum of fifty dollars. To Elias Williams, the sum of fifty dollars. To Amos Williams, the sum of fifty dollars. To Elisabeth Pedicord (wife of Humphrey Pedicord), the sum of twenty five dollars. I also devise that fifty square feet of my land be reserved for the family graveyard which already exists on my property. I bequeath my land called "Caryall" to Urith Barnes and Amos Williams to share jointly between them. My arm chair to Mary Hooker and at her decease the chair should be returned to Ann Willis. To Elias Williams, my large red chest. To Levan Williams, my small white chest. To Elisabeth Manning (daughter of Jesse Manning (of A)), six silver tea spoons. To Mary Ann Willis, one pepper box and one trunnel bed. To Joseph Willis, my watch.

Renunciation
Moses Barnes, Levi Williams and Jesse Manning refuse to accept the executorship and desire that the role be granted to Flin Garner, the other mentioned executor. Witnessed on October 2, 1837 by William Jameson and John Armagast.

Witnesses: John Parrish, Elijah Wooden, William Griffee
Executor(s): Flin Garner and Moses Barnes (if either should die then I appoint Jesse Manning (of R) and Levan Williams to take their place)
Signed with his signature

Peters, Veronica   of Carroll County

                                     August 27, 1838

                                     October 8, 1838

Number 38, Folio 64   October 8, 1838

To my two daughters, Veronica and Rachel, fifty dollars each for services rendered to me during my sickness and if they should marry before my death then they are to be given household furnishings in the amount of fifty dollars. To my daughter, Anne (wife of David R. Mause), twenty five dollars. To my daughter, Veronica, my saddle and bridle. To my daughter, Rachel, my bed and bedding. To my daughters, Veronica, Anne, Catharine and Rachel, all my clothes. Any surplus money should be divided equally among my children, namely: Lewis, Henry, Jacob, Veronica, Catherine, Anne and Rachel. The legacy to my daughter, Anne, shall be solely for her use and to not fall into the hands of her husband (David R. Mause) and if she should die and have issue then her legacy is to be kept in trust of my executors for the use of her children.

Witnesses: Anthony Wivel, Frances J. Baumgartner
Executor(s): Lewis Peters (son)
Signed by her mark

Poulson, Rachel   of Carroll County

                                     August 27, 1840

                                     October 21, 1850

Number 335, Folio 580   October 21, 1850

All my estate should go to my two daughters, Ann Poulson and Elizabeth B. Evans (wife of Samuel Evans) provided that they pay the sum of one hundred dollars to Cornelius Lee Poulson by the time he reaches age twenty one.

Witnesses: David Cassell, Abraham Cassell (of D), Ellen Geatty
Executor(s): not named
Signed with her signature

Powder, Jacob (senior)   of Carroll County

                                        January 28, 1840

                                        March 21, 1842

Number 127, Folio 212   March 21, 1842

To my son, Jacob Powder, ten acres of land in Carroll County called "Addition to Narrow Bottom" which adjoins the land of Thomas Wills. The residue of my real estate should go to my two daughters, Polly Powder and Margaret Powder. The residue of my estate should be divided equally among: my son Jacob Powder, my daughter Elisabeth, my daughter Sally, my daughter Susan, my daughter Catharine, my daughter Polly, my daughter Margaret, one part to my grandchildren (Henrietta Powder, Christina Powder, Andrew and Elisabeth Powder) who are the children of my son Andrew.

Witnesses: Jacob Grove, William Zepp, Jesse Manning
Executor(s): Polly Powder (daughter)
Signed with his signature

Powel, Esther   of Carroll County

                                        March 4, 1850

                                        June 9, 1851

Number 356, Folio 607   June 9, 1851

To my grandchildren, namely: Mary Byers, my queensware, iron pots and ten dollars; Elizabeth Byers, my bedstead with bedding and ten dollars; John Byers, ten dollars; Henry Byers, ten dollars; Susan Byers, five dollars; one dollar to be equally divided among the children of my son, Jacob Powel. To my son, Peter Byers, one hundred and fifty dollars. To my son, John Powel, ten dollars. The residue of my estate should be sold and the proceeds should go to my son, John Powel.

Witnesses: Edward Lynch, Daniel Coltrider, Adam Bower
Executor(s): Daniel J. Geiman (my esteemed neighbor)
Signed by her mark

Prugh, Frederick   of Carroll County
                        February 17, 1849
                        August 11, 1851
Number 358, Folio 610   August 11, 1851

To my daughter, Rachel Bennett, six hundred and eighty dollars in order to make her equal with my other children. To my daughter, Rachel Bennett, my colored girl called Eliza Jane to serve her until said Eliza reaches the age of twenty four and at that time should be freed. To my grandson, Levi Manahan, a mortgage I hold against the late William Demmits estate in the amount of twelve hundred dollars which is to be given to him when he reaches the age of twenty six. To each of my children four hundred dollars, namely: my daughter Mary Farver, my son John Prugh, my daughter Rachel Bennett, my son Abraham Prugh, my son Peter Prugh and my son David Prugh. The residue of my estate both real and personal should be sold and the proceeds are to be equally divided among my children herein named and my grandson, Levi Manahan (Levi should have a portion equal to my children).

Witnesses: Joshua C. Gist, George W. Belleson, Joseph Frizzell
Executor(s): Abraham Prugh (son), David Prugh (son)
Signed with his signature

Pusey, George   of Carroll County
                     August 15, 1840
                     September 24, 1847 (codicil)
                     July 15, 1850
Number 329, Folio 572   July 15, 1850

To my beloved wife, Sarah Pusey, my house and lot in Carroll County as well as all contents at McKinstry's Mill on Sam's Creek. After her death or marriage, this house and lot should be sold and the proceeds equally distributed among my four children, namely: Thomas Pusey, Catherine Jameson (wife of Robert J. Jameson), Elizabeth Pusey and Margaret Pusey. My lot and ground in New Market, Frederick County and the residue of my personal estate should be sold and the proceeds equally divided among my four children above named.

Codicil
"My daughter Margaret has since...intermarried with a certain Clempson Stevens who has since said marriage wantonly and cruelly deserted her first striping her of all she had then in her possession and leaving her with one child, a daughter named Sarah." I declare that said Stevens should be "debarred" of all benefit from my estate.

Witnesses: George Yandis, Evan McKinstry, Samuel McKinstry
Executor(s): Robert J. Jameson (son in law), Elias Grimes (trusty friend)
Will signed with his signature and codicil by his mark

Rait, Basil   of Carroll County
                                         May 30, 1839
                                      August 19, 1839
Number 56, Folio 100   August 19, 1839

My horse, surveying compass, books and personal property should be sold and the proceeds should be applied to repairing the house where my father currently resides. My interest in the farm where my father currently resides should be divided equally among my siblings, namely: Nathan Rait, Hanson C. Rait and Margaret Rait. I ask that my executors purchase a pair of tombstones (tombstones similar to those at the grave of my deceased brother, John) and place them at my grave.

Witnesses: Isaac Dern, Nimrod Norris, William Hiner
Executor(s): Nathan Rait (brother)
Signed with his signature

Reaver, Philip   of Carroll County
                                      September 10, 1838
                                      December 4, 1843
Number 164, Folio 288   December 4, 1843

To my beloved wife, Christina Reaver, two beds with bedsteads and bedding, one table, one cow, two chairs and as much kitchen and household furniture as she requires. To my son, Frederick Reaver, my plantation where I currently reside called "Owens" which adjoins the lands of Ulrick Reaver and John B. Boyle containing one hundred acres on condition that he provide my wife with the room that she currently occupies, and use of the house, kitchen and cellar, plus annually ten bushels of wheat, five bushels of rye, five bushels of corn, five bushels of potatoes, two hundred pounds of pork, one hundred pounds of beef, one third of the garden, maintenance of her cow, fire wood delivered to her room and twenty five dollars annually. I also desire that my son, Frederick Reaver, pay my debts. To my son, Frederick Reaver, half of my horned cattle, half of my sheep, my clock and case and all my money. To my grandson, James Wolf, twenty five dollars. The residue of my personal estate should be sold and the proceeds should go to my son, Frederick Reaver.

Witnesses: Joseph Reever, John Reaver, Henry Boyle
Executor(s): John B. Boyle (friend)
Signed by his mark

Reaver, Ulrich   of Carroll County
                                      November 2, 1847
                                      February 4, 1850
Number 314, Folio 551   February 4, 1850

All my real and personal property should be sold and the proceeds should be distributed as follows: to my son, Joseph Reaver, eight hundred dollars; to my granddaughter, Catherine (wife of Frederick Hawk), two hundred dollars; to my daughter,

170

Mary (wife of Isaiah Caskey), twenty five dollars; to Eliza Golley (wife of my grandson David S. Golley), fifty dollars; to my grandson, David S. Golley, fifty dollars; to my granddaughter, Sarah (wife of Joseph Bower), one hundred dollars; to my granddaughter, Elizabeth Golly, one hundred dollars; to my grandson, Abraham Golly, one hundred dollars; to my great grandson, Joseph Bower (son of my granddaughter Mary Caskey), one hundred dollars. The residue of my proceeds should be equally divided among my previously mentioned legatees.

Witnesses: John Longley, James Thomson, John Reindollar
Executor(s): John Thomson (trusty friend)
Signed by his mark

Reed, Jacob   of Carroll County
                                                   January 7, 1838
                                                   October 29, 1838
Number 42, Folio 72   October 29, 1838

To my daughter, Mary Reed, two hundred dollars, two beds with bedsteads and bed clothes, one cow of her choice, two sheep, three hogs, one spinning wheel, one chest, half of all the flax and linen, half of all the coverlets and half of my kitchen furniture. To my daughter, Frana Reed, two beds with bedsteads and bed clothes, one cow of her choice, two sheep, three hogs, one spinning wheel, one chest, half of all the flax and linen, half of all the coverlets and half of my kitchen furniture. To my daughters, Mary Reed and Frana Reed, my clock and case, stove and pipe, copper kettle, woolen wheel, clock reel, churn, bucking tub, table, six chairs and pewter ware which should be divided equally. To my daughters, Mary and Frana, all the wheat, rye and corn growing in the fields at the time of my death and four hundred pounds of bacon. To my daughters, Mary and Frana, my large Dutch Bible, one testament, two hymns books and two other German books. To my grandson, Andrew Smeach, all my English books and one chest. To my daughters, Mary and Frana Reed, the plantation where I currently reside for the term of three years after my death. Also for the term of three years after my death, to my daughters Mary and Frana, the use of the best of my stock, two set of horse gears, two cows, one wagon, one plough, one harrow, one shovel plow, one winnowing mill, one cutting box and all my poultry. The remainder of my personal estate should be sold and the proceeds should be equally divided among my four children, namely: George Reed, Mary Reed, Elizabeth Smeach and Frana Reed. After three years of my death my real estate and personal property allotted to my daughter, Mary and Frana, should be sold and the proceeds should be equally divided among my four children with one exception that one hundred dollars of the money going to my daughter, Elizabeth Smeach, should go to grandson, Andrew Smeach (Andrew who is currently living with me).

Witnesses: Michael Sullivan, Michael Ritter, Frederick Ritter
Executor(s): George Reed (son)
Signed with his signature

Reid, Margaret   of Frederick County
                                                   August 6, 1824
                                                   October 8, 1838
Number 37, Folio 61   October 8, 1838

My executors should sell my real estate which adjoins the lands of Elizabeth McIlhenny (the land that was given to Elizabeth McIlhenny by Doctor Upton Scott of Annapolis). To my daughter, Margaret Reid, one sixth of my real estate proceeds and first choice of my bed and bedding. To my daughter, Elizabeth McIlhenny, one sixth of the proceeds and one bed with bedding. To my daughter, Mary Reid, one sixth, one bed and bedding, and my negro woman called Esther. To my daughter, Catherine Darby, one sixth and one clock with case.

One sixth of the proceeds to my grandchildren, Margaret and Catherine Henderson. The remaining one sixth should be used to purchase stock in the Frederick County bank for my two grandchildren, Alexander Hamilton Reid and James Reid.

Renunciation
John Darby renounced his right as executor and requested that Mr. Philip Hann be appointed which was approved by the heirs of Margaret Reid. Witnessed October 3, 1838 by Elizabeth MIlhenny, Margaret Reid and Mary Reid.

Witnesses: Samuel Naill, James Maloney, A. B. R. McLine
Executor(s): John Darby (son in law)
Signed with her signature

Reiszle, John   of Carroll County
                                         January 27, 1843
                                         August 7, 1843
Number 159, Folio 276   August 7, 1843

To my wife, Margaret Reiszle, half of my estate for her life. After the death of my wife, her share should be divided among her son, Michael, and her daughter, Catharina (wife of John Dorfler). The other half of my estate should be divided among my three children, namely: Daniel Reiszle, Maria and Rosina.

Witnesses: Joseph Sharrer, Adam Eszig, Goring Sindel
Executor(s): Daniel Reiszle (son)
Signed with his signature

Ridinger, Peter   of Carroll County
                                         May 8, 1842
                                         May 23, 1842
Number 131, Folio 218   May 23, 1842

All my property both real and personal should go to my wife, Catherine Ridinger.

Renunciation
John Bishop resigns his executorship. Witnessed on May 21, 1842 by James Thomas.

Witnesses: James Thomas, David Kephart, Jacob Feeser
Executor(s): John Bishop
Signed by his mark

Rinedollar, George   of Carroll County

                                               January 23, 1838
                                                  March 3, 1851
Number 351, Folio 599   March 3, 1851

To my beloved wife, Mary Rinedollar, one bed with bedstead and bedding, bureau, barouche and as much furniture as she requires. The residue of my personal estate should be sold and two thirds of the proceeds should go to my son, Samuel Rinedollar, and the remainder to my son, George Rinedollar. To my son, George Rinedollar, fifty acres of the plantation where I currently reside in Carroll County along the public road from Frederick City to York, Pennsylvania which adjoins the lands of Abraham Koons and the heirs of Blasins Noel. The residue of my property where I currently reside which contains one hundred acres and all buildings should go to my son, Samuel Rinedollar on condition that my son, Samuel, maintains my wife and pays the following legacies: to my daughter, Margaret, five hundred dollars; to my daughter, Lydia (wife of Michael Stier), four hundred dollars such that the money to Lydia does not fall into the hands of her husband.

Renunciation
George Rinedollar (son of George Rinedollar, testator) renounces his executorship of said will. Witnessed March 3, 1851 by John Joseph Baumgardner.

Witnesses: Joseph Wivel, Lewis Peters, Jacob Peters
Executor(s): Samuel Rinedollar (son), George Rinedollar (son)
Signed with his signature

Rinehart, Magdalena   of Carroll County

March 11, 1840
May 24, 1841

Number 104, Folio 172   May 24, 1841

To my son, George Rinehart, all the land which was conveyed to me by Josiah Brown, also the land which was conveyed to me by the heirs of "Beaver" and the land that was conveyed to me by Michael Morelock. To my son, George, the rent and profits of my house and land in Gettysburg provided that he pays my estate the two hundred dollars that he owes me. To my granddaughter, Elizabeth Weaver, my house and lot in Gettysburg after the death of her father (George Rinehart). To my grandsons, John Rinehart and Peter Masonhimer, my land called "Rumlers Place" to be kept in trust for the children of my daughter Barbara Lippy (Elizabeth, Ann, Joseph, Magdalena, William and David Lippy). To my grandsons, John Rinehart and Peter Masonhimer, my land called "Stones Place" and the land which was conveyed to me by Frank Houses to be kept in trust for the children of my grandson Frederick Masonhimer. To my grandsons, Peter Masonhimer and Daniel Masonhimer, my land called "Feasant's Place." To my grandson, John Masonhimer, the eighty acres of land that I own in the state of Illinois and three hundred dollars. To my grandsons, John Rinehart and Peter Masonhimer, my land called "Stannors Place", three cows each and one hundred dollars each all of which should be kept in trust for my granddaughters Susan Masonhimer and Mary Masonhimer. To my grandchildren, John and Susan Lippy (children of my deceased daughter Mary Lippy) one hundred and sixty acres in the state of Illinois and I give to them the sum of seven hundred dollars. To my granddaughters, Rebecca Lippy and Catherine Lippy (daughters of my deceased daughter Mary Lippy), an equal share in the house and eleven lots in Manchester as well as the lot that was conveyed to me by "Steffee and Weaver." To my grandsons, John Rinehart and Peter Masonhimer, my land called "Lingenfellers Place" and one cow all to be kept in trust for my granddaughter, Susan Feiser. To my grandsons, John Rinehart and Peter Masonhimer, my land called "Montz Place" to be kept in trust for my granddaughter, Isabella Sentz. To my grandsons, John Rinehart and Peter Masonhimer, my land called "Stevensons Place" and four cows all to be kept in trust for my granddaughters, Sarah Sentz and Catherine Ellen Sentz. To my grandsons, John Rinehart and Peter Masonhimer, my house and land in Reisterstown and my eight day clock to be kept in trust for my daughter, Sally Sentz. Upon the death of my daughter, Sally Sentz, this property should go to my grandson, Joshua Sentz. To my daughter, Elizabeth Everly, the "Mill Place" which was conveyed to me by Andrew Ebaugh, all the land which was conveyed to me by John Murray which adjoins "Mill Place", a note I hold against David Everly for the sum of seven hundred dollars and also two hundred and fifty dollars provided that after the death of my daughter, Elizabeth Everly, fifty dollars of which should go to the church formerly known as "Cryders Church." To my daughter, Elizabeth Everly, my home place known as "Klines Place" provided that she shall pay half of the fair market value to my grandsons, John Rinehart and Peter Masonhimer, and pay the other half of the value to my daughter, Sally Sentz. My clothes and furniture should be equally divided among my daughters, Barbara, Elizabeth and Sally. The balance of my estate should be sold and the proceeds equally divided among my three children, namely: George Rinehart, Elizabeth Everly and Sally Sentz. If anyone questions or brings suit against my estate, then they will forfeit their share.

Witnesses: Joshua Smith (junior), Daniel Baumgartner, Jacob Young
Executor(s): George Rinehart (son), Levi Everly, Joseph Hesson (of Peter)
Signed with her signature

Roberts, Sarah

widow of Carroll County (relict
of Richard Roberts late of
Frederick County)
September 23, 1848
October 21, 1850

Number 336, Folio 581

October 21, 1850

To my step daughter, Rachel Ann Haulk (wife of Edward Haulk), one large looking glass, one bureau, one bed with bedstead, two pair of sheets with pillow cases and a table clock. I bequeath to my three nieces (daughters of my brother Benjamin Hibberd), the following: to Sarah Jane Hibberd, a half dozen silver table spoons; to Alice Ann Hibberd, a half dozen silver tea spoons; to Tacy Hibberd, a half dozen silver tea spoons. To my said nieces, all my clothes. The residue of my personal property should be sold and divided equally among my three named nieces.

Witnesses: Silas Hibberd, Samuel Gilbert, Job Hibberd
Executor(s): Joseph Hibberd (nephew and son of my brother
Silas Hibberd)
Signed with her signature

Robosson, Ann

of Carroll County
May 14, 1842
January 26, 1846

Number 217, Folio 400

January 26, 1846

To my daughter, Martha Carr, all the land that I own on the South River in Anne Arundel County and after the death of my daughter, Martha Carr, this land should go to her children [not named].

Witnesses: Nicholas Harden, N. Browne, Barbara Bennett
Executor(s): John Robosson (son)
Signed by her mark

Robosson, Elijah

Number 93, Folio 157

of Carroll County
November 19, 1840
March 3, 1841
March 3, 1841

"For as much as my son Benjamin Robosson has received as much of my estate as I think he ought to have and since being suspected of having joined a certain secret association had become an infidel and despiser of the saviour of the world...for the reasons aforesaid..." I give to my son, Benjamin Robosson, twenty five cents. I give to my son, John Robosson (after the death of his mother), my tract of land in Allegheny County where he currently resides, and my tract of land called "Collins Farm" as well as my tract of land called "Polished Mountain." To my grandson, Thomas P. Robosson (after the death of his grandmother), my tract of land called "Flintstone" and "Resurvey on Flintstone" both lying in Allegheny County near the waters of Flintstone creek. After the death of my wife, my tract of land called "Rapho" in Baltimore County should go to my daughter Martha Carr and after her death it should be equally divided among the children and legal heirs of said Martha Carr [not named]. My son, John Robosson, and my son in law, Joshua H. Shipley, should inspect this land called "Rapho" and make certain that it is not wasteful and is sufficient to maintain the children of my daughter, Martha Carr. To my daughter, Mary Ann H. Shipley (after the death of her mother), the plantation where I currently reside with the rights to the quarry limestone. To my daughter, Mary Ann H. Shipley, the lot on the northwest corner of Const and Allisannd Streets in Fells Point (city of Baltimore) plus all my household and kitchen furniture in my current dwelling house. To my son, Francis Robosson (after the death of his mother), all my remaining tracts of land. To my daughter in law, Hamutal Weir, during her widowhood the use of my negro woman called Ann along with Ann's negro children called Polly, Adaline and George. To my daughter in law, Hamutal Weir, all the other chattel such as furniture, sheep, horses, hogs that are currently in the care of my said daughter in law. After the death of my daughter in law, Hamutal Weir, these items should be equally divided among her children, namely: Elijah, Lemuel, Benjamin and Rachel Robosson. To my granddaughter, Mary Ann Robosson, my negro girl called Josephine. It is my will that Margaret Tevis should remain at my home for the rest of her natural life and continue to live with the privileges as if she had been a member of our family. I desire that my colored people, namely: Harry (commonly called Miller), Henny, Henny's daughter (Rebecca), Deborah, James Trimble and Lloyd should be retained by my son, John, as his portion and the portion of his nephew, Thomas P. Robosson. My negro people, namely: Riley, Dennis and Sall should go to my daughter, Mary Ann Shipley. My negro boy, David, should go to my daughter, Martha Carr. My negro man, George, should go to the heirs of my deceased son, Oneal Robosson [not named]. My older negroes (Sarah, James, Parrish, Rebecca and Flora) should be retained on my current farm unless they desire to go with any of my children. The rest of my personal estate and all the remainder of my negroes (that I own in Carroll, Baltimore, Anne Arundel and Allegheny Counties) should be sold after the death of my wife and the proceeds should be divided into five equal parts and distributed as follows: one part to my son, John Robosson; one part to my grandson, Thomas P. Robosson; one part to my daughter, Mary Ann Shipley; the other two parts should remain in the hands of my son, John Robosson, and my son in law, Joshua H. Shipley, in trust for the children of my daughter, Martha Carr, and the children of my deceased son, Oneal Robosson.

Witnesses: John B. Devries, Nicholas Dorsey, Joshua Kerby
Executor(s): John Robosson (son), Francis Robosson (son)
Signed with his signature

Rodkey, George   of Carroll County
October 30, 1851
November 10, 1851 (codicil)
January 12, 1852
Number 374, Folio 631   January 12, 1852

One horse to each of my sons, namely: John Rodkey, Jacob, George Washington, Joshua Westly, and William Henry. To my daughter, Susan Rodkey, two cows, one feather bed with bedstead and bedding, six chairs, stand, table, bureau, looking glass, two buckets, two iron pots, one chain, two flat irons and one skillet or pan. To my daughter, Elisabeth Emeline, the same as my daughter, Susan, and one additional item (a side saddle). To my son, William Henry Rodkey, one hundred dollars once he arrives at the age of twenty one. To my dear and beloved wife, Elizabeth Rodkey, the residue of my personal property and all my real estate in Carroll County during her natural life. After the death of my wife, I give to my son, John Rodkey, the farm where I currently reside (containing one hundred acres, adjoining the lands of Augustine Arnold and John Lingwell) on for the sum of one thousand dollars. This payment of one thousand dollars from my son, John Rodkey, should be paid out as follows: two hundred to my daughter, Mary Ann (wife of Jacob Feeser), after one year of my wife's death; two hundred dollars to my daughter, Susan Rodkey, after two years of my wife's death; two hundred dollars to my daughter, Catherine (wife of Isaac Hyder), after three years of my wife's death; two hundred dollars to my daughter, Elisabeth Emily, after four years of my wife's death; two hundred dollars to my daughter, Mary Ann (wife of Jacob Feeser), after five years of my wife's death. After the death of my wife, I give to my son, Jacob Rodkey, the corner track of land near Eck's Mill (containing eighty three acres) for the sum of five hundred dollars. This payment of five hundred dollars from my son, Jacob Rodkey, should be paid in equal parts to my other children, namely: Susan Rodkey, Catherine Hyder and Elizabeth Emaline. After the death of my wife, I give to my son, George Washington Rodkey, the part of the farm where I currently reside (containing eighty five acres) for the sum of six hundred dollars. This six hundred dollar payment from my son, George Rodkey, should be paid equally to my other children, namely: Elisabeth Emaline, Mary Ann Feeser, Susan, Catherine Hyder and William Henry. After the death of my wife, I give to my son, Joshua Westley Rodkey, a tract of land in the upper part of the farm where I currently reside (containing eighty three acres) for the sum of five hundred. This five hundred dollar payment from my son, Joshua Westley Rodkey, should be paid to my son, William Henry. If my daughter, Susan, marries Henry Eck then she should have nothing of my estate.

Codicil
I appoint my worthy friend, Jacob Zumbrun, to be my executor in place of my son, George Washington Rodkey.

Renunciation
John Rodkey renounces his right as executor. Written July 12, 1852.

Witnesses: Thomas Jones, Jacob Zumbrun, Samuel Bean, Jesse Shafer
Executor(s): John Rodkey (son), Jacob Rodkey (son), Jacob Zumbrun (friend)
Signed with his signature

Rogers, Hannah   of Baltimore City
                                        November 27, 1850
                                        January 13, 1851
Number 346, Folio 593   January 13, 1851

I give to my niece, Adeline Linville, all my property.

Witnesses: M. G. Cockey, George Jacobs, Richard Jacobs
Executor(s): Adeline Linville (niece)
Signed with her signature

Royer, Peter   of Carroll County
                                December 5, 1841
                                August 1, 1842
Number 133, Folio 221   August 1, 1842

To my wife, Anne Royer, the brick part of my house on Farm
No. 1 where I currently reside for her during her widowhood as
well as the use of the spring house, wash house, wood house,
carriage house, the new granary and any part of the stabling,
pasture and hay in order to maintain four cows and a horse. My
son, John Royer, should provide my wife the following items
on an annual basis: two hundred bushels of oats, one hundred
bushels of corn, and as much fire wood, use of garden, wheat
flour, bacon, lard and fruit as may be needed. My wife should
also have the use of the carriage, bedding, furniture, desk
(except the contents), clock and kitchen utensils. To my
daughter, Catherine Wampler, "the one seventh part of all my
Bank Stock, with the sum of six thousand four hundred and
forty dollars including the book of account of money which I
have and may give her myself." To my son, Christian Royer,
my Farm No. 3 which was conveyed to me by George Widder
in 1822, also two thousand nine hundred and forty dollars and
one seventh of my bank stock. To my son, Jesse Royer, my
Farm. No. 2 which was conveyed to me by Frederick Arthur in
1810, also two thousand nine hundred and forty dollars and one
seventh of my bank stock. To my daughter, Mary Merring, one
half of my Farm No. 4 and half of my wood lot No. 2, also two
thousand three hundred and twenty dollars and one seventh of
my bank stock and after the death of my daughter, Mary, this
legacy should go to her heirs. If my daughter, Mary Merring,
should have no heirs and after her death and the death of her
spouse, her estate should be sold and equally divided among my
six other children, namely: Catherine Wampler, Christian
Royer, Jesse Royer, Ann Waybright, Louisa Englar and John
Royer. To my daughter, Ann Waybright, my Farm No. 5 which
was conveyed to me by William Koontz (trustee of Frederick
Merring) in 1835, also two thousand four hundred and forty

dollars and one seventh of my bank stock. To my daughter, Louisa Englar, the other half of my Farm No. 4 and the other half of my wood lot No. 2, also two thousand three hundred and twenty dollars and one seventh of my bank stock. To my youngest son, John Royer, my Farm No.1 where I currently reside and my wood lot No. 1 and one seventh of my bank stock. My colored boys and girls should be freed at the age of twenty one as well as be given fifty dollars each as they reach age, namely: Henry Pompey, John, Amos, Oscar, Lewis, Ellen and Jane. To Abraham Caylor and John Hess, "five hundred dollars to be disposed by them according to the verbal directions I have given them." To John Bucher and Henry Bucher, five hundred dollars to be disposed according to the verbal directions I have given them. The notes that I hold against my sons, Christian Royer, Jesse Royer and John Royer, should be paid to my wife. As my daughter, Catherine Wampler, has not been given any real estate she should be paid one thousand dollars of the final distribution of my estate. The balance of my estate should be equally divided among my remaining children. The family graveyard should be enlarged so as to contain one quarter of an acre (which was agreed upon by myself and John Roop).

Witnesses: David Roop, Jacob Royer, Philip Boyle
Executor(s): Christian Royer (son), Jesse Royer (son), Jacob Merring, John Royer (son)
Signed with his signature

Rudisel, Ludwick   of Frederick County
                                        August 19, 1830
                                        August 1, 1842
Number 132, Folio 219   August 1, 1842

It is my desire that my beloved wife, Nancy, and all my children should remain as one family until all my children reach age and that my wife should have complete ownership and control of my property both real and personal provided that she remains my widow. If my wife should remarry, then she should have one third of my estate. My sons should remain with their mother until they reach the age of twenty one, and after they reach age they should be compensated an allowance. After the death of my wife, my estate should be sold and equally divided among my children [not named]. If either of my sons should leave home and go into business for themselves, my wife should provide assistance.

Witnesses: Henry Swope, Abraham Lichtenwalter, James Smith
Executor(s): William Rudisel (son), Thomas Rudisel (son)
Signed with his signature

Rup, Michael   of Baltimore County
                                              March 3, 1814
                                              April 18, 1816
Number 286, Folio 512   September 4, 1848

To my beloved wife, Mary Rup, the use and proceeds of my house in Manchester where I currently reside (which includes a total of five lots) for her use during her widowhood. After the death or marriage of my wife, my property in Manchester should be sold and one half of the proceeds should be equally distributed among my ten children, namely: Jacob Rup, Michael Rup, Samuel Rup, George Rup, Henry Rup, Barbara (wife of John Earlick), Elizabeth (wife of Stephen Lowall), Mary (wife of George Dahofe), John Rup and Frederick Rup. The remaining half of the proceeds from my property in Manchester should be equally distributed to the five children of my wife, namely: Samuel Weaver, Philip Weaver, Elizabeth Weaver, David Weaver and Susanna (wife of Philip Shriver). To my wife, one kitchen cupboard, spinning wheel, stove, my horse, one cow and two beds with bedsteads. My remaining real and personal property should be sold and one half of the proceeds should go to my wife and the other half should be equally divided among my ten children. I also direct that the share to my daughter, Mary, should not go to the hands of her husband, George Dahofe. If my daughter, Mary Dahofe, should die before her husband then her share shall go to my granddaughter, Elizabeth Dahofe.

Witnesses: George Matter, George Linewaver, John Steiffer
Executor(s): Jacob Rup (son)
Signed by his mark

Sawyer, John   of Carroll County
                                              June 5, 1837
                                            March 21, 1842
Number 125, Folio 209   March 21, 1842

To my beloved wife, Margaret Sawyer, all my personal property, my house and lot where I currently reside (which adjoins the lands of Henry Reindollar and the heirs of Samuel Thomson) and my house and lot in the town of Petersburg (Littletown) in Adams County, Pennsylvania. After the death of my wife, my personal and real property should be sold and one half of the proceeds should go to the children of my deceased siblings, namely: the heirs of Daniel Sawyer, the heirs of Mary Miller, the heirs of Catherine Arthur, "to the heirs of Margaret Monshower by Arbaugh one share to be equally divided amongst them that is to say to Mary Wickert one share of her share, Henry Abaugh one share and Elizabeth Rose one share." The other half of the proceeds of my estate should be divided equally among the following: to Peter Kessler (son of Jacob Kessler), Peter Geatty, Elizabeth David, Molly Geatty, Mary Ritter, the heirs of Mary Geatty, Peter Bankard, Catherine Bankard and David Kessler.

Witnesses: Abraham Lichtenwalter, Samuel Slagenhaupt, John Reindollar
Executor(s): John Thomson
Signed with his signature

Sellars, Jacob   of Baltimore County

May 2, 1836
March 15, 1841
Number 94, Folio 161   March 15, 1841

To my dearly beloved wife, Barbara Sellars, feather bed with furniture (in my largest room). To my daughter, Sarah Sellars, cow, bed with bedstead and furniture, bureau, table, tray, and twenty five dollars. The remainder of my estate should be sold and (after my wife's thirds) the proceeds should be equally divided among my children, namely: Jacob Sellars, Elizabeth (wife of William Albaugh), Catherine (wife of David Deal), Rachel (wife of Joshua Richards) and Sarah Sellars.

Witnesses: John Stansbury, Henry Steffey, Jacob Schaeffer
Executor(s): Jacob Sellars (son)
Signed with his signature

Seller, John   of Carroll County

December 11, 1838
October 25, 1841
Number 114, Folio 189   October 25, 1841

To my beloved wife, Elizabeth, all my personal estate.

Witnesses: Jacob Gitt, George Matters, George Everhart
Executor(s): Henry Krantz (son in law)
Signed by his mark

Sellers, George (junior)   of Carroll County

August 1, 1850
August 19, 1850
Number 331, Folio 575   August 19, 1850

My personal estate should be sold and the proceeds to my wife, Malinda, for support and education of my children [not named].

Witnesses: David C. Frankforter, Jesse Shultz, Elias Myerly
Executor(s): James Bosley (brother in law)
Signed with his signature

Sentz, Sally   of Carroll County
                                         November 2, 1848
                                                January 1, 1849
Number 287, Folio 514   January 1, 1849

To my daughter, Susanna Feiser, half of my clothes. To my daughter, Susanna Feiser, the interest on two hundred dollars which should be paid to her annually. If my daughter, Susanna Feiser, should become a widow then she shall have the principal of two hundred dollars. Should my daughter, Susanna Feiser, die before her husband then the principal should be equally divided among her children, namely: Sarah Ann and Susanna Feiser (my granddaughters). To my daughter, Mary McMaster, the sum of five dollars. To my son, Joshua Sentz, the sum of five dollars. To my daughter, Essibella Yisser, the sum of five dollars. To my daughter, Sarah Jain Sentz, the sum of five dollars, two cows, one bureau, one bed with bedstead and six chairs. To my daughter, Allen Catherine Sentz, my home place where I currently reside to be held in trust by my executors until my daughter, Allen Catherine Sentz, reaches the age of twenty one. To my executor, the sum of one hundred dollars for his trouble and efforts. Should my daughter, Allen Catherine Sentz, die then the farm should be sold and the proceeds divided equally between my daughter, Sarah Jain, and my granddaughter, Sarah Ann Feiser. To my daughter, Allen Catherine Sentz, my carriage, side saddle, all my beds with bedsteads, household furniture of every description and the other half of my clothes. The residue of my estate should be sold and the proceeds equally divided among my three daughters, namely: Susannah Feiser, Sarah Jain and Allen Catherine.

Witnesses: James Grace, Daniel Matthias, Joseph Lippy
Executor(s): Joseph Heisson of Peter (friend)
Signed with his signature

Shaffer, David   of Carroll County
                                        March 1, 1844
                                        March 25, 1844
Number 171, Folio 304   March 25, 1844

After my real estate debts are paid to John Lammott, I give all my real and personal property to my wife, Catherine Shaffer, and Henry Masonhimer (Henry currently resides with me).

Witnesses: Abraham Wampler, Joshua Plowman, Jacob Trump, William T. Shaffer
Executor(s): Lewis Reigle (brother in law)
Signed with his signature

Shaffer, John   of Carroll County
                                        December 1, 1847
                                        April 30, 1849
Number 298, Folio 530   April 30, 1849

To my beloved wife, Elizabeth Shaffer, two cows, two bedsteads with furniture and bed clothes, case of drawers, my cupboard, all the cups with saucers and plates, ten plate stove, cooking stove, clock, table, six chairs, six knives, six forks, six spoons, linens, all my kitchen furniture and one hundred dollars. After the death of my wife, these items should be sold and the proceeds equally divided among my children. To my beloved wife during her widowhood, a sufficient room in the house where I currently reside as well as use of kitchen, cellar, spring house, half of garden, and a yearly quantity of fifteen bushels wheat, ten bushels corn, one hundred pounds pork, one hundred pounds beef and sufficient amount of cut fire wood and fruit. To my son, Samuel Shaffer, my broad tread wagon with cover, feed trough, one cow, one bed and bedstead and all my blacksmith tools. To my son, Jacob Shaffer, one large narrow tread wagon, one cow, one bed and bedstead and my thrashing machine. To my son, Samuel Shaffer, one desk. To my sons, Samuel Shaffer and Jacob Shaffer, my negro man named Jesse to serve them both until December 25, 1845 at which time Jesse should be freed. To my wife, Elizabeth Shaffer, my two negro girls called Rachel and Lett until December 25, 1845 at which time Rachel and Lett should be freed. To my two sons, Samuel Shaffer and Jacob Shaffer, my home plantation containing tracts of land called "North Canton" and "Addition to North Canton" containing one hundred and ninety four acres plus my wood lots on condition that my two said sons maintain my wife as previously described. Five thousand dollars to be equally divided among the rest of my children, namely: Henry Shaffer, Mary (wife of Aaron Crumrine), Elizabeth (wife of Fanual Wentz), David Shaffer and George Shaffer. The residue of my estate should be sold and the proceeds equally divided among all my children.

Witnesses: Jacob Schaeffer, Lewis Shafer, Michael Sullivan
Executor(s): Samuel Shaffer (son), Jacob Shaffer (son)
Signed with his signature

Shauck, John   of Carroll County (formerly
                                     Baltimore County)
                                                August 19, 1838
                                                August 19, 1839
Number 59, Folio 102   August 19, 1839

To my wife, Mary Magdalena, two beds with bedsteads and bedding, one spinning wheel, chest of drawers, bureau, all the flax and tow and linen, sewing threads, factory stuff and muslins, all the dried fruit, honey, preserves, pots and garden seeds. To my daughter, Mary Magdalena (wife of Micajah Stansbury), my plantation on the tracts of land called "Plowmans Fancy", "Plowmans Addition", "Bite the Bitter" and "Canton Bearon" containing about one hundred and eighty acres in Carroll County (formerly Baltimore County) and adjoining the lands of Richard Richards and Ulrick Zerbeichen for the sum of sixteen hundred dollars. My current dwelling plantation and mill in Carroll County (formerly Baltimore County) and in York County, Pennsylvania containing five hundred and fifty acres (adjoining the lands of John Brodbeck, Yoderus Messimer and George Fair) as well as my tract of land in Shrewsbury, Hopewell township, York County, Pennsylvania containing one hundred and forty six acres should be sold. The residue of my personal estate should be sold. To my eldest son, Henry Shauck, in consideration of his birth right and other services, five hundred dollars. My wife, Mary Magdalena, one third of the residue of my estate. My son, John Shauck, has already received money from me and should not be charged interest for such. My son in law, John Brodbeck (husband of my deceased daughter Catherine), has borrowed money from me and should be charged interest. The residue of my estate should be equally divided among my children, namely: Henry Shauck, John Shauck, Mary Stansbury and the children of my deceased daughter Catherine Brodbeck (namely Jeremiah, John, Mary Anne, Nimrod, George and Eliza Brodbeck).

Witnesses: David Jones, Jacob Bollinger, Loder Messemer
Executor(s): Aaron Shauck (grandson)
Signed with his signature

Shauck, Mary   of Carroll County
                                                      June 14, 1843
                                                      April 8, 1844
Number 174, Folio 309   April 8, 1844

All my personal and real property should be sold and the proceeds should be distributed as follows: to my son, John Shauck, three hundred dollars for his kindness; to the children of my daughter, Catherine (wife of John Brobeck), one hundred and eighty dollars to be equally divided; one share of the residue to my son, Henry Shauck, one share to my son, John Shauck; one share to the children of my daughter, Catherine Brobeck, to be shared equally; one share to my daughter, Mary

190

(wife of Micajah Stansbury), after money owed to me.

Witnesses: George D. Klinefeller, George Fisher
Executor(s): John Shauck (son)
Signed by her mark

Shaw, Moses   of Carroll County
                                                    March 20, 1846
                                                 February 26, 1849
Number 292, Folio 522   February 26, 1849

To my daughter, Frances Lauver, two hundred dollars. To my
grandchildren, Moses Thomas, Braxton Thomas and Mary L.
Thomas, one hundred and eight seven dollars to be placed at
interest and divided equally among them as they arrive at age.
To my granddaughter, Grizelda Thomas, all the goods that she
brought to my house and the cow that she raised while living
with me. To my granddaughter, Frances Thomas, one good bed
and bed furniture. To my grandson, William Martin, my silver
watch that formerly belonged to his father. The residue of my
estate should be divided among the following: my son, William
Shaw; my daughter, Martha Currey; my daughter, Nancy
Wright; my daughter, Mary Roberts; my daughter, Ann
Thomas, or the heirs of Ann Thomas.

Witnesses: Henry H. Herbaugh, John M. Ferguson, John Gore
Executor(s): William Shaw (son)
Signed with his signature

Shilling, Murray   of Carroll County
                                                    March 19, 1841
                                                     June 22, 1846
Number 229, Folio 421   June 22, 1846

To my dearly beloved wife, Rachel Shilling, a residence and an
ample support from my crops to be provided by my son, Josiah

Shilling as I have given the property where I currently reside to Josiah. To my son, Nicholas Shilling, the land where he resides on Beaver run (which adjoins the land of Mrs. McCrery and Allen Baker). To my son, Josiah, my negro boy called Richard, all the household goods and furniture, stock and cattle and every other thing on my property where I currently reside. I leave to my son, Nicholas Shilling, house and lot on Deer Park road. To my son, Nicholas, a tract of land near Westminster containing four acres (adjoining the lands of Thomas Hillen, Andrew Powder and Mrs. Colgate). These two pieces of property given to my son, Nicholas, should be kept in trust for my daughter, Ruth Yingling, and should not fall into the hands of her husband (Benjamin Yingling). The land conveyed to me by Bazil D. Stevenson containing seventy nine acres should be sold and the proceeds should go to my daughter, Ruth Yingling (to be held in trust by my son Nicholas). A deed should be provided to Thomas Hillen (heir of James McHaffe) for the land that I bartered to James McHaffe.

Renunciation
Josiah Shilling renounces his role as executor and that the role should go to Nicholas Shilling as mentioned the will of Murray Shilling. Witnessed August 3, 1846 by John M. Yingling.

Witnesses: Shadrack Bull, George Trumb, J. S. Shipley, William Shipley (junior)
Executor(s): Nicholas Shilling (son), Josiah Shilling (son)
Signed by his mark

Shipley, Denton   of Carroll County
                                                June 12, 1844
                                                July 15, 1844
Number 180, Folio 321   July 15, 1844

To my son, William E. Shipley, one dollar. All my of my estate including all of my personal property including cash in hand, book accounts, notes of hand, stock, household furniture, farming utensils and the grain growing in the ground should be equally divided among my children, namely: Joshua S. Shipley, Denton R. Shipley and Susannah E. Shipley. My estate should go the above named children on condition that they pay off my debts.

Witnesses: Burgess Nelson (junior), William J. Grumbine
Executor(s): Joshua S. Shipley (son), Denton R. Shipley (son)
Signed with his signature

Shoemaker, Peter   of Frederick County
                                                    March 15, 1836
                                                    December 31, 1839
Number 46, Folio 79   December 31, 1839

To my granddaughter, Barbara Martin, the sum of one hundred dollars. All my slaves should be manumitted and freed after my death, namely: John Sater, Anna Sater, Sarah, Samuel, Elizabeth, Jacob, Mariah and John. To my colored woman called Anna Sater (wife of John Sater), eight acres including all buildings and improvements thereon in Frederick County being part of a tract of land called "Look About" and "Fathers Aduce" (which are contiguous to one another and were conveyed to me by George Stary with the deed dated March 14, 1825). I give to all my negroes, the beds and bedding used by them. I give to my colored man, John Sater, a small ten plate stove and pipe, one chest, one axe, hatchet, scythe, cradle hand saw, two small saws, four planes, nine chisels, brace and bits, five auger, screw cutter, drawing knife, lathing hammer and table, plus my corner cupboard. The residue of my estate should be sold and the proceeds should be divided into four equal parts, namely: one part to be equally divided among the sons and daughters of my deceased daughter, Susanna Rinehart, upon reaching lawful age; one part to be equally divided among the sons and daughters of my deceased daughter, Mary Martin, upon reaching lawful age; to my daughter, Sarah Barnhart, the interest on one fourth until her sons and daughters are to come of lawful age at which point the principal should be equally divided among my grandchildren (the children of Sarah Barnhart); to my daughter, Elizabeth Sprinkle, the interest on one fourth until her sons and daughters are to come of lawful age at which point the principal should be equally divided among my grandchildren (the children of Elizabeth Sprinkle). To the extent that some of my legatees may live at a great distance from me, my executors should not incur any costs associated with neglect or refusal on the part of my legatees.

Witnesses: John Nusbaum, Abraham Hesson, Jacob Sell, Peter Dehof
Executor(s): Jacob Mathias, Joshua Smith
Signed with his signature

Shoey, Rosanna   widow of Daniel Shuey,
                                        Frederick County
                                            December 11, 1830
                                                April 22, 1839
Number 50, Folio 87   April 22, 1839

To my son, Henry Shoey, the sum of one hundred and thirty eight dollars which should put him at equal footing as his siblings. The remainder of my estate should be divided equally among my six living children, namely: Henry Shoey, Mary Cook (widow of Mathias Cook), Barbara Greenwood (wife of John Greenwood), Elizabeth Hining (widow of Thomas Hining), Catherine Greenwood (wife of Ludwick Greenwood) and Daniel Shoey.

Witnesses: Noah Worman, Joseph Greenwood, George Yandis
Executor(s): John Greenwood (trusty friend and son in law)
Signed by her mark

Shriner, Peter   of Carroll County
                                               January 22, 1838
                                               September 4, 1838
Number 35, Folio 59   September 4, 1838

I have already given my son, Abraham Shriner, his part of my
estate. To my son, Jacob Shriner, my plantation where I
currently reside in Carroll County (containing fifty five acres)
on condition that he pay my estate two thousand dollars after
one year of my decease. To my son, Jacob, my eight day clock,
stove and pipe and the long table in the kitchen. To my
daughter, Mary Perry, my plantation called "Resurvey on Small
Beginning" containing one hundred acres, my mulatto girl
called Matilda to serve until the age of twenty five (refer to the
records of manumission of Frederick County) and one thousand
dollars to be paid from my estate after one year of my death.

Witnesses: Evan McKinstry, David Engler, John P. Shriner
Executor(s): William Dudderer
Signed with his signature

Shriner, Peter   of Carroll County
                                               February 16, 1849
                                               August 25, 1851
Number 360, Folio 612   August 25, 1851

To my son, John Shriner, my wheat fan. To my daughter,
Mary, all my horn cattle, the dishes with plates and spoons and
bed with bedstead and bedding. The remainder of my personal
property and my farm lying in Carroll County called "Brothers
Agreement" (containing one hundred and fifty five acres)
should be sold. If the farm does not sell within the first year of
my death, then my son, John Shriner, should have it for fifty
dollars on condition that he keep it in good repair and rents it
out. The proceeds of my estate should be divided equally
among: my son, John Shriner; my son, Peter Shriner; my
daughter Catherine Ridinger (widow of Peter Ridinger); my

daughter, Elizabeth (wife of Elias Sowers); my daughter, Nelly (wife of Daniel Fleegle); my daughter, Mary Shriner; my daughter, Lydia (wife of Daniel Frock); my grandson, Samuel Newcomer, when he arrives at the age of twenty one.

Witnesses: William Rudisel, Levi Buffington, William Fisher
Executor(s): John Shriner (son), Daniel Frock
Signed by his mark

Shunk, Joseph   of Carroll County
                                         March 27, 1848
                                         April 10, 1848
Number 278, Folio 502   April 10, 1848

To my mother, Aberilla Shunk, all my clothes and silver watch. My executors should sell the remainder of my personal estate and the interest that I have with my brother, Jeremiah, in the land in Tanytown where he now resides as well as the unimproved lot that I own in Taneytown. The residue of the proceeds of my estate should go to my mother, Aberilla Shunk.

Witnesses: William Rudisel, William Burk, Israel Hiteshue
Executor(s): Benjamin Shunk (brother)
Signed with his signature

Shunk, Rebecca   of Carroll County
                                         April 16, 1848
                              September 22, 1851
Number 365, Folio 619   September 22, 1851

To my niece, Mary Shunk (daughter of my brother Daniel), my bed with bedding. The residue of my estate should go to my brother, Daniel Shunk.

Witnesses: William Shepherd, Job C. Haines
Executor(s): Daniel Shunk (brother)
Signed by her mark

Sire, John   of Carroll County

                                              April 1851

                                        May 19, 1851

Number 353, Folio 604   May 19, 1851

To my illegitimate son, William Corbin, and to Daniel L. Hoover, a land warrant for one hundred and sixty acres issued to me by the Commissioners of Pensions on February 15, 1851 (Number 1113).

Witnesses: Henry Zipp, Joshua Corbin, Kissier Evans
Executor(s): William Corbin (son)
Signed by his mark

Slyder, John   of Baltimore County

                                          March 5, 1847

                                 November 1, 1847

Number 264, Folio 481   November 1, 1847

To my beloved wife, Catherine Slyder, all my estate until the time that my youngest child, Sarah Jane Slyder, should arrive at the age of eighteen at which point all my estate should be sold. The proceeds of my estate should be equally divided among: my wife, Catherine Slyder; my son, Frederick Slyder and my daughter, Sarah Jane Slyder.

Witnesses: Michael Sullivan, Joshua Tipton, Jonas Deal
Executor(s): Catherine Slyder (wife)
Signed with his signature

Slyder, Peter   of Carroll County

                                        May 14, 1839

                                        June 1, 1840

Number 76, Folio 135   June 1, 1840

My clothes should be equally divided among my sons: William Slyder, John Slyder, Jacob Slyder, Henry Slyder and Josiah

Slyder. My tract of land called "Unions Mill" in Carroll County and Hanover, York County, Pennsylvania (containing sixty acres and conveyed to me by my son John) should be sold. One thousand and twenty two dollars should be equally distributed among the following children: William Slyder, John Slyder, Jacob Slyder, Henry Slyder, Josiah Slyder, Anna Mary Slyder, Catherine (wife of John Hillesbrock), Barbara (wife of Jacob Warnes), Susan (wife of Samuel Babylon), Rachel Slyder, the children of my deceased daughter Elizabeth Eck and her husband Peter Eck (Nancy, Levi, William, Eli, Jacob, Josiah and James Eck). To my son, John Slyder, the balance of the proceeds from the sale of my real estate. To my daughter, Anna Mary Slyder, one bed with bedstead and bedding, spinning wheel and one cow. To my daughter, Rachel Slyder, one bed with bedstead and bedding, spinning wheel and one cow. The residue of my estate should be sold and the proceeds should be distributed as follows: to my daughter, Anna Mary Slyder, fifty dollars; to my son, Henry Slyder, one hundred dollars; to my son, Josiah Slyder, one hundred dollars; the residue should be equally divided among my children, namely: William Slyder, John Slyder, Jacob Slyder, Henry Slyder, Josiah Slyder, Anna Mary Slyder, Catherine Hillterbrick, Barbara Warnes, Susan Babylon, Rachel Slyder and the children of my deceased daughter Elizabeth Eck.

Witnesses: Benjamin Shunk, Joseph Eck, John Baumgartner
Executor(s): William Slyder (son)
Signed with his signature

Smiech, John   of Carroll County
                                    January 28, 1841
                                    April 8, 1841
Number 98, Folio 165   April 8, 1841

To Elizabeth Messemer (daughter of Samuel Messemer), her choice of a bed with bedstead and twenty five dollars. To my daughter, Lydia, one bed with bedstead and one hundred and fifty dollars. To Jacob Sterner, one hundred and fifty dollars. The residue of my estate should be sold and the proceeds should be equally divided among my children [not named].

Witnesses: George Stegner, John Fuherman, Daniel Peterman
Executor(s): Henry Houck, Jacob Stoner
Signed by his mark

Smith, James   of Carroll County
                                                                July 23, 1840
                                                             January 31, 1842
Number 122, Folio 202   February 7, 1842

To my dear and beloved wife, Sarah Smith, all my property (except the legacies to my children). Each of my nine children should be given fifty cents, namely: Nancy, Ann, William, Robert, Elizabeth, Mary, Charlotte, Susan Jane and Jerusa.

Renunciation
Nicholas H. Browne renounces his executorship and asks that the letters testamentary be granted to Sarah Smith, widow of the deceased. Witnessed February 7, 1842 by Nimrod Frizzell.

Witnesses: Adam Gilbert, Horatio Price, Amon Tipton
Executor(s): Sarah Smith (wife), Nicholas Hall Brown (friend)
Signed with his signature

Smith, John   of Carroll County
                                                                 June 5, 1841
                                                          September 5, 1842
Number 135, Folio 231   September 5, 1842

To my daughter, Mary Barnes, the plantation where she currently resides (which was conveyed to me by the late James Denning) and contains seventy eight acres. To my son, Richard

Smith, the balance of my farm formerly occupied by him which contains seventy six acres. To my son, George Smith and his wife Nancy, the farm where I currently reside containing one hundred and forty acres. After the death of George and Nancy Smith, this land should go to my grandson, Thomas Smith (son of George Smith), provided that Thomas pay his sister, Rebecca Smith, one hundred and fifty dollars. If Rebecca Smith survives Thomas Smith, then this land belongs to her. To my granddaughter, Rebecca Smith (of George), my large family chest. To my granddaughter, Mary Smith (of George), my bedstead with bedding. The balance of my estate should go to my son, George Smith.

Witnesses: Joshua Smith, Joseph Smith, John Smith
Executor(s): George Smith (son)
Signed with his signature

Smith, John Frederick   of Carroll County
                                              June 5, 1838
                                          December 19, 1842
Number 143, Folio 245   December 19, 1842

To my beloved wife, Christena, all my estate. After the death or marriage of my wife, my estate should be sold and the proceeds should be distributed as follows: to my daughter, Rebecca (wife of Andrew Pfeifer), twenty five dollars; to my daughter, Polly, one seventh; to my daughter, Elizabeth (wife of Jacob Wagonner), one seventh; to my daughter, Catherine (wife of John Klinedents), one seventh; to my daughter, Rachel, one half of one seventh; to the eldest heir of my daughter Rachel, one half of one seventh; to my daughter, Rebecca (wife of Andrew Pfeifer), one seventh; to my son, George, one seventh; to the heirs of my deceased daughter, Sarah, one seventh.

Witnesses: Jacob Gitt, Henry E. Beltz, William Crumrine
Executor(s): George Shower (good friend)
Signed with his signature

Smith, Joshua   of Carroll County

March 31, 1841

December 24, 1841

Number 116, Folio 191   December 27, 1841

To my son, Thomas Smith, the plantation where I currently reside (containing ninety acres) called "The Five Sisters" on condition that my son, Thomas Smith, should pay my daughter, Mary Smith, eleven hundred dollars. To my son, Joseph Smith, the plantation where he now dwells in Carroll County (containing one hundred and eighty acres) on condition that my son, Joseph Smith, pays my daughter, Mary Smith, fifteen hundred dollars. To my daughter, Mary Smith, sixty one acres in Carroll County which was conveyed to me by Joshua Howard. To my daughter, Mary Smith, the ten acres that were conveyed to me by Samuel Carr and the wood lot (containing fifty two acres) which was conveyed to me by George H. Waesche. To my son, John Smith, the fifty acres that were conveyed to me by George Henry and Catherine Waesche in 1834. To my son, John Smith, the one hundred and ninety four acres conveyed to me by Michael Smith on condition that my son, John smith, should pay my other son, Richard Smith, six thousand and five hundred dollars. I manumit and free my two negro girls called Catherine and Darkey. To my son, John Smith, and to my daughter, Mary Smith, my negro boy called Nick and the son of my negro woman Beck (Beck's son's name being Jeremiah) to share equally, however, as Nick and Jeremiah reach the age of twenty five they should be freed. The residue of my personal property should be sold and the proceeds equally divided among my son, John Smith, and my daughter, Mary Smith, on condition that they pay the following legacies: to my son, Richard Smith, two hundred dollars and to my son, Joshua Smith, one hundred dollars.

Witnesses: Isaac Haines, John Baumgartner, Eli Haines
Executor(s): John Smith (son)
Signed with his signature

Snader, Jacob   of Carroll County
                                      May 7, 1840
                                      December 20, 1847
Number 265, Folio 482   December 20, 1847

To my daughter, Margaret Snader, the use of room that she currently occupies which is the largest upper room in the brick portion of the house as well as all the privileges of the kitchen so long as she remains single. I give to my daughter, Margaret Snader, three thousand dollars provided that she pays my sons, Philip and Jacob Snader, each fifty dollars a year until she has paid a total of fifteen hundred dollars (half of the amount she received). My son, Jacob Snader, shall provide my daughter, Margaret, as much flour, meat, vegetables and wood as required as long as she is to remain single and at my residence. Should my daughter, Margaret, marry then my sons should pay her fifty dollars a year until they have paid the sum of fifteen hundred dollars less the amount that she paid them during her stay at my house. To my son, Philip Snader, the recently divided part of farm where I currently reside (containing one hundred and seventy acres) and the wood lot (containing thirty acres) near Bethel Meeting House. To my son, Jacob Snader, the recently divided part of the farm where I currently reside (containing one hundred and twenty five acres) and twenty five acres of my wood lot.

Witnesses: Daniel Engel, David W. Naill, David Engel
Executor(s): Philip Snader (son), Jacob Snader (son)
Signed with his signature

Snider, Peter   of Carroll County
                                      June 25, 1838
                                      April 29, 1844
Number 175, Folio 311   April 29, 1844

To my wife, Margaret Snider, my property both real and personal for her life. After the death of my wife, my estate should be equally divided among my sons, John Snider and Peter Snider, on condition that they should pay one hundred dollars to each of my daughters, namely: Catherine (wife of Samuel Jones), Elizabeth (wife of Abraham Sentz) and Anna Mary (wife of Jacob Pensil).

Witnesses: Henry Eckard, John Troxel, Moses Eckard
Executor(s): Peter Snider (son)
Signed with his signature

Snyder, Christian   of Carroll County
                                                        March 3, 1838
                                                        March 7, 1842
Number 123, Folio 203   March 7, 1842

To my beloved wife, Magdalena Snyder, two cows, two feather beds with bedsteads and bedding, my corner cupboard which is standing the front room, six cups and saucers, one pewter basin, one pewter dish, six plate stove, small table, six chairs, six knives, six forks, six spoons, one teapot, linens, all the kitchen furniture she requires and the sum of fifty dollars. The residue of my personal property should be sold and the proceeds should be divided among eight of my children and among my grandchildren, namely: Jacob Snyder, Michael Snyder, Henry Snyder, Magdalena Yingling (wife of John Yingling), Barbary Witter (wife of Samuel Witter), Catherine Yingling (wife of Jacob Yingling), Leah Glase (wife of Henry Glase), Rachel Keller (wife of Philip Keller), the children of my deceased son George Snyder, the children of my deceased daughter Elizabeth Rockey and the children of my deceased daughter Anna Maria Whiteleather. I give to my beloved wife, the use of the front room in my house, the kitchen, half of the garden, half of the spring house, half of the cellar, half of the apple orchard plus annually eight bushels wheat, four bushels rye, four bushels corn, five bushels potatoes, two hundred pounds pork, twenty five pounds beef, ten pounds flax, ten pounds tow and sufficient cut firewood. It is my desire that my son in law, Samuel Witter, farms the plantation where I currently reside and maintains my wife as described previously as well as pays my wife forty dollars annually. The residue of my estate should be sold and the proceeds should be equally divided among my heirs as mentioned. After the death of my wife, my farm should be sold and equally divided among my heirs as mentioned.

Witnesses: Frederick Ritter, Michael Ritter, Michael Sullivan
Executor(s): Henry Glase (son in law)
Signed with his signature

Snyder, Jacob (senior)   of Carroll County

May 21, 1846

February 11, 1850

Number 316, Folio 554   February 11, 1850

To my son, Jacob, fifty dollars. To my daughter, Magdalain, fifty dollars, bed with bedstead, bureau and one cow. Fifty dollars to the children of my daughter, Susanna, which should be equally divided among them. Fifty dollars to the children of my daughter, Beggy, which should be equally divided among them. Magdalena's share should be put at interest for her maintenance during her life and after her death this money should be equally divided among the rest. With the exception of my son, Jacob's share, and my daughter, Magdalain's share, the balance should be equally divided among all: Jacob, Magdalain, Susanna, Beggy and George Lambert.

Renunciation
George Lambert refuses to act as executor and defers to the other named executor. Dated February 11, 1850.

Witnesses: John Lichly, Michael Harner, Ephraim Jones
Executor(s): Jacob Snyder, Jr. (son), George Lambert (son in law)
Signed by his mark

Snyder, Magdalena   of Carroll County

February 7, 1850

June 23, 1851

Number 357, Folio 608   June 23, 1851

My personal property should be sold and the proceeds should be divided into ten equal portions, namely: to my son, Jacob Snyder, one share; to my son, Michael Snyder, one share; to my son, Henry Snyder, one share; to my daughter, Magdalena Yingling, one share; to my daughter, Barbara Witter, one share; to my daughter, Catherine Yingling, one share; to my daughter, Leah Glase, one share; to my daughter, Rachel Heller, one share; two shares are to be equally divided among seven of my grandchildren, namely: David A. Snyder, George W. Snyder, Daniel Snyder, Magdelina Steffon (wife of George Steffon), Catherine Snyder, Martin Witeleather, Rebecca Witeleather. To my daughter, Barbary Witter, my large rocking chair and "all my cupping apparatus and lancet for bleeding."

Witnesses: David E. Reigal, John Stephan, Michael Sullivan
Executor(s): Samuel Witter (son in law)
Signed by her mark

Speelman, Anna Mary   of Carroll County

January 3, 1845

April 21, 1845

Number 200, Folio 369   April 21, 1845

To Tillila Welk (wife of George Welk), all my real and personal property (which amounts to one hundred and fifty dollars). To Tillila Welk also one bed with bedding, my ten plate stove, table and chairs.

Witnesses: John Hesson, Adam Masonheimer, Charles Devilbiss
Executor(s): Tillilia Welk (niece)
Signed by her mark

Stansbury, Mary of Carroll County
October 12, 1850
November 18, 1850
Number 340, Folio 587 November 18, 1850

All my estate should be equally divided among my brothers: Jared Stansbury, Isaac Stansbury, Caleb Stansbury, Joseph Stansbury and William Stansbury. After the deaths of my brothers, I give to my nephew, John L. Stansbury (son of Emanuel Stansbury), sixty dollars and to my niece, Elizabeth Ruth Taylor (daughter of my sister Rebecca Taylor), sixty dollars.

Witnesses: John Sweeden, William Arbaugh, Stephen Oursler
Executor(s): not named
Signed by her mark

Stansbury, Richard of Carroll County
October 1, 1838
May 8, 1848
Number 281, Folio 506 May 8, 1848

To my daughter, Creasy Stansbury, one hundred dollars, French bedstead with furniture, six chairs, chest and one cow. To my son, Josiah Stansbury, one hundred dollars, French bedstead with furniture, six chairs, chest, one cow and a horse. The residue of my personal and real estate (excluding one quarter of an acre to be used as a burying ground with privilege of a road from the burying ground to the York road) should be sold. The proceeds of my estate should be equally distributed among the following: John Stansbury, Richard Stansbury, Cresy Stansbury, Kesiah (wife of Joshua Spindle), heirs of Ellen Faes (wife of Lewis Faes), Joshua Stansbury and Josiah Stansbury. "Whereas the said Lewis Faes has left this part of the country in a mysterious way leaving my sons Richard Stansbury Joshua Stansbury and Josiah Stansbury in debt, it is my will...." that the said money come out of the share to the heirs of Ellen Faes.

The crops growing at the time of my death should go to my daughter, Creasy Stansbury, and to my son, Josiah Stansbury.

Witnesses: Thomas Sater, John Sneck, Jacob Kerlinger
Executor(s): John Stansbury (trusty son)
Signed by his mark

Steele, James   of Carroll County
                                              March 20, 1838
                                                April 2, 1838
Number 27, Folio 45   April 2, 1838

To my dear mother, Mary Denning, the plantation where I currently reside called "Eppington Forest" (containing two hundred acres) and "Red Oak Ridge" (containing seventy acres). After the death of my mother, this land should go to my brother, Joseph Steele. After the death of my brother, Joseph, this land should go to my nephews, namely: John Thomas, James Henry, William Robert and Joseph Wesley Steele (sons of my brother Joseph Steele). To my nephew, James Henry Steele, my negro woman called Beck and her son called Hiram (Hiram should be a slave for life). To my nephew, James Henry Steele, any issue that Beck may have, however, Beck should be freed on January 8, 1844. To my nephew, John Thomas Steele, my gold watch. The residue of my estate and my lands (adjoining Nelly Demmit and Abner Baile on the Old Liberty Road) called "Resurvey Fathers Gift", "Hawkins Fancy" and "Lawrence's Industry" and a tract of land in Huntington County, Springfield township, Pennsylvania (containing fifty three acres) should be sold. The proceeds should be equally divided between my three brothers, namely: Robert, Joseph and Thomas Steele.

Witnesses: Nathan Browne, Beale Buckingham, Vachel Buckingham
Executor(s): Joseph Steele (brother)
Signed with his signature

Steever, Mary   of Carroll County
                                      October 4, 1841
                                   February 13, 1843
Number 146, Folio 251   February 20, 1843

My estate should be sold and the proceeds should be equally divided among my grandchildren, namely: Andrew Dewees and Mary Sharrer (wife of David Sharrer and sister to Andrew).

Witnesses: Jacob Gitt, Henry N. Brinkman, Jacob Linaweaver
Executor(s): Andrew Dewees (grandson)
Signed by her mark

Steffee, Michael   of Carroll County
                           1838 [only year given]
                                     May 27, 1850
Number 327, Folio 569   May 27, 1850

To my beloved wife, Christina, all of my estate. After the death of my wife, my estate should be sold and the proceeds equally divided among my children and grandchildren, namely: Jacob Steffee, heirs of Peter Steffee, Barbara (wife of Henry Rhule), Polly (wife of David Frankforter) and Henry Steffee.

Witnesses: Jacob Gitt, Jacob Shower, Samuel B. Fuhrman
Executor(s): David Frankforter (son in law), Henry Steffee (son)
Signed by his mark

Stevenson, Nancy   of Uniontown, Carroll County
                                      April 20, 1846
                                       June 12, 1848
Number 283, Folio 509   June 12, 1848

To my nephew, Frederick Devilbiss, four hundred dollars. To my grand niece, Emma Devilbiss (daughter of my nephew Frederick Devilbiss), my bureau and bed with bedstead. The residue of my estate should go to my sister, Jemima Stevenson.

After the death of my sister, my estate should be equally divided between my nephew, Frederick Devilbiss, and my sister, Elizabeth Devilbiss (wife of Charles Devilbiss). My sister's share to held in trust by my nephews, James Devilbiss and Charles S. Devilbiss. After the decease of my sister, Elizabeth, her portion should go to her children [not named].

Witnesses: Samuel A. Lauver, Jacob Christ, John Roberts
Executor(s): Frederick Devilbiss (nephew)
Signed by her mark

Stevenson, Sarah   of Union Town, Carroll County
                                          January 6, 1838
                                               May 5, 1845
Number 201, Folio 371   May 5, 1845

My estate should go to my two sisters, Nancy Stevenson and Jemima Stevenson.

Witnesses: James Devilbiss, Frederick A. Devilbiss, Charles S. Devilbiss, John Roberts
Executor(s): John Roberts (friend)
Signed with her signature

Steward, Sarah   of Carroll County
                                          January 12, 1846
                                           August 10, 1846
Number 233, Folio 427   August 10, 1846

My estate should be equally divided among: my eldest son, Washington Wilson, my daughter, Matilda Wilson, and my daughter, Mary Bowars. Five dollars should go to my youngest son, Lewis Stewart, as he was the heir to his father's estate.

Witnesses: Daniel Stoner, Joseph Myers
Executor(s): Stephan Bowers (trusty friend and son in law)
Signed by her mark

Stocksdale, Edward (of John)   of Carroll County
December 9, 1841
March 14, 1842

Number 124, Folio 206
March 14, 1842

To my daughter, Nelly Hanes, the sum of five hundred dollars. Also to my daughter, Nelly, one three year old (will be four years old by next June) negro girl called Amanda Ann and two cows. Also my daughter, Nelly, should keep a home with my son, Solomon Stocksdale, however I forbid that Nelly's husband, Edward Hanes, should have any interest in the legacy that I have given to her. To the children of my deceased son, John Stocksdale, each one hundred dollars, namely: Emily Jane, Edward and Ellen Stocksdale. To my son, Noah Stocksdale, the plantation (on the turnpike road and on a plat made by William Whalen) containing one hundred and thirteen acres provided that the Mill Road be kept open. To my son, Solomon Stocksdale, the residue of my real estate (which is drawn on the plat made by William Whalen) which contains one hundred and ninety six acres called "Point Intelligence" as well as the lot of land conveyed to me by William Jameson (William Jameson who was acting as trustee for the estate of Jacob Hooker). To my son, Solomon Stocksdale, the residue of my personal property. I ask that my son, Solomon Stocksdale, maintain my afflicted daughter, Rachel, in an affectionate and decent manner and in doing so I give to my son, Solomon Stocksdale, my negro girl named Harriet. I also expect that my daughter, Nelly, should help with maintaining my daughter, Rachel. My sister, Elizabeth Lane, should be able to keep her home with my son, Solomon Stocksdale, as long as she desires.

Witnesses: William Jameson, Louis L. Dickson, Jacob Cakle
Executor(s): Solomon Stocksdale (son)
Signed with his signature

Stoner, Elizabeth of Carroll County
September 6, 1849
December 8, 1851
Number 371, Folio 626 December 8, 1851

Whereas I advanced to my nephew, John Englar (the son of my brother), the sum of one hundred dollars to be applied to building a comfortable room adjoining his house where I plan to spend my remaining days, and whereas I hold a note for eight hundred dollars assigned to my by Daniel Haines and due to me from his son William M. Haines, I give to said John Englar the note for eight hundred dollars with interest on the condition that he has claimed to provide for me during my life. I give all my remaining personal property to John Englar.

Witnesses: John Weaver, William A. Smelser, David W. Naill
Executor(s): John Englar (friend)
Signed by her mark

Stoner, John of Frederick County
March 20, 1832
June 3, 1835 (codicil)
March 1, 1841
Number 92, Folio 155 March 1, 1841

However there was an agreement between myself and my current wife [not named] that I was not to have anything of her estate which she had previous to our marriage and she was not to have any claim on my estate, yet I bequeath to her fifty dollars as a present to be taken out of my estate. My mill and property in Linganore should be equally divided among the seven children of my deceased son, Abraham Stoner, namely: Samuel Stoner, John Stoner, Ezra Stoner, Abraham Stoner, Eleanor Stouffer, Mary Stoner and Sophia Stoner. To my son, John Stoner, the mill and property where I currently reside and the land which was conveyed to me by William Farquhar and Joseph Biggs and one half of the wood lot which was conveyed to me by Casper Devilbiss and one half of the wood lot in Baltimore County which was conveyed to me by Phillip Engler. To my eldest daughter, Mary Englar, and to my youngest daughter, Elizabeth Schriner, the plantation where my son John now resides and one half of the wood lot which was conveyed to me by Casper Devilbiss and one half of the wood lot in Baltimore County which was conveyed to me by Phillip Engler. I give my plantation now occupied by Isaac Landes which was conveyed to me by David McDaniel, David Eves and James Muneford and the land which was conveyed to me by John Ferguson and Jacob Yon to my daughter, Hannah Landes. All my personal property should be sold including the stock that I have in Frederick County Bank and the remaining proceeds of my personal estate should go equally to my daughters, Mary Engler and Elizabeth Schriner.

Codicil
Given that my daughter, Mary Engler, is now deceased, I devise that her share should be divided equally among her children, namely: Ephraim Engler, Eliza Stouffer, Julian Slingluff, John Engler, Hannah Engler, Mordecai Engler and Levina Engler.

Witnesses: Evan McKinstry, Jacob Landes, Samuel McKinstry
Executor(s): John Stoner (son), Philip Engler, Jacob Schriner
Signed with his signature

Stonesifer, Daniel   of Carroll County
                                          October 11, 1842
                                          January 29, 1844
Number 166, Folio 291   January 29, 1844

To my wife, Catherine Stonesifer, one cow, two beds with bedsteads and quilts, one case of drawers, one corner cupboard, one leaf table, six Windsor chairs, all the linens, chest and stove. To my son, Joshua Stonsifer, my plantation where I currently reside in Carroll County (containing one hundred and fifty three acres) on condition that he allows my wife the use of one third of the house, kitchen, cellar, spring house, garden, and pay my wife fifteen dollars annually as well as provide her annually with twenty five bushels wheat, twenty five bushels oats, twenty five bushels corn, three hundred pounds pork, fifty pounds beef, sufficient potatoes, apples and cut firewood plus pasture and care for her cows. I also require that my son, Joshua Stonesifer, pay my two daughters each one thousand dollars, namely: Cazza (wife of Benjamin Matthias) and Elizabeth Stonesifer. To my daughter, Elizabeth Stonesifer, two cows, one heifer, two sheep, three hogs, one dining leaf table, six windsor chairs, large bureau, middle sized chest, one complete bed and French bedstead, one common bed and bedstead and spinning wheel (as fit as that given to her sister Cazza). I give to my son, Joshua Stonesifer, the residue of my personal property.

Witnesses: William Bachman, David S. Bankert, J. Henry Hoppe
Executor(s): Joshua Stonesifer (son)
Signed with his signature

Stouffer, John   of Carroll County
                                         August 4, 1838
                                      November 26, 1840
Number 86, Folio 148   January 3, 1842

To my sister, Elizabeth Chew, all my personal and real property which includes the interest that I have in the farm where my mother now resides near Uniontown and the land that I recently purchased of David Yingling lying on the road from Uniontown to Union Bridge. If my sister, Elizabeth Chew, should die before me then my estate should be equally divided among her children [not named].

Witnesses: John Roberts, Benjamin Hahn, John Gore
Executor(s): William Roberts (friend)
Signed by his mark

Strevig, John   of Carroll County
                                                       January 7, 1844
                                                         March 4, 1844
Number 169, Folio 298   March 4, 1844

All my real and personal property should be sold. I ask that my executors set aside enough money to maintain my beloved wife, Margaret, for her life. The residue should be equally divided among my children, namely: Jacob Strevig, John Strevig, George Strevig, Mary (wife of John Warehime), and Susanna (wife of George Walker). As my daughter, Catherine (wife of Valentine Manche), has received previous assistance, I consider her share paid. I have sold property to George Wentz, and my executors should claim the money owed to my estate.

Witnesses: Henry Kautz, Adam Rohrbach, Jacob Kerlinger
Executor(s): John Strevig (son)
Signed with his signature

Stultz, Conrad   of Carroll County
                                                          May 19, 1837
                                                  May 18, 1839 (codicil)
                                                     September 16, 1839
Number 61, Folio 112   September 16, 1839

To my wife, Mary Stultz, one feather bed with bedstead and bedding, one cow, spinning wheel, one bureau and all the furniture that she has bought that is in my house. The residue of my personal estate and all my real estate should be sold. One third of the proceeds should go to my wife, Mary Stulz, in lieu of her dower. The balance of my estate should be equally divided among my children, namely: the children of my daughter Catherine Otto, Ann Dayhoof (widow of Jacob Dayhoof), Elizabeth Wilson, Margaret Rempyone, David Stultz, Abraham Stultz, Sarah Shriner (wife of John Shriner), Hannah Stultz, Sophia Leas and Mary (provided that Mary comes for her share within three years of my death).

Codicil
Whereas my daughter, Sarah Shriner (wife of John Shriner), has since departed this life since I wrote my will, I direct that her share be divided as follows: one third to her husband (John Shriner) and the remaining two thirds should be equally divided among her children [not named].

Witnesses: Daniel Shunk, John Koons, Jacob Hann
Executor(s): Thomas Hook (friend), David Stultz (son)
Signed with his signature

Stultz, David   of Carroll County
                                    July 30, 1849
                                August 13, 1849
Number 305, Folio 538   August 13, 1849

To my wife, Ann Stultz, the farm where I currently reside (containing one hundred and twenty five acres), also three horses, four cows, five hogs, my wagon, all the farming implements and all the kitchen and household furniture for her use during her widowhood until that time when my youngest daughter, Sarah Jane, should arrive at the age of twenty one. My executors should provide my wife ample grain until the next crop comes in. The residue of my personal and real estate including that lot adjoining my land called "Brothers Agreement" (containing seventeen acres) should be sold. After the marriage of my daughter Sarah Jane or after the date of her arriving at age, the real and personal property mentioned herein should be sold. The proceeds of my estate should be equally divided among my wife and children, namely: Ann Stultz (wife), Sophia Otto (wife of Herbert Otto), William Stultz, Eliza Ann Stultz, Samuel Franklin Stultz, Catharine Stultz and Sarah Jane Stultz.

Witnesses: Benjamin Shunk, John Reck, Tobias Rudisel
Executor(s): James Crouse
Signed by his mark

Stultz, Elizabeth   of Carroll County

June 9, 1847

September 6, 1847

Number 259, Folio 472   September 6, 1847

To my third son, Henry Stultz, twenty eight dollars. Twelve dollars should be equally divided among my three sons, namely: David, Abraham and Ephraim Stultz. The balance of my estate should be equally divided among my four daughters, namely: Anne, Margaret, Susannah and Elizabeth Stultz.

Witnesses: Andrew Haines, George Wilson, John Eckerd
Executor(s): Margaret Stultz (daughter)
Signed by her mark

Sulivan, Mary   of Frederick County

November 28, 1832

January 6, 1851

Number 345, Folio 592   January 6, 1851

To William Durbin and his wife, Elizabeth, the house and lot where I currently reside. After their death, this house and lot should go to Hannah Durbin (daughter of said William and Elizabeth). If Hannah dies without heirs, the house and lot should go to Ruth Durbin (sister of said Hannah). To my niece, Mary Catherine Sulivan (daughter of my brother William), my silver tea spoon set. To my nephew, Cornelius Sulivan (son of my brother Abraham), my silver watch. To my sister, Margaret Bear, my clothes. To my niece, Polly Bear (daughter of my sister Margaret), a bed quilt. To Catherine Durbin, a bed quilt. To Elizabeth Durbin (daughter of William), my china cups and saucers. The residue should go to my brother, William Sulivan.

Witnesses: William Durbin, Joshua Smith (junior), Nicholas Durbin
Executor(s): William Sulivan (brother)
Signed by her mark

Sullivan, Herod F.   of Carroll County
                                        February 11, 1848
                                        March 6, 1848
Number 271, Folio 491   March 6, 1848

To my beloved wife, Rebecca Sullivan, all of my estate.

Renunciation
Rebecca Sullivan, widow of Herod F. Sullivan, renounces her
title as executor and requests that the letters of administration
be granted to George Everhart. Witnessed March 6, 1848 by
William G. Stansbury.

Witnesses: Jacob Kerlinger, Henry E. Beltz, James Stansbury
Executor(s): Rebecca Sullivan (wife)
Signed with his signature

Swartzbaugh, John   of Carroll County
                                        May 7, 1847
                                        September 6, 1847
Number 258, Folio 470   September 6, 1847

My executors should sell my land lying on the road from
Manchester to York and the proceeds should be applied to my
debts. If this is not sufficient to cover my debts then lots
should be sold to cover such. The residue of my real and
personal estate should remain in the hands of my wife,
Elizabeth, including three beds and bedsteads, stove, clock,
corner cupboard and contents, chest, spinning wheel, copper tea
kettle, baking pans, churn, iron kettle, iron pots, two horses,
four cows, five hogs, five sheep, one wagon, two ploughs, one
harrow, log chains and all the pewter ware for her widowhood.
If my wife should remarry, then I give her one cow, one bed
and bedstead, one table, one set of chairs and spinning wheel.
To my adopted son, William Kealer (a son of my wife
Elizabeth), my negro boy called Peter as a slave for life, my
rifle, my bay colt and fifty dollars. To my daughter, Amanda

(wife of Jacob Berwager), my negro girl called Sevilla. I direct that my son adopted son, William Kealer, and my daughter, Amanda Berwager, pay my son, Edmund, fifty dollars as he reaches age. To my son, Edmund, the sum of two hundred dollars and my best silver watch when he reaches age. After the death of marriage of my wife, my estate should be equally divided among my children: William Kealer, Amanda Berwager and Edmund Swartbaugh. My son, Edmund, should be educated and maintained out of the profits of my real estate.

Witnesses: Jacob Kerlinger, George Shower, Jacob Houck
Executor(s): Adam Shower (friend), William Crumrine (friend)
Signed by his mark

Swope, Henry   of Carroll County
                                     January 26, 1842
                                     August 7, 1843
Number 158, Folio 275   August 7, 1843

To my beloved wife, Elizabeth Swope, all my real and personal property plus the interest of three hundred dollars for her until her death. After the death of my wife, my property both real and personal should be divided equally among my children (net of their debts owing to me), namely: my daughter Eliza (wife of Samuel Forney), John Swope, Samuel Swope, William L. Crapster (husband of my daughter Mary), Daniel H. Swope, Henry Swope and Clarissa Swope. To my daughter, Clarissa A. Swope as long as she remains single, the proceeds arising from the lot that I have taken from my brother, Adam Swope (as satisfaction for my part in my brother, George Swope's, estate). My servant, James Matthews, shall not serve more than ten years and when freed should be given all the tools belonging to the shop.

Witnesses: Ludwick Rudisel, Hugh Shaw, Tobias Rudisel
Executor(s): Samuel Swope (son)
Signed with his signature

Tawney, Elizabeth   widow of Carroll County
                                           February 27, 1837
                                               April 10, 1837
Number 1, Folio 1   April 10, 1837

To my granddaughter, Margaret (daughter of Catherine) my
bed, bed clothes, bedstand, bureau and a cow. To my son,
George, more than his share of my estate to include one horse
of his choosing and his father's (the late Frederick Tawney)
desk. After the sale of my remaining property, the proceeds
should be divided into seven shares: to my son, Jacob Tawney;
to my son, John Tawney; to my son, David Tawney; to my son,
George Tawney; to my daughter, Sally; and two shares to my
daughter, Catherine.

Witnesses: David Roop, John Schweigart, John Roop, Jr.
Executor(s): Jacob Shriver
Signed by her mark

Tawney, Jacob   of Carroll County
                                           January 19, 1844
                                           December 30, 1844
Number 191, Folio 343   December 30, 1844

To my wife, Abigail, and my ailing daughter whom resides with
us, Lucretia, my land and dwellings where I currently reside
(which is situated on the road leading from Westminster to
Tawneytown) for use during my wife's natural life. Should my
daughter, Lucretia, out live her mother then I give said land to
my friends, Samuel L. Swermstedt and John Royer, to rent out
and the proceeds should go to the support of my daughter,
Lucretia. If in the case of the death of both my wife, Abigail,
and my daughter, Lucretia, I direct my friends, Samuel L.
Swermstedt and John Royer, to sell my property and give the
proceeds to my daughters, Margaret J., and my step daughter,
Elizabeth Matchel, to share alike. To my daughter, Margaret,
ten dollars after a year of my decease; to my step daughter,

Elizabeth Matchel, ten dollars after a year of my decease. To my wife all my remaining personal estate and property.

Witnesses: Francis Mathias, Caleb Boring, Richard Brown
Executor(s): Samuel L. Swernstedt
Signed by his mark

Taylor, George of Carroll County
August 26, 1842
November 28, 1842
Number 140, Folio 241 November 28, 1842

To my wife, Catherine Taylor, the tract of land conveyed to me by Amos Evans and part of a tract of land called "Aspen Hill."

Renunciation
Amos Evans refuses to accept the executorship. Witnessed on November 8, 1842 by John Bowman.

Witnesses: George Arbaugh, John Bowman
Executor(s): Amos Evans
Signed with his signature

Taylor, John of Carroll County
December 13, 1848
March 19, 1849
Number 294, Folio 524 March 19, 1849

To my son, Kinzy Taylor, one hundred and twenty five dollars. To my daughter, Isabella (wife of Adam Kelbaugh), all the land and buildings south of the County road leading from Browns Meeting House to Sandy Mount (where Rachel Taylor resides) also twelve acres of land across from said land called "The Mill Site." To my four sons (Elijah, Johnsey, Noah and Jesse Taylor) the balance of my estate equally divided (except that the two eldest have an additional fifteen dollars each).

Renunciation
Johnzey Taylor, Noah Taylor and Jesse Taylor refuse to accept the executorship and they desire that the role be granted to the first named executor, Elijah Taylor. Witnessed on March 20, 1849 by Samuel Taylor (of M) and Kinzey Taylor.

Witnesses: George W. Matthews, Jesse Matthews, George Richards, Jr.
Executor(s): Elijah Taylor (son), Johnsey Taylor (son), Noah Taylor (son), Jesse Taylor (son)
Signed with his signature

Tener, George   of Carroll County
                                                    July 9, 1838
                                                    July 30, 1838
Number 33, Folio 54   July 30, 1838

To my daughter, Mary Ann Tener, all of my land and dwelling adjoining that of Thomas Condon (beyond my lime kiln and my saw mill, across the dam until it intersects the land of Ezekiel Pickell). To my daughter, Caty Ann Tener, all the land north of the Liberty Road and three hundred dollars the latter to be paid by my daughter, Mary Ann Tener, and my executors. To my son, Joseph Tener, the residue of my real estate subject to the legacies to my daughter, Caty Ann Tener. To my son, Samuel Tener, one hundred dollars provided he return home in two years after my death and if he does not return home then the money should be shared between my son, Joseph Tener, and my daughter, Caty Ann Tener. All my personal property should be shared between my son, Joseph Tener, my daughter, Mary Ann Tener, and my daughter, Caty Ann Tener.

Renunciation
Joseph Tener, son of George Tener, "refuse to take out letters Testamentary on the estate of said deceased and do therefore renounce my title and claim to said executorship desiring at the same time that letters of administration may be granted to

myself and Joshua C. Gist jointly both of the county aforesaid."
Witnessed on August 13, 1838 by Joseph H. Gillis.

Witnesses: Joshua C. Gist, Thomas Condon, Richard A. Kirkwood
Executor(s): Joseph Tener (son)
Signed with his signature

Thomas, John H.   of Carroll County
                                        November 16, 1842
                                        December 5, 1842
Number 141, Folio 242   December 5, 1842

By the account of Francis Shriver, John H. Thomas had been living at the Shriver home for the past year while in ill health. On the night before his death (November 16, 1842), John H. Thomas told both Francis and Isaac Shriver that he desired fifty dollars to go to George W. Thomas. The balance of his estate should be equally divided amongst his sister, Mary, and his two brothers, William and George. If William and George could not be found, then the balance should all go to his sister, Mary.

Witnesses: Francis Shriver, Isaac Shriver (Francis Shriver's father)
Executor(s): Francis Shriver
Verbally given to Francis Shriver

Townsend, Thomas   of Carroll County
                                        March 19, 1844
                                        December 1, 1851
Number 370, Folio 625   December 1, 1851

To my wife, Elizabeth, an upper room in the house we now occupy and part of the garden during her natural life and she should be supported comfortably in sickness and health by my son, Thomas Townsend. I also give the following specific items to my wife during her natural life: one bedstead, clothes, one cow, one colt. To my son, John Townsend, a horse valued at seventy dollars or the value of the horse. To my son, Thomas Townsend, a grey horse, colt, bridle and saddle, cooking stove, desk, bed and clothes that he now uses. To my son, Thomas Townsend, the use of my home farm and wood lot provided that he cares for his mother including items such as paying for doctor's bills, property taxes and items necessary for her comfort. That my son, Thomas Townsend, should pay the taxes on the land for his privilege and that he should buy three hundred chestnuts each year while his mother is living and that he should not cut firewood from the home farm, but he should cut the wood and haul it from the wood lot and he is to farm the land as I have been doing of late and keep it in good repair. To my daughter, Mary Ann Townsend, the value of two cows, one bed stead and clothes, one bureau, one table, half a dozen Windsor chairs, one pot and kettle being in amount what my married daughters have received. I request that my executors sell the residue of my estate and that the proceeds by equally divided among my seven children, namely: Dorothy Danner, John Townsend, Anna Crowl, Sarah Shelenburger, Thomas Townsend, Elizer Engleman, Mary Ann Townsend and Sarah Crowl. However Sarah's share should be equally divided between herself and (my grandchildren) her children, namely: Elizabeth Crowl, Jesse Crowl, Mary Crowl, John Crowl, William Crowl and George Crowl. Whereas I hold notes against my son, John Townsend, my son in law, Abraham Danner, my son in law, Henry Crowl, and Daniel Crowl this money should be taken out against their inheritance. It is my desire that my daughter, Mary Ann Townsend, shall have her home with her mother and brother, Thomas Townsend, until her marriage or the death of her mother. I express my wish that my children visit their mother as frequently as the can and that they pay her attention as is their duty.

Witnesses: William Baile, Henry Baile, James Smith
Executor(s): Thomas Townsend (son), William Engleman (son in law)
Signed with his signature

Towson, James   of Baltimore County
                                            February 6, 1835
                                              April 17, 1837
Number 3, Folio 4   April 17, 1837

To my wife, Kerenhappuch, all my real and personal estate, cattle, houses and land belonging to me in Baltimore County for her natural life. After the decease of my wife, all my estate belonging in Baltimore County should go to my grandson, William F. Taney. To my daughters, Rebecca and Nancy, all my lands in the state of Ohio which should be equally divided among them, however Rebecca should have her first choice. After the decease of my daughter, Rebecca, I desire that her half of the land should go to her son and my grandson, Thomas Taney.

Witnesses: John Trine, Philip Trine, Jacob Trine
Executor(s): Kerenhappuch Towson (wife)
Signed with his signature

Trine, Jacob   of Carroll County
                                                July 8, 1843
                                      December 16, 1844
Number 190, Folio 342   December 16, 1844

To my wife [not named] all my real and personal property for her use during her lifetime (or she may sell it as she sees fit). After the decease of my wife, all my property should be sold and the proceeds should be equally divided among my five children [not named].

Witnesses: George Richard, Jesse Brown, Joshua Algire (son of George Algire)
Executor(s): Samuel Trine (son), John Trine (son), William Lockard (son in law)
Signed with his signature

Utz, George   of Carroll County

                                          May 1, 1841

                                      January 31, 1842

Number 120, Folio 198   January 31, 1842

My possessions should remain in the hands of my beloved wife, Magdelena, for the term of one year after my death and then my property (not bequeathed to my wife and heirs) should be sold. To my wife, Magdelena, one bed, bedding, stove, dining table, chest, two benches, clock, three chairs, Starks prayer book, kitchen cupboard, flat irons, two tubs of butter, churn and stand, meat tub, coffee mill, bread baskets, spinning wheel, axe, cow, pots, tongs, shovel, all the meat, hogs lard and tallow, hogs, sheep, flax, yarn, vinegar barrel, salt barrel, soap, dried fruit, apple butter, rye wheat, corn, potatoes, flour and all the grain growing the ground. As long as my wife is a widow she is to enjoy all the items above mentioned during her lifetime. If she remarries, then my executor should sell all the above mentioned articles at public auction and she should leave my premises immediately upon marriage and the proceeds from the auction are to be equally divided among my children. If she remains my widow, then the said items should only be sold at her death and the proceeds equally divided among my children. To my son, John Utz, one hundred and eighty dollars, one bed with bedstead and bedding, small table, one Bible and Hymn book. To my son, Frederick Utz, two hundred and sixty dollars. To my son, David Utz, three hundred dollars, bed with bedstead and bedding, chest and my great book. To my son, David Utz, three hundred dollars. To my son, George Utz, seventy dollars. To my daughter, Sarah, ten dollars, bed with bedstead and bedding, spinning wheel, six new chairs, new bureau, cow, leaf table, two table clothes, two hand towels, six knives, six forks, six cups and saucers and eight earthen plates. To my daughter, Rachel, thirty dollars, bed with bedstead and bedding, spinning wheel, six new chairs, new wing table, two table clothes, three hand towels, six knives and forks, six cups and saucers and eight large earthen plates. After one year of my death, all my property should be sold and the proceeds should be divided as follows: one third to my wife, Magdalena; the remaining balance should be divided into nine equal shares, namely: to my son, George Utz; to my son, Frederick Utz; to my son, John Utz; to my son, David Utz; to my daughter, Elisabeth (wife of Frederick Face); to my daughter, Catherine (wife of George Zepp); to my daughter, Magdalena (wife of Philip Arter); to my daughter, Rachel; to my daughter, Sarah.

Renunciation
George Weaver (of Henry) and Philip Arthur renounce their title as executors and request that the letters of administration be granted to George Utz (junior) who is one of the sons of the deceased. Witnessed on January 31, 1842 by Michael Sullivan.

Witnesses: Jacob Stonesifer, David Utz, Daniel Peterman
Executor(s): George Weaver, Philip Arter (son in law)
Signed with his signature

Wagers, William   of Carroll County
                                    March 11, 1845
                                    April 10, 1848
Number 279, Folio 503   April 10, 1848

To my wife, Nancy Wagers, all my personal property and the use of all my real estate for her life. After the death of my wife, the use of my real estate should be divided between my daughters, Mary Criswell (wife of Elijah Criswell) and Rachel Roach (wife of Caleb Roach). After the death of my daughters, Mary Criswell and Rachel Roach, this property should go to my grandsons, William Wagers Criswell (son of Elijah and Mary Criswell) and Owen Pennington.

Witnesses: George Ogg (junior), John Ogg, William Caple
Executor(s): Nancy (my dear wife)
Signed by his mark

Waggoner, John   of Carroll County

                                              April 3, 1850

                                              October 14, 1850

Number 333, Folio 578   October 14, 1850

To my son, Michael Waggoner, all the personal property he has
received from me and the farm where he currently resides
(containing one hundred and ninety six acres). To my daughter,
Elizabeth, one half of all my bedding, clothing, carpeting,
household furniture, kitchen utensils, two clocks and two
stoves. I give to my daughter, Rachel, the other half of my
personal property not given to Elizabeth. Both my daughters,
Elizabeth and Rachel, should have use of the farm and stock for
one year after my death including all profits arising from said
farm. To my grandson, Upton Decker, one half of my ten acre
lot called "Mollys Fancy." To my daughter, Elizabeth, the
other half of "Mollys Fancy." After one year of my death, my
farm and livestock should be sold and the proceeds should be
equally divided among my six daughters, namely: Mary, Anna,
Margaret, Elizabeth, Sarah and Rachel.

Witnesses: Henry H. Herbaugh, Daniel Roop, John Babylon
Executor(s): Michael Babylon (friend), Daniel Benner (son in law)
Signed by his mark

Wagner, Michael   of Meadow Branch, Frederick
                                            County

                                              November 9, 1835

                                              March 4, 1839

Number 48, Folio 83   March 4, 1839

To my wife, Sophia Wagner, (in lieu of her dower) my dwelling
house and land containing all appurtenances in Uniontown,
Carroll County. After the death of my wife, this land should be
sold. The residue of my personal and real property should be
sold after my decease. To my grandchildren who are now
residing in the state of Ohio (the children of my deceased

daughter Catherine who was the former wife of David Warner), the sum of fifty dollars each "except Thomas Warner who has been unkind to me and treated me in a manner unbecoming a grandchild and I therefore bequeath to him one dollar only if he ever calls upon my executors and demands it." To my grandson, John You (son of my deceased daughter Barbara), the sum of fifty dollars. The residue of my estate should be equally divided among my five heirs, namely: my only son, Jacob Wagner; my daughter, Susanna (wife of Andrew Babylon); my daughter, Elizabeth (wife of George Warner); to my daughter, Mary (wife of John Swigart); to my daughter, Lydia (widow of David Leister). Whereas I paid for the land deeded by Peter Hafley to my daughter, Barbara (wife of George McClean), I consider this to be her full share of her legacy. My executors should set aside three hundred dollars of the share to my daughter, Lydia Leister, and give to my infant granddaughter, Julia Barbara Leister, when Julia reaches the age of eighteen years and that the annual interest of said money should be used towards her education.

Witnesses: John Nusbaum, John Smith, John Hyder
Executor(s): Jacob Wagner (son), Andrew Babylon (son in law)
Signed with his signature

Walker, Daniel   of Carroll County
                                                      May 15, 1844
                                                      August 12, 1844
Number 183, Folio 326   August 12, 1844

I give to my beloved wife, Catherine, all my estate (except my cash and distillery) to be used for the support and education of my minor children until the time that my youngest son, Emanuel, reaches twenty one. If my wife should remarry and die before my youngest reaches twenty one, then all my estate should be sold and that the proceeds equally distributed among my children, namely: John, George, Daniel, Joseph, Noah,

Emanuel, Elizabeth, Polly, Catherine, Sally, Susanna, Peggy, Harriet and Maudy. If my wife should remain my widow at said time (when my youngest son, Emanuel, turns twenty one), then I give her the following: two good beds with bedsteads, one stove and pipe, table, four chairs, case of drawers, corner cupboard, one cow with feed and pasture, the east room of my dwelling house, a portion of the garden and as many apples as she likes. The remainder of my personal property at said time should be sold and the proceeds equally divided among my children. After the death of my wife, my plantation should be sold and the proceeds should be equally divided among my children. The outstanding money owed to me should be collected and my distillery should be sold and the proceeds to be kept in the hands of my executors to be paid out to my minor children for an allowance as they reach age.

Witnesses: Henry Williams, Yoder Messemehr
Executor(s): John Walker and Daniel Walker (my trusty sons)
Signed with his signature

Wampler, Hannah   of Westminster, Carroll County
                                              June 1838 [no day given]
                                                    October 15, 1838
Number 40, Folio 68   October 29, 1838

To my nephew, Augustus G. Grove (a minister of the Holy Gospel of Christ), my eight day mantle clock. To my nephew, Lewis Grove, six chairs, candle stand and mahogany table. To my niece, Hannah Grove, six silver table spoons and five silver tea spoons. To my brother in law, Jacob Grove, one hundred dollars. To my niece, Elizabeth Lammott, six silver tea spoons, one silver ladle and pair of silver sugar tongs. To my niece, Angaline Lammott, one bureau, one bed with bedstead and bed furniture, and one hundred dollars with the latter to be held in the hands of my executors to be used for her education. To my nephews, George Wesley Lammott, William Henry Lammott and Lewis J. A. Lammott, each twenty five dollars to be paid to them at the age of twenty one. To my sister, Mary Lammott, all my clothes. To my beloved brother, George Trumbo, one bed with bedstead and bed furniture, one looking glass and the rest of my furniture. To my brother, George Trumbo, my one third interest in my mother's estate, one third of the interest in the estate of my uncle, Henry Neff (brother to my mother), and one third of the interest in the estate of my grandmother Neff's estate. To my sister, Mary Lammott, my one third interest in my mother's estate, one third of the interest in the estate of my uncle, Henry Neff (brother to my mother), and one third of the interest in the estate of my grandmother Neff's estate which is all to be held in trust by my brother, George Trumbo. To my brother in law, Jacob Grove, one hundred dollars which should be paid from the remaining one thirds of my interest in the mentioned estates as well as the moneys to my nieces and nephews which should be paid from the same. The residue of my estate should go to my brother, George Trumbo.

Witnesses: Jacob Yingling, William Yingling, William Zepp
Executor(s): George Trumbo (brother)
Signed with her signature

Ward, Richard   of Carroll County
                                              May 18, 1847
                                              July 12, 1847
Number 253, Folio 462   July 12, 1847

To my sister, Jane Day (of the state of Ohio), five hundred dollars. To my niece, Jane Ward (youngest daughter of my brother Thomas), six hundred dollars. To my niece, Levina Ward (daughter of my brother Thomas), two hundred dollars. To my niece, Eliza Stocksdale (daughter of my brother Thomas and wife of Solomon Stocksdale), four hundred dollars. To my niece, Caroline Ward (daughter of my brother Thomas), four hundred dollars. To my niece, Cynthia Ann Whittle (daughter of my brother Thomas and wife of John Whittle), four hundred and twenty five dollars. To Martha Litsinger (wife of George Litsinger), three hundred and fifty dollars. To Ann Stocksdale of Ohio (daughter of the late Richard Richards and widow of Eli Stocksdale), thirty dollars. The residue of my real estate should be sold and the proceeds equally divided among the three sons of my brother Thomas Ward (nephews not named other than John T. Ward). The legacy for my nephew, John T. Ward, should be kept in trust by my executors until said John engages in a suitable business or calling whereupon he may succeed, otherwise said legacy should only be used for him during times of sickness or any other necessity. My bank stock in the savings institution at Westminster should remain under the direction of Jacob Reese until my death and at which time should go to my executors to execute said legacies.

Witnesses: Samuel L. Swormstedt, Francis Shriver, Noah Stocksdale
Executor(s): Solomon Stocksdale and Washington H. Ward (my trusty and faithful friends)
Signed with his signature

Wareham, Henry   of Carroll County
                                              July 4, 1837
                                              July 22, 1837
Number 10, Folio 14   August 14, 1837

The debt of sixteen hundred dollars that my son, John Wareham, owes me is exonerated on consideration of any claims he may hold against my estate. To my daughter, Margaret (wife of John Schaeffer), my land in Harrison County, Virginia containing nine hundred and twenty acres. After the death of my said daughter, Margaret, the land should be equally divided among her children. To my son, Conrad Wareham, the plantation where I currently reside in Carroll County containing whole or parts of the following tracts of land called "North

Canton", "Resurvey on Wells Care Enlarged", "Ormly" and "Iron Intention" all containing one hundred and eighty acres. To my son, Conrad Wareham, the following tract of land in Carroll County part of "Iron Intention" containing fifty acres conveyed to me by Peter Sentz recorded in Baltimore County on May 20, 1813. To my son, Conrad Wareham, the following part of a tract of land called "Winfaw" containing six acres conveyed to me by John Ritter recorded in Baltimore County on November 13, 1819. I give all these lands to my son, Conrad Wareham, on condition that he allows my wife, Charity Wareham, to keep her dwelling on my plantation along with use of the kitchen, one third of the garden, one third of the cellar, one third of the spring house and on condition that he pays her provides her the following on an annual basis: one hundred dollars, twenty bushels of wheat, ten bushels of Indian corn, one hundred pounds of good pork, one hundred pounds of good beef, as much fruit as needed and sufficient quantity of cut firewood delivered to her front door. Also my son, Conrad Wareham, should pay my executors after the death of my wife the sum of twenty two hundred dollars to be made in equal annual payments and to be divided equally among them. To my son, George Wareham, my plantation where my son Conrad now resides in Carroll County on a tract of land called "The Resurvey on Lime Pitt" containing one hundred and eighteen acres conveyed to me by David R. Gist recorded in Frederick County on April 2, 1817 and a part of the tract of land called "Resurvey on Lime Pitt" containing two acres conveyed to me by Jacob Steinciferd recorded in Frederick County on April 12, 1816. To my son, George Wareham, a part of a tract of land called "Iron Intention" containing twenty five acres conveyed to me by Greenberry Magers recorded in Baltimore County on October 7, 1811. I give these lands to my son, George Wareham, on condition that he pays my wife, Charity, fifty dollars per year. Also my son, George Wareham, should pay my executors after the death of my wife the sum of twenty two hundred dollars to be made in equal annual payments and to be divided equally among them. To my wife, Charity, two cows, two beds with bedsteads and bedding, my corner cupboard with contents, ten plate stove and pipe, dining table, six chairs, clock and case, six knives, six forks, six spoons, six table cloths, six hand towels, my large German Bible, my Hymn book, as much kitchen furniture as desired, and all the linens and thread in the house at my time of death. The residue of my estate should be sold and the proceeds to be distributed as follows: to my wife, Charity, two hundred dollars; to my grandson, Albert Wareham, sixty dollars; to my son, Henry, five hundred dollars; to my son, Conrad, one hundred dollars; to my daughter, Sarah (wife of Andrew Weisleather), five hundred dollars; to my granddaughter, Mary Yeiser (daughter of my deceased daughter Elisabeth), five hundred dollars.

Witnesses: J. Henry Hoppe, Jacob Matthias (of George), Daniel Stonesifer, John Baumgartner
Executor(s): George Wareham (son), Conrad Wareham (son)
Signed with his signature

Warfield, George Fraser   of Carroll County
                                   April 17, 1847
                                   February 4, 1850
Number 315, Folio 552   February 4, 1850

To my son, William Henry Warfield "who has been dutiful, kind and affectionate to me", half of all my interest in the schooner called "Nancy" and her cargo of coffee "which vessel and her cargo was taken by the French government, and condemned by said government in the year 1797 on her voyage home to Baltimore from a port on the Island of St. Domingo laden with coffee...Bartholomew Putman Jr. was captain and Felix Coune supercargo, to which vessel and cargo I am one third owner Henry Messonier and Lewis Pascault (both of whom have since deceased) owners of the other two thirds." The other half of my interest in the schooner "Nancy" and her cargo should be equally divided among my children, namely: Susanna Warfield, George Washington Warfield and Ann Elizabeth Wade (wife of John Wade Jr.). If my executor is successful in obtaining my claim and interest in said schooner and cargo from either the French or American government, I give him five percent of the net proceeds as payment for his efforts. If either of my daughters should die without lawful issue, then their portion should go to my grandson, Lewis Marshal Warfield (son of my son, George Washington Warfield). To my son, William Henry Warfield, my negro woman called Jane and all her children with the exception of Sophia (daughter of Jane). I give to my daughter, Ann Elizabeth Wade, [illegible] which is now in her possession in Baltimore. The residue of my estate should go to my son, William Henry Warfield.

Witnesses: Howes Goldsborough, Charles W. Hood, Nicholas Owens
Executor(s): William Henry Warfield (son)
Signed with his signature

Warfield, Jemima   of Carroll County
                                    October 15, 1847
                                    January 31, 1848
Number 269, Folio 488   January 31, 1848

To my daughter, Mary Catherine Warfield, one feather bed, three pairs of blankets, one set of china, silver sugar tongs, one dozen silver dessert spoons, one set of castors and my mahogany bureau. To Betty Sanders (a colored woman formerly to me), her little daughter Margaret. My colored woman, Lucy Ann, should be freed at my death if her servitude does not expire before my death. I give to my colored woman, Lucy Ann, her little son called Levi. To my son, Joshua Warfield, my colored man called Alexander to serve him until said Alexander reaches the age of twenty five at which time said Alexander should be freed. The residue of my estate should go to my son, Joshua Warfield.

Witnesses: John Danner, Jesse L. Warfield
Executor(s): Jesse L. Warfield (son)
Signed with her signature

Warfield, Sarah   of Carroll County

                                        May 8, 1846
                                        February 8, 1847
Number 243, Folio 445   February 8, 1847

To my daughter, Mary E. Evans (wife of Levi Evans), such personal property of mine that she currently has in her possession. To my daughter, Louisa Yingling (wife of John Murray Yingling), such personal property of mine that she currently has in her possession. To my daughters, Mary Evans and Louisa Yingling, my clothes, beds and bedding, all my household furniture and all my kitchen furniture to be shared equally. To my sons in law, Levi Evans and John M. Yingling, my cow and my household furniture which my son, William Warner Warfield, has in his possession. The residue of my personal estate should be sold including my carriage with harness. My negro man called Wesley Cook and my negro woman called Eliza Cook are both to be sold for a term ending April 1, 1844 at which time they should be liberated (also they should not be sold out of the state) and any issue of my negro woman called Eliza Cook for a term ending at the age of twenty five at which time they should be liberated (also they should not be sold out of the state). I order that my executors collect all money owed to me, including money still owed to the estate of my first husband, George M. Sellman, who is now deceased. Out of the proceeds, my debts should be paid including funeral expenses and the purchase of two tombstones, one for myself and one for my deceased husband, Thomas J. Warfield. A fence should be put up around the burying ground on the farm where Washington Barnes now resides near Warfieldsburg. The proceeds left from my personal estate should be divided into five equally parts to the following: to my son, Henry A. Sellman (by my first husband); to my son, Alexander Warfield; to my daughter, Louisa Yingling (wife of John M. Yingling); to my daughter, Mary E. Evans (wife of Levi Evans); to my son, William Warner Warfield. To my son in laws, John M. Yingling and Levi Evans, the land situate in Frizzelburg, Carroll County where my son, William Warner Warfield, now resides which contains the land conveyed to me by John Rinehart and his wife Mary Rinehart and all that parcel of land conveyed to me by Levi Fleagle and his wife Susan Fleagle. I ask that my son in laws keep this land in trust for my son, William Warner Warfield and his wife Jemima M. Warfield, and allow said William and Jemima to continue occupying said land with all contents.

Witnesses: William King, William Grumbine, John Baumgartner
Executor(s): John M. Yingling and Levi Evans (both sons in law)
Signed with her signature

Webster, Isaac   of Carroll County
                                      September 29, 1850
                                      February 17, 1851
Number 350, Folio 597   February 17, 1851

To my beloved wife, Clemency H. Webster, my real estate in Carroll County on the northeast end of the city of Westminster and on the northeast side of the road leading from Westminster to Littlestown, Adams County, Pennsylvania containing four acres and part of a larger tract of land called "Kellys Range" conveyed to me by my son, George Webster, and his wife, Mary Ann Webster in 1843. Also to my wife, one acre of the larger tract of land called "Kellys Range" conveyed to me by Joshua Smith (acting as trustee for the heirs of George Rinehart) in 1849. I also give to my wife all improvements and appurtenances on said real estate. To my wife, Clemency H. Webster, my negro girl called Grace plus all my other personal property of every description.

Renunciation
Clemency H. Webster refuses to act as executrix and requests that all letters of testamentary be granted to Michael G. Webster, the other named executor. Witnessed on February 17, 1851 by C. W. Webster.

Witnesses: Jacob Mathias, Jesse L. Warfield, William Shreev
Executor(s): Clemency H. Webster (wife), Michael G. Webster (son)
Signed with his signature

Wells, Thomas   of Carroll County
                                     March 26, 1841
                                     August 16, 1841
Number 111, Folio 184   August 16, 1841

To Thomas W. Durbin, all my clothes. I liberate and manumit my slaves after my death, namely: Jesse, John, Luke, Henry, Ann and Margaret. I give to my negro men (Jesse, John, Luke and Henry), fifty dollars and I give to my negro woman (Margaret), one hundred dollars. I give my negro boy, George, to my nephew, Thomas Stevenson (son of my sister Margaret Stevenson who is now deceased) until said George should reach the age of twenty five years. I give my negro boy, Josiah, to my nephew, Joshua Smith, until said Josiah should reach the age of twenty five years. I give my negro girl, Mary, to my niece, Mary Smith, until said Mary (negro) reaches the age of twenty five. I liberate and manumit my said slaves, George, Sarah and Mary at their age of twenty five years and I give to them at the time of their liberation fifty dollars each. I direct that my negro girls Ann and Margaret and children born to Ann, Margaret or Mary (mentioned herein) should not be taken or sold out of the state of Maryland and that they should be liberated at the age of twenty five years. I direct that all my bank stock and bonds be sold and all debts owing to me be collected. My land and real estate should be sold provided that the lands containing my Mill should not be sold in a manner or to a purchaser that would allow or permit the existing watercourses to be diverted from their present course nor dammed up or impeded in any way. I request that my executor put one thousand dollars at trust and that the annual interest should be paid to my housekeeper, Molly Wilson, for the faithful manner in which she has served me. To James, Charity, William, Augustus Washington, Sarah, Catherine, Thomas, Washington, Samuel and John (all children of Thomas W. Durbin), the sum of three hundred dollars each. If James Durbin fails to pay my estate the money that he owes me, then he will not receive his legacy. My executors should put one thousand dollars at trust and the annual interest should be paid to Thomas W. Durbin and his wife Sarah. After the decease of Thomas and Sarah (or the marriage of Sarah), the said legacy should go to aforementioned children of Thomas Durbin. The balance of my estate should be divided into three equal parts: to the children of my deceased sister, Nancy Owings, one third of my balance to be equally divided among them; to the children of my deceased sister, Margaret Stevenson, one third of the balance to be equally divided among them; to the children of my deceased sister, Susannah Smith, one third of the balance to be equally divided among them. Except for the portion that is to go to Henry Stevenson, son of Margaret Stevenson, who has not been in these parts for some time, his share should be kept in trust by my executors for ten years after my death and if he does not collect this money then it should be equally distributed among my other legatees.

Witnesses: John Baumgartner, Otho Shipley, Charles W. Webster
Executor(s): Joshua Smith, Jr. (nephew)
Signed with his signature

Wentz, Rachel   of Carroll County
                                      May 2, 1838
                                      May 14, 1838
Number 29, Folio 48   May 14, 1838

My estate should be sold including the house and lot where I currently reside (containing four acres) called "Kelly's Range" on the turnpike leading from Westminster to Petersburgh (Littlestown), Adams County, Pennsylvania. The proceeds should pay funeral expenses and the debt I owe Jacob Reese (for the purchase of said property recorded in Frederick County on April 28, 1838). To my son, George Washington Wentz, the residue of my estate.

Witnesses: Jesse Reifnsider, Horatio Price, George Shriver
Executor(s): Jacob Reese
Signed with her signature

Wentz, Valentine   of Carroll County
                                      January 28, 1843
                                      March 6, 1843
Number 148, Folio 254   March 6, 1843

My plantation which was conveyed to me by J. Henry Hoppe called "Stullers Place" (containing eighty acres) should be sold and any personal property that my wife, Rachel, does not need should be sold. The proceeds should be used to pay debts. The residue of my property should go to my wife, Rachel, for her widowhood. After the death or marriage of my wife, my estate should be sold and the proceeds equally divided among my children, namely: David, John, Valentine, Elizabeth, Jacob, Samuel, Eve, Nancy, Rachel and Susanna Wentz.

Witnesses: Adam Feiser, Michael Lynch, John Rinehard, J. Henry Hoppe
Executor(s): Valentine Wentz (son)
Signed with his signature

Werble, Andrew of Carroll County
March 13, 1849
May 7, 1849
Number 299, Folio 532 May 7, 1849

To my sister, Mary Grammer, and her husband, John Grammer, my lot and brick house (containing one acre) situated in Westminster as well as the residue of my estate.

Witnesses: Henry H. Herbaugh, Charles Hiteshaw, John Garber
Executor(s): John Grammer (brother in law)
Signed by his mark

Whiteleather, David of Carroll County
September 27, 1849
October 15, 1849
Number 307, Folio 540 October 15, 1849

The Nuncupative will of David Whiteleather taken at his bedside by Alexander Whiteleather and Mrs. Lippy (wife of Henry Lippy):

My property should not go to my brothers and sisters [not named]. My property should go to my wife [not named].

Witnesses: David Whiteleather, Rebecca Lippy (wife of Henry Lippy), Henry E. Betz, David C. Frankforter
Executor(s): not named
Signed [given orally]

Willet, Jacob of Carroll County
January 27, 1852
February 16, 1852
Number 377, Folio 638 February 16, 1852

To my wife, Sarah Willet, as much of my personal property not to exceed one hundred dollars in value. To my son, Abraham

Willet, one horse saddle and bridle. To my daughters, Amanda F. C. Willet and Rebecca Willet, each one bed with bedstead and bedding. The residue of my estate should be sold including the tract of land and farm where I currently reside in Carroll County (containing one hundred and forty acres) plus my wood lot (containing five acres) which lies near the turnpike near Silver Run Church. To my wife, Sarah Willet, nine hundred dollars as her dower. The residue should be equally divided among my children, namely: Abraham, Amanda F. C., Rebecca, Carolina, Susannah and Josephena A. Willett.

Witnesses: Samuel Myers, Henry Brown, Samuel Stonesifer
Executor(s): Benjamin Shunk
Signed with his signature

Williams, George   of Carroll County
                                          October 15, 1850
                                          December 23, 1850
Number 342, Folio 589   December 23, 1850

To my wife, Naomy Williams, all my property of every description.

Witnesses: Mordecai G. Cockey, Samuel Wildesen, Franklin Finley Horner
Executor(s): Naomy Williams (wife)
Signed with his signature

Williams, John   of Carroll County
                                          February 3, 1848
                                          February 9, 1849 (codicil)
                                          November 26, 1849
Number 310, Folio 543   November 26, 1849

To my beloved wife, Rebecca Williams, her right dower of my lands but she should not clear any new fields or down any timber. To my wife, one feather bed with bedding and furniture, six chairs, two cupboards with contents, tea kettle, dinner pot, large boiler, two stoves, my clock, my desk, all the silverware and plates, the small folding leaf table, breakfast table, my riding mare, her side saddle, my horse called Starling, my horse wagon and cover, horse harness, one cow, six sheep, all the contents of my barn, two bushels wheat, twenty bushels corn and one hundred pounds of bacon. I release my daughter, Rachel Fringer (wife of George Fringer) from the debt she owes my estate. To my son, Washington Williams, fifty eight dollars and I release him from the debt he owes my estate. To my son, George Williams, fifty two dollars and I release him from the debt he owes my estate. I release my daughter, Charcilla Kelley (wife of John C. Kelley) from the debt she owes my estate. To my daughter, Ruth Ann Bushey (wife of Henry Bushey), fifteen dollars and I release her from the debt she owes my estate. To my daughter, Sarah Williams, one hundred dollars. To my son, Benjamin Williams, one hundred dollars. To my son, Louis Williams, one hundred dollars. To my son, James Williams, one hundred dollars. To my son, Charles Williams, one hundred dollars. To my son, John Williams, one hundred dollars. The residue of my estate should be sold the proceeds should be equally divided among my children, namely: Benjamin Williams, Sarah Williams, Charcilla Kelley, George Williams, Ruth Ann Bushey, Louis Williams, James Williams, Charles Williams and John Williams.

Codicil
I bequeath to my sons, James, Charles and John, the crop presently growing on my farm to be equally divided among them.

Witnesses: Amon Richards, David Abbott, John F. Richards, George Burk, Washington Jones
Executor(s): Benjamin Williams (son), Henry Bushey (friend)
Signed with his signature

Williams, Prudence   of Carroll County
                                                    February 11, 1847
                                                    May 3, 1847
Number 249, Folio 456   May 3, 1847

To my son, James Williams, all my real estate and farm where I currently reside. To my grandson, Benjamin Williams, one silver cup and eight dollars. To my granddaughter, Cassander Williams, one thread wheel and one reel. To my grandson, Joshua Williams, one feather bed with furniture. To my granddaughter, Prudence Williams, my silver table and tea spoons and my cups and saucers. To my grandson, Nathan Williams, eight dollars. To my grandson, Thomas Williams, five dollars. To my grandson, Absolom Williams, one feather bed with furniture. The balance of my estate should be equally divided among my children [not named].

Witnesses: George Ogg, John M. Blizzard, Elijah Criswell
Executor(s): James Williams (son)
Signed by her mark

Willis, Joseph   of Carroll County
                                                    March 27, 1842
                                                    April 26, 1847
Number 248, Folio 454   April 26, 1847

To my wife, all my real estate called "Caledonia" containing one hundred and thirty eight acres. To my wife, all my personal estate which includes two horses, four head of cattle, one wagon plus all other personal effects.

Witnesses: Moses Parrish, Grove Shipley (junior), James Parrish
Executor(s): Ann Willis (my wife)
Signed with his signature

Wilson, John   of Carroll County
                                     April 14, 1845
                                     May 21, 1849
Number 300, Folio 533   May 21, 1849

To my beloved wife, Polly, all my estate both real and personal. After the death of my wife, my estate should be sold and the proceeds equally divided among my four children, namely: Nancy (wife of Samuel Bowers), Hannah Wilson, John Wilson and David Wilson.

Witnesses: John Hartzell, John Reck, Ephraim Bower
Executor(s): John Wilson (son)
Signed with his signature

Winck, Jacob   of Carroll County
                                     April 2, 1850
                                     April 15, 1850
Number 324, Folio 565   April 15, 1850

To my wife, Polly, all that I inherited with her being one hundred and forty two dollars, one bed and bedding, stove, all the queens ware and glass ware, kitchen furniture to keep one house, one cow, two hogs, two sheep, one spinning wheel, five chairs, one Dutch Bible and any other items she had when we married. The residue of my estate should be sold and the proceeds divided into four equal shares with one fourth going to my son, Samuel, and the other three shares to the legal heirs of my son, Samuel. I ask that the court appoint guardians for said minor grandchildren and that they should only come into their inheritance at marriage or as they come of age (whichever happens first).

Witnesses: Henry Falkenstein, George Winck, Jacob Feather
Executor(s): David Brilhart, David C. Frankforter
Signed by his mark

Wine, Henry   of Carroll County
                                              July 2, 1850
                                             April 7, 1851
Number 352, Folio 602   April 7, 1851

To my son, Jacob Wine, all my clothes and my large German
Bible. To my daughter, Elizabeth (wife of Jacob Frock), seven
hundred dollars to be held in trust at interest. If my daughter
Elizabeth should die before her husband, then the principal
should be divided among her siblings. The remainder of my
estate should be distributed as follows: one sixth share to my
son, Jacob Wine; a sixth to my daughter, Catherine (wife of
Jacob Geething); a sixth to my daughter, Anna Mary (wife of
John Stonesifer); a sixth to my daughter, Sarah (wife of Jacob
Baum); a sixth to my daughter, Elizabeth (wife of Jacob Frock),
in addition to the mentioned legacy; a sixth to the children of
my daughter, Rachael (wife of John Lippy), to be kept in trust
by executors and paid to each grandchild as they come of age.

Witnesses: Isaac Biehl, Philip Arter, David B. Earhart
Executor(s): Jacob Wine (son), Jacob Geething (son in law)
Signed with his signature

Winters, Catherine   of Carroll County
                                         November 4, 1843
                                              May 4, 1846
Number 224, Folio 409   May 11, 1846

To my daughter, Margaret Simmons, and her son, William
Simmons, the house and lot where I currently reside in New
Windsor, Carroll County. To my daughter, Elizabeth Ecker
(residing in Ohio), thirty dollars. All my personal property
should be sold to pay my debts.

Witnesses: Jonas Ecker, James Erhard
Executor(s): John Lambert
Signed by her mark

Winters, Catherine   of Carroll County
                                        May 1, 1842
                                        September 15, 1851
Number 362, Folio 615   September 15, 1851

To my son, Samuel Winters, my eight day clock, my one horse wagon, and all my interest in the tract of land where I currently reside (containing two hundred) plus twenty five dollars on condition that he pays my daughter, Esther Lambert, the sum of six hundred dollars and that he pays my daughter, Judith Appler, the sum of six hundred dollars and that he pays my son, Martin Winters, the sum of six hundred dollars. The latter should be kept in trust for my son, Martin Winters, by my executor. If my son, Martin Winters, should die then his legacy should be distributed equally to my children, namely: Samuel Winters, Esther Lambert, Rebecca Warner and Judith Appler. I give to my granddaughter, Elizabeth Winters (daughter of my son Samuel), my red chest. I give to the Trustees of the Lutheran Church near my home, the sum of twenty dollars. The remainder of my estate should be sold and equally divided among my herein named children.

Witnesses: David W. Naill, William Engleman, George Geiselman
Executor(s): Samuel Winters (son)
Signed by her mark

Yohn, Mary   of Carroll County
                                        January 16, 1847
                                        March 1, 1847
Number 247, Folio 453   March 1, 1847

To my daughter, Elizabeth Sundergill, the interest of twelve hundred dollars and after her death this should go to my three granddaughters, namely: Henrietta Powder, Christian Deal and Mary Elizabeth Powder. To my son, William Yohns, the sum of twelve hundred dollars. To my daughter, Elizabeth Sundergill, one eight day clock now in her possession and after

246

my daughter's death the clock is to go to my granddaughter, Mary Elizabeth Powder. One hundred dollars to my granddaughters: Henrietta Powder, Christian Deal and Mary Elizabeth Powder. Fifty dollars to my grandsons John Lewis Sundergill and Joshua Hamilton Sundergill. Fifty dollars to my granddaughter, Adaline Virginia Sundergill. To my son, William Yohn, seventeen hundred and fifty dollars. To my son, William Yohn, my negro woman called Eliza and her children (Moses, John, Ann Rebecca, Jeremiah). To my son, William Yohn, all my household furniture and provisions. To my daughter, Mary Smith, my colored girl called Henrietta and the balance of my estate. Fifty cents to my grandchildren: William T. Smith, Susannah Smith and Joshua Smith. To my daughters, Elizabeth Sundergill and Mary Smith, enough money to buy a full dress of mourning.

Witnesses: Joseph Frizzell, George W. Belleson, Joshua C. Gist
Executor(s): Thomas Smith (son in law)
Signed with her signature

Yost, John   of Carroll County
                                              April 3, 1843
                                              May 15, 1843
Number 154, Folio 267   May 15, 1843

One year after my death my beloved wife, Anamaria, shall have my furniture as deemed necessary for her use. My children my take any furniture provided that they can support my wife during her lifetime. My youngest children should have their home in mine until they arrive of age. My daughters, Margarith and Elizabeth, shall have their furniture. After my wife's death, my sons should sell my property and have the proceeds should be shared alike [legatees not named].

Witnesses: George Leese, Daniel Rhinehart, Pruitt Peterman
Executor(s): Jacob Yost (son)
Signed with his signature

Zacharias, Susan   of Carroll County

June 13, 1851
February 23, 1852
Number 379, Folio 640   February 23, 1852

To my son, Jacob Zacharias, and to my daughter, Elizabeth Brown, my three negroes called Samuel, Willy and Beck. To my daughter, Elizabeth Brown, my bureau and leaf table (which I purchased at N. H. Brown's estate sale), bedstead and bedding. To my son, Conrad Zacharias, after five years from my death one negro named Isaac. After the death of my son, Conrad Zacharias, the same negro named Isaac should go to my son, Jacob Zacharias. To my daughter, Sevilla (wife of Jacob Royer), all the goods, lands and chattel given to me by Jesse Reifsnider. To my son, Jacob Zacharias, and daughter, Elizabeth Brown, all my household and kitchen furniture for all of Elizabeth Brown's widowhood and should Elizabeth remarry then her half should go to my son Jacob. To my son, Jacob Zacharias, all the residue of my personal property and the tracts of land in Carroll County called "Keys Industry", "Covers Adventure", "Zacharias Lot" and "Lookabout" (the latter being adjacent to the lands of John A. Byers and John Roop). To my daughter, Elizabeth Brown, fifty dollars two years after my death. My executors should pay Jesse Reifsnider one hundred dollars for property herein mentioned which has been given to my daughter, Sevilla Royer. To my son, Jacob Zacharias, fifty dollars. To my daughters Ellen Byers, Appalona Reifsnider, Susan Shaffer and Polly Hoover each fifty dollars after two years from my death. If any of my children are dissatisfied with the amount given them then they are to be given twenty five cents.

Witnesses: Henry B. Grammer, John Beggs, J. Henry Hoppe
Executor(s): Jacob Zacharias (son)
Signed with her signature

Zile, Barbary (Barbara)   of Carroll County
                                   November 12, 1838
                                   April 3, 1843
Number 149, Folio 256   April 3, 1843

To my son, Abraham Zile, my desk. To my daughter, Eve Bellison, five dollars. To my daughter, Margaret Grimes, five dollars. The remainder of my property should be equally divided among my children, namely: Jacob Zile, Elizabeth Smith, John Zile, Rachel Zile, Eve Bellison, Abraham Zile, Mary Smith and Margaret Grimes.

Witnesses: Benjamin Dudderar, Frederick Prugh, Joseph Frizzell
Executor(s): Abraham Zile (son)
Signed by her mark

Zimmerman, Christiann   of Carroll County
                                   November 28, 1851
                                   January 12, 1852
Number 373, Folio 630   January 12, 1852

To my daughter, Caroline (wife of Samuel Zepp), all my personal property and all my real estate in Carroll County (which adjoins the lands of Jacob Sellers and John Ruby) on the condition that she maintains me comfortably during my natural life. At my death all my other property should be sold and after all debts paid, the balance should be distributed equally among my children, namely: Elizabeth (wife of Henry Keller), Polly (wife of Henry Miller), George Zimmerman, John Zimmerman, Lydia (wife of William Runk), Christian Zimmerman, Henry Zimmerman, Sarah Ann (wife of Jacob Rumler), Adam Zimmerman and Caroline (wife of Samuel Zepp).

Witnesses: James Kelly, Joseph Lippy, Samuel Snyder
Executor(s): Samuel Zepp (son in law)
Signed by her mark

Zocchi, Nicholas   Pastor of Taneytown, Carroll
                                        County
                                        January 17, 1843
                                        January 19, 1846
Number 373, Folio 398   January 19, 1846

I desire to "be buried in the front of the door of the Catholic
Church at Taneytown at the place indicated by the circle in the
fence." My tombstone should say, "Nicholas Zocchi Pastor the
year month and day of death Christian say Lord have mercy on
his soul," and my body should remain twenty four hours in the
house, twenty four hours in the Catholic Church so that
Catholic Priests be united to celebrate mass, and the third day I
should be buried without any solemnity. My house and lot
should go to the Trustees to the Roman Catholic Church at
Taneytown (for the benefit of my successors) with the
"obligation that the said Trustees will cause to be said for the
benefit of my soul, three masses, yearly in the month in which I
die." I give to my housekeeper, Sophia Wright, one bed with
bedstead and a portion of my furniture (the other portion as
designated by the Trustees should be kept for the benefit of my
successors). To the Rev. Francis Vespre, of Georgetown
College, fifty dollars which he should, in turn, send to Angelo
Gallic for assistance that is much needed. I give to Sophia
Wright, four hundred and fifty dollars. To Henrietta Boyle, one
hundred dollars, in consideration of my respect for her. To
Miss Frances Weems fifty dollars. My executor should dispose
of my horse and carriage. My clothes should go to Lewis Cash
in case he may be in my service at the time of my death and,
and if not, then the Boy who may so be. Half of my estate
should go to charity as jointly approved by my executor and my
housekeeper, Sophia Wright. The other half of my estate
should go to the Rev. G. Flaut to be used for masses.

Witnesses: William Burk, Daniel Snovell, William Short
Executor(s): John B. Boyle (my friend)
Signed with his signature

Zollickoffer, Caroline   widow of Uniontown

                                        April 23, 1850

                                        January 6, 1851

Number 344, Folio 591   January 6, 1851

To my granddaughter, Caroline Dulin, six table spoons and pair of sheets. To my granddaughter, Maria L. Shriver, the bedstead and carpet in the room upstairs with the new pillows also a large chest. To my grandson, William Henry Keener, my eight day clock. To my granddaughter, Mary E. Button (of my son Daniel), the new bedstead in the front room upstairs and one dozen Liverpool dinner plates. To my granddaughter, Annie M. Zollickoffer, a bedstead, feather bed, pair muslin sheets, quilt, pair store blankets, pillows in my room, china tea set, dozen tea plates, sugar tongs and six teaspoons. To my granddaughter, Caroline S. Zollickoffer (of my son Daniel), the Mahogany low posted bedstead, feather bed, pillows, pair store blankets, quilt, pair muslin sheets, the bureau in the room upstairs, cherry breakfast table and stair carpet. To my granddaughter, Ann Louisa Zollickoffer, mahogany tea table and pair of brass candle sticks. Twenty five dollars each to my granddaughters (of my son William Zollickoffer) when they turn eighteen. To my son, William Zollickoffer, cook stove, dining table, seven chairs and the split bottom chairs in the parlor. To my daughter, Mary Keener, the remainder of my clothes, sheets, pillow cases, quilts, table linens, "my deceased husband's likeness", a silver soup ladle and red chest. To Emily V. Brown a small dining table. To Henrietta Bond, twenty five dollars. The residue of my personal property should go to my son, Daniel Zollickoffer. My house and lot in Uniontown where I now reside should be sold and proceeds equally divided among my children: Henry Zollickoffer (of Philadelphia), Daniel Zollickoffer (of Carroll County) and Mary Keener (of Baltimore).

Witnesses: John Smith, John Roberts, Henry H. Herbaugh
Executor(s): Daniel Zollickoffer (my son)
Signed with her signature

INDEX

Slaves are listed under the surname of the testator unless a surname is provided for them. All land grants are in italics. Women are listed by their married names where possible.

James, 138
Joseph, 6
Lydia [slave], 6
Polly [slave], 6
Rebecca [slave], 6
Samuel [slave], 6
Samuel, 6
William [slave], 6
Zacharias [slave], 6
Arnolds Desire, 22
ARTER, Magdalena, 226
Philip, 226, 245
Solomon, 64
ARTHUR, Catherine, 6, 7, 185
Frederick, 182
Joseph, 7
Lydia, 6, 7
Philip, 226
Solomon, 6, 7
Aspen Hill, 220
ATLEE, Frank [slave], 8
Gabriel [slave], 8
Isaac, 8
James C., 8, 11, 91
Mary, 8
Samuel J., 8
BABYLON, Andrew, 8, 228
David, 9
Elisabeth, 9
Elizabeth, 9
Jacob, 9, 10
Jesse, 9
John, 9, 10, 227
Michael, 9, 227
Philip, 9
Samuel, 198

Susan, 198
Susanna, 8, 228
William, 10
Bachelors Chance or Choice, 52
Bachelor's Refuge, 20
BACHMAN, David, 147
Mary Ann, 147
Peter, 10
William, 213
BACKMAN, Henry, 155
Mary, 155
Bagdad, 110
BAILE, Abner, 207
Abraham, 42, 118
Henry, 223
Mary, 98
William, 223
BAKER, Allen, 44, 192
Charles G., 10
Elener, 10
Jesse, 10
John, 80
Moris, 10
Morris, 10
Naomey, 10
Simeon, 10
William, 10
BANKARD, Catherine, 185
Peter, 185
BANKER, Hannah, 57
Peter, 57, 100
BANKERT, David S., 213
Jacob, 71
BANKS, Elizabeth, 118
Barbados, 134
BARNES, Airey, 11

Alfred, 11
Amelia, 12
Andrew P., 12, 102
Anna, 78
Aquilla G., 97
Archibald, 11, 12
Belinda, 36
Elizabeth, 12
Francina, 13
Garretson, 159, 164
Garrison, 165
James P., 12
Levi T., 12
Margaret, 163
Mary, 14, 199
Moses, 159, 165
Narcissa, 12
Prudence, 12
Rachel, 12
Sally Elizabeth, 11, 12
Slingsby L., 12
Slingsly L., 12
Thomas, 11
Thomas E. F., 12
Urith, 164, 165
Violette, 12
Violette E., 11
Washington, 236
William, 36, 37
William P., 46
Zachariah, 78
Zadock, 12, 78
BARNHART, Sarah, 194
BART, Rosannah, 92
BARTHOLOW, John, 14
Michael, 13, 14

Nancy, 13, 14
Thomas, 14
BASEMAN, Sarah, 16
Bashan, 159
BATES, Francis Henry, 94
John, 87
BAUGH, John, 157
BAUGHER, Mary Ann, 9
BAUMGARDNER, Daniel, 3
Elizabeth, 14
Jacob, 14
John, 14
John H., 3
John Joseph, 39, 174
Josiah, 14
Magdalene, 14
Mary Magdalene, 14
Samuel, 14, 162
BAUMGARTNER, Amanda, 144
Ann Mary, 15
Daniel, 15, 16, 176
Elizabeth, 15, 144, 147
Frances J., 166
Francis, 108
Francis J., 106, 107
Henry, 15, 144, 147
Jacob (junior), 15
Jacob (senior), 15
Jacob, 15, 107, 127
John, 6, 15, 18, 57, 63, 66, 80, 106,
    161, 198, 201, 233, 236, 238
John J., 84
Joshua, 144
Josiah, 96, 106
Lewis, 144
Peter, 15

Samuel, 144
BAURN, Jacob, 245
  Sarah, 245
BAUST, Cornelious, 50
Baxters Choice, 38
BAYPLOT, Lavinia, 99
BEAN, Samuel, 181
  William, 72
BEAR, Margaret, 216
  Polly, 216
BEASMAN, Charity [slave], 16
  Eliza Ann, 16
  Johnze, 16
  Joseph, 159
  Joshua, 16, 45
  Mary, 16, 17
  Patience [slave], 16
  Phebe [slave], 16
  Sarah, 16
  Thomas, 60
  William, 159
Beasman's Discovery, 159
Beasmans Discovery Corrected, 45
BEAVER, Adam, 17
  Jacob, 17
  John, 18
  Nancy, 17
  Susannah, 17
  Unknown, 175
  William, 17
BECHTEL, Catherine, 56, 57
  Henry, 57
  Mary Ann, 17
  Samuel, 17
BECKER, David, 120
  Polly, 120

BEECHER, John, 73
BEGGS, Eleanor, 18
  John, 114, 248
BEHO, Mary, 18
  William, 19
BELLESON, George, 168, 247
BELLISON, Eve, 249
BELTZ, Henry E., 200, 217
BENNER, Daniel, 227
BENNETT, Aaron [slave], 23
  Alice [slave], 21
  Allen, 20, 23
  Ann [slave], 21, 23
  Barbara, 177
  Belinda, 19
  Ben [slave], 21
  Benjamin, 11, 19, 20, 21, 22,
    23, 72
  Benjamin Franklin, 20, 23
  Charles [slave], 21
  Charles W., 21, 131
  Charlotte, 131
  Eleanor Ann, 23
  Eli, 20
  Elisha, 20, 21, 22, 61
  Emma [slave], 21
  Fanny [slave], 19
  Francis Lewis, 22
  George [slave], 21
  Harriott [slave], 23
  Jesse, 21
  Kitty Helen, 20, 23
  Larkin, 19, 23
  Lewis Henry, 23
  Margaret, 23
  Mary, 131

David, 116
George, 26, 144
Jeremiah, 26
Black Oak Hill, 128
BLACK, Joseph, 60
BLIZZARD, George, 137
James, 139
John M., 243
Margaret, 139
Rachel, 160
BOLLENCY, Mary, 79
Thomas, 79
BOLLINGER, Andrew, 27
Barbara, 27
Catherine, 27
Daniel, 27, 129
Elizabeth, 27
George, 27
Jacob, 27, 190
John, 73
Joseph, 27
Margaret, 72
Molly, 27
Peter, 27
Sarah, 27
Susanna, 27
BOND, Andrew Jackson, 28
Charles, 28
Christopher, 27
Edward, 28
Eliza Ann [slave], 28
Henrietta, 27, 251
Joshua, 28
Julia Ann [slave], 28
Larkin, 28
Peter, 28

Samuel, 28
BONECKER, Catherine, 29
George William, 29
William, 29
BONHAM, Milly, 86
Richard, 86
BORING, Caleb, 220
Ezekiel (senior), 29
Ezekiel, 29, 56, 112, 125
Hester, 29
Jacob W., 55, 56, 78
John, 29, 30
Mary, 29
Thomas, 29
BORNS, George, 150
Lydia, 150
BOSLEY, Ann, 30
James, 30, 186
Joshua, 30
Sarepta, 31
Shadrack, 30, 31
Thomas, 30
BOULINGER, Elizabeth, 127
Samuel, 127
BOWARS, Mary, 209
BOWER, Adam, 167
David, 31
Esther, 31
Joseph, 171
Rachel, 163
Samuel, 163
Sarah, 171
Stephen, 31
BOWERS, George, 154
Jacob, 105
Joseph, 51

258

N., 23
N. H., 248
Nancy, 34
Nat [slave], 32
Nathan, 21
Neilson, 36
Nicholas Hall, 28, 36, 199
Noah, 35
Peter [slave], 32
Peter, 37
Poll [slave], 32
Rachel, 33, 34
Rebecca, 35
Richard, 220
Ruth, 35, 36, 37
Samuel, 34
Sevelley, 37
Sofid, 37
Susan, 36
Susannah E., 32
William, 32
William Stansbury, 36
BROWNE, N., 72, 177
Nathan, 133, 207
Nicholas H., 199
BRUNGARD, Amos, 38
Jacob, 38
Mary, 38
Susanna, 38
BUCHANAN, Jane, 71
John, 72
BUCHER, Abraham, 38
Christian, 38
David, 38, 39
Henry, 183
Jesse, 39

John, 183
Mary, 38, 39
Noah, 38
Rachel, 38
BUCHON, Sarah Z., 129
BUCKER, Christian, 38
BUCKINGAM, William, 149
BUCKINGHAM, Beale, 112, 207
Elisha, 160
Louisa, 11, 12
Nicholas, 39
Obadiah (junior), 17
Obadiah, 39
Owen F., 73
Pat [slave], 39
Vachel, 207
BUFFENTON, Abraham, 123
BUFFINGTON, Abraham, 82
Anne, 82
Levi, 196
BULL, Shadrack, 192
BUNTING, James, 24
BURGESS, Emily Jane, 40
Henrietta, 40
Margaret Elizabeth, 40
Richard Bonaparte, 40
Richard H., 40
Theodocia Virginia, 40
BURGOON, William, 64
BURK, George, 242
William, 196, 250
BURLY, Elisabeth, 129
BUSBY, Rachel, 45
BUSHEY, Henry, 242
Ruth Ann, 242

BUTTON, Mary E., 251
BYERS, David, 3
    Elizabeth, 167
    Ellen, 248
    Henry, 167
    Jannett, 18
    John, 167
    John A., 248
    Mary, 167
    Peter, 142, 143, 167
    Rebecca, 142
    Susan, 167
CAKLE, Jacob, 210
Caladonia, 137
Caledonia, 243
CALTRIDER, Kesiah, 30
CAMPBELL, Jacob, 38, 125
Canton Bearon, 189
CAPLE, Jacob, 131
    William, 226
CARL, Sarah, 66
CARLYLE, Ann, 40, 41
    Anna, 73
    David R., 41, 73
    Ebenezer, 40, 73
    Mary, 73
CARR, Martha, 177, 178, 179
    Mary, 60, 61
    Samuel, 201
CARTER, Henry, 32
    William, 138
Caryall, 165
CASE, George, 42
CASH, Lewis, 250
CASKEY, Isaiah, 171
    Mary, 171

CASSADY, Susan, 94
    Thomas, 94
CASSELL, Abraham, 166
    D., 166
    David, 42, 166
    George, 41
    Henry, 41
    Isaac, 42
    Jacob, 18, 41, 42
    Joseph, 42
    Mary Diehl, 58
CATTRIDER, Joshua, 30
    Kesiah, 30
CAYLER, Levi, 98
CAYLOR, Abraham, 41, 51, 68,
    83, 183
    Margaret, 41
CHALFANT, James, 42
    Martha, 42
    Mary Ann, 42
Chance, 163
CHAPMAN, Ann, 43
    Eliza Jane [slave], 43
    Henry [slave], 43
    James, 43
    Mary E., 43
    Rachel, 43, 44
    William, 43
Charles and Adams Choice, 26
CHENOWETH, John B., 38
Chestnut Ridge, 15
CHEW, Elizabeth, 213
    John H., 139
CHILCOTE, Hester, 118
CHOATE, Samuel, 88
CHRIST, Elizabeth, 3

264

Henry W., 59
Jacob, 58, 59, 117
John, 58, 59
Jonas, 58, 59
Samuel, 58, 59
DIFFENDAL, Samuel, 151
DIFFENDALL, Mary, 151
DILL, Nicholas, 56
DISE, Elizabeth, 88
DITZLER, Jacob, 141, 161
DIXON, Elenora, 93
George, 93
DODS, Margaret, 59
Sarah, 59
DOLL, Catherine, 55
DORFLER, Catharina, 173
John, 173
DORITY, Caleb, 93
DORSEY, Archibald, 60, 61
Beal, 61
Elisha, 54
Eliza C., 60
Ely C., 60, 61
Gustavus, 55
Henry C., 60, 61
John H., 61
Jonathan, 60, 61
Mary, 60
Mary C., 61
N., 32
Nicholas, 17, 22, 32, 44, 60, 61, 136, 179
Nimrod B., 60
Otho, 60, 61
DOWNEY, Anna, 104
Thomas, 104

Dry Works, 36
DUDDERAR, Benjamin, 249
DUDDERER, William, 195
DULIN, Caroline, 251
DUNN, Rebecca, 72
William, 72
DURBIN, Augustus Washington, 238
Catherine, 62, 216, 238
Charity, 62, 238
Comfort, 62
Elizabeth, 216
George, 157
Hannah, 216
James, 238
John, 238
Margaret, 62
Nicholas, 62, 216
Ruth, 216
Samuel, 57, 238
Sarah, 238
Thomas, 238
Thomas W., 62, 237, 238
Washington, 238
William, 42, 157, 216, 238
Durbins Mistake, 133
DUVALL, Mary, 120
EADINGER, Christina, 127
John, 127
EARHART, Catherine, 63, 64
David D., 10, 13, 34, 64, 81, 95, 127, 128, 135, 152, 245
George, 64
Jacob, 64
Jacob B., 64
John, 63, 64

Mary Ann, 67
Nathan, 67, 68
Octavious Augustus, 66
Phebe, 67
Philip, 68
Samuel, 69
ENGLEMAN, Elizer, 223
  William, 41, 98, 223, 246
ENGLER, David, 195
  Ephraim, 212
  Hannah, 212
  John, 212
  Levina, 212
  Mary, 212
  Mordecai, 212
  Philip, 212
  Phillip, 212
EPAUGH, Henry, 91
  Mary Catherine, 91
EPHRAIM, Bower, 244
Eppington Forest, 207
ERB, Abraham, 94
  Barbara, 94
  Christopher, 134
  Jacob, 94, 134
  Peter, 94
ERHARD, James, 245
ESZIG, Adam, 173
EVANS, Amos, 220
  Elizabeth B., 166
  Kissier, 197
  Levi, 235, 236
  Mary, 89, 235
  Mary E., 235, 236
  Samuel, 12, 57, 109, 166
EVENS, Amos, 70

Catherine, 70
John, 70, 138
Joseph, 70
Levy, 70
Lewis, 70
Susannah, 70
William, 70
EVERHART, George (the elder),
  162
  George, 129, 145, 186, 217
EVERLY, David, 6, 176
  Elizabeth, 176
  Levi, 71, 176
  Rebecca, 71
Everything Needful, 30
EVES, David, 212
EWING, William, 71, 72
EWINGS, William, 20
FACE, Elisabeth, 226
  Frederick, 226
FAES, Ellen, 206
  Lewis, 206
FAIR, Ephraim, 72
  George (junior), 72
  George, 32, 72, 190
  Henry, 73
  Peter, 72
  Samuel, 32, 72
  Sarayann, 72
  William, 72
FALKENSTEIN, Henry, 244
FANNING, William, 73
FARQUHAR, Deborah, 102
  Joel, 102
  William, 211
FARVER, Mary, 168

FROCK, Catherine, 80, 81
Daniel, 196
Elizabeth, 245
Henry, 81
Jacob, 80, 81, 151, 245
John, 122
Lydia, 196
Michael, 80, 81
Rachel, 151
Rebecca, 81
Sarah, 151
Susannah, 81
William, 80, 81
FUHERMAN, John, 199
FUHRMAN, Margaret, 124
Samuel B., 124, 208
FULKERTH, Ebenezer, 41
Michael, 41
FULKES, Henry, 8
FUSS, J. Adam, 43
Mary, 82
GAITHERS, Henry, 60, 61
GALLIC, Angelo, 250
GALT, Ann Eliza [slave], 82
James, 82
Mary, 82
Moses, 82
Samuel, 82
Sterling, 82, 106
GARBER, Catherine, 82, 83
John, 83, 240
Michael, 83
Solomon, 83
GARDNER, Freeborn, 39
Joseph, 112, 125, 132
L., 39

Lovelace, 139, 158
GARFIELD, Asbury O., 113
GARNER, Cary, 165
Flin, 165
GARRET, Ann Mary, 15
Nicholas, 15
GARRETTSON, Aquila, 84
James Aquila, 84
Richard, 84
Richard Freeborn, 84
Thomas Henry, 84
William Edward, 84
GEARING, Ezekiel, 102
GEATTY, Ellen, 166
Mary, 185
Molly, 185
Peter, 185
GEETHING, Catherine, 245
Jacob, 64, 245
GEIGER, Charlotte, 128
Peter, 128
GEIMAN, Abraham, 85
Christian, 85
Daniel, 85
Daniel J., 64, 85, 86, 167
David, 85, 86
Jacob, 85
John, 85
Joseph, 85
Samuel, 85
GEISELMAN, George, 246
George's Purchase, 2
GERNAND, Joseph, 151
GETTHING, Jacob, 64
GETTIER, George, 125
Margaret, 125, 126

270

Michael, 136, 140, 141
Peter, 79
GILBERT, Adam, 199
Adam C., 56
Catherine, 56
Samuel, 177
Susannah, 56
GILLIS, Alexander, 89
Jerusa, 86
John, 86
Joseph H., 86
GIST, David R., 232
Federal Ann Bonaparte, 87
George W., 87
Harriet, 86, 87
Henry Clay, 87
Joshua, 86
Joshua C., 8, 11, 12, 22, 87, 88,
89, 142, 168, 222, 247
Margaret Amelia, 8
Mary S., 87
Mordecai, 87
Rachel, 87
Richard [slave], 87
Richard, 87
States, 87
Thomas, 87
GITT, Jacob, 74, 78, 79, 104, 186,
200, 208
GITTIER, Jacob, 155
Margaret, 155
GLASE, Henry, 203, 204
Leah, 203, 205
GLASSGE, Ann Bartholow, 13
William K., 13
GOLDSBOROUGH, Howes, 234

GOLLEY, David S., 171
Eliza, 4, 171
GOLLY, Abraham, 171
Elizabeth, 171
GOOD, Matilda, 94
GORE, John, 4, 191, 213
Philip, 74
Samuel, 21
GORSUCH, Ann, 88
Benjamin, 57
Clorosa [slave], 88
Eliza Ann, 88
Georg [slave], 88
George W., 149
Harriett [slave], 88
Honour [slave], 88
Jacob, 128
James H., 130
John W., 88, 149
John Washington, 88
Lovelace, 88
Lovelace M., 39
Manerva [slave], 88
Nathan, 88
Nathan J., 39
Perrygrine, 88
Polly [slave], 88
Stephen, 12
Thomas Jefferson, 88
William, 88
GOSNELL, Amos, 89
Charles A., 90
Comfort, 88, 89
David, 89
Enoch [slave], 90
Eurith, 90

271

Hannah [slave], 90
Harriett, 90
Herod, 89
James, 78
John [slave], 90
John, 89
Joseph, 89
Lewis [slave], 90
Lydia [slave], 90
Mariah [slave], 90
Matilda, 90
Nimrod, 89
Peter, 89
Rachel [slave], 89
Reuben [slave], 89
Rooney, 89
Samuel, 89
Sarah, 88, 89
William, 89, 90
William S., 90
Gotham, 74
GOUGER, Jacob, 152
GRACE, James, 137, 187
GRAMMER, Andrew, 91
 Ann Mary, 90, 91
 Dorratha, 91
 Henry, 90
 Henry B., 248
 John, 240
 Mary, 240
 Rachel, 90, 91
 Rebecca, 91
 Simon Jonas, 91
GREEN, Isaac, 77
 James [slave], 73
GREENFIELD, Jacob, 84

Mary, 84
GREENHULT, Samuel, 113
GREENWOOD, Barbara, 194
 Barbary, 91, 92, 93
 Catherine, 92, 194
 Daniel, 91, 92
 David Henry, 92
 Eliza Jane, 93
 Elizabeth, 92
 Harry [slave], 91
 Isaiah, 92
 Jeremiah, 92
 John (senior), 93
 John, 91, 194
 John W., 91, 92, 93
 Joseph, 91, 92, 194
 Josiah, 92
 Ludwick, 92, 194
 Magdalena, 92
 Margaret, 92
 Philip, 93
 Uriah, 92
 William H., 93
 William Henry, 92
GRIFFEE, William, 165
GRIMES, Cornelius, 55
 Elias, 82, 169
 Gassaway S., 55
 Margaret, 93, 249
GROFF, Catherine, 94
 Dorus, 26
 Francis, 94
 Jacob, 94
 John, 94
GROGG, Eve, 72
 Jacob, 72

HEADDINGTON, James O., 45
HEADINGTON, James O., 159
HEBBARD, Ann Robinson, 103
  Lydia, 103
  Moses B., 103
  Susan, 103
  Susan F., 103
  William A., 103
  William B., 103
HECK, Mary, 101
HEISSON, Joseph, 187
  Peter, 187
HELDEBRIDLE, Eve, 100
  John, 100
Heller Noell, 15
HELLER, Rachel, 205
HENDERSON, Catherine, 173
  Henry [slave], 103
  John, 103
  Lydia, 103
  Margaret, 173
HENESTOFFLE, Anna, 103
  Henry, 104
  John, 104
  Samuel, 104
  Ulrick, 104
HENNEMAN, Charles, 57
  Charles W., 141
HENRY, George, 201
HERBAUGH, Henry H., 191, 227,
  240, 251
HERNER, Amanuel, 104
  Catherine, 104
  Elizabeth, 104
  Jacob, 104, 105
  John, 104, 105

  Lydia, 104
  Magdalena, 104
  Michael, 104, 105
  Peter, 104, 105
  Rebecca, 104
  Susanna, 104
  Susannah, 104, 105
HESS, Ann, 48, 49
  Charles, 105
  Daniel, 106
  Henry, 106, 158
  Jess, 49
  John, 51, 83, 106, 158, 183
  Magdalena, 105
  Samuel, 48, 49, 106
HESSON, Abraham, 106, 194
  Baltzer, 106
  Barbara, 106
  Benjamin, 107
  Daniel, 106
  Elizabeth, 107
  Isaac, 95
  Jacob, 106
  John, 106, 107, 205
  Joseph, 176
  Louis, 106
  Margaret, 106, 107
  Peter, 95, 106, 176
HESSONE, Daniel, 105
  Magdalena, 105
HEWITT, Nancy, 19
HIBBERD, Alice Ann, 177
  Benjamin, 177
  Job, 177
  Joseph, 177
  Sarah Jane, 177

Silas, 47, 177
Tacy, 177
HICKINGER, Hester, 6
HICKS, Mary Ann, 148
HIDE, Joshua, 128
  Polly, 128
HILDERBRAND, Barbary, 2
HILL, Hannah, 107
  Lydia, 107
  Nancy, 45
HILLEN, Thomas, 192
HILLESBROCK, Catherine, 198
  John, 198
HILLTERBRICK, Catherine, 198
HILTABRIDEL, Jacob, 142
HINDS, Easters, 108
  Patrick, 108
HINER, William, 169
HINES, James, 81
HINING, Elizabeth, 194
  Thomas, 194
HITESHAW, Caroline, 113
  Charles, 113, 240
HITESHEU, Charles, 83
HITESHEW, Mary, 108
HITESHUE, Israel, 79, 196
  William, 51
Hockstadt, 74
HOFFMAN, Fredericka, 109
  Jacob, 109
  Samuel, 59
HOFFOCKER, David, 109
  Elisabeth, 150
  George, 109
  Henry, 150
  Henry M., 109

Jacob, 109
John, 109
Samuel, 109
HOLBERSTAR, Eli, 83
  Eliza, 83
  Lydia, 83
HOLLINGSWORTH, Hester
  [slave], 110
  Horace [slave], 109
  Jesse, 110, 133
  John, 109
  Mary Ann R., 109, 110
HOLMES, Jacob, 164
Honours delight, 117
HOOD, Charles W., 121, 234
  James, 110, 111
  John, 110, 111
  Sarah, 110
  Sarah L., 111
  Thomas, 89, 102, 111
  William, 110, 111
HOOK, Thomas, 26, 215
HOOKER, Amos, 164
  Jacob, 210
  Johnathan Greenbury, 164
  Mary, 111, 164, 165
  Mary Ann, 111
  Richard, 50
Hookers Meadow Resurveyed, 38
HOOKEY, Lloyd, 111
HOOPER, Ann Bartholow, 13
  Elizabeth, 13
  John, 13
  John Thomas, 13
  Michael Hanson, 13
  Uritha, 13

276

HOOVER, Catherine, 129
Daniel L., 130, 197
Joseph, 163
Polly, 248
Sally, 163
HOPPE, J. Henry, 3, 7, 37, 64, 114, 143, 144, 145, 147, 213, 233, 239, 248
John Henry, 100, 120
HORATIO, Price, 37
HORN, Elizabeth [slave], 94
HORNER, Franklin Finley, 241
William, 114
HORTON, Isaac, 112
Nelly, 112
Thomas, 112
William, 112
HOSHAL, Caleb, 1
HOUCK, Catherine, 112
David W., 2
Elizabeth, 35
George, 35, 112
Henry, 15, 199
Jacob, 218
Rachel, 2
William, 112
HOUCKER, David, 155
HOUSES, Frank, 175
HOWARD, Elizabeth Ann, 112
Jemima, 112
Joshua, 201
HOWARDS, Joshua, 67
HUGHES, Deborah, 102
Elizabeth, 102
HULL, David, 123
Peter, 107

Veronica, 107
HUMBERT, Adam, 81
Elisabeth, 81
George, 128
John, 81
Susannah, 81
HYDE, Isaac, 8
HYDER, Adeline Delaplane
Euclid, 113
Ann Lucinda, 113
Caroline, 113
Catherine, 113, 114, 180, 181
Elizabeth, 113
Isaac, 180
Jacob, 114
John, 4, 113, 114, 228
John Franklin, 113
Mary Carmack, 113
Sophia, 113
HYLE, Elizabeth, 114
Joseph, 114
INGELS, Thomas, 12
Inglers Addition, 26
IRELAND, Edward, 72
Iron Intention, 232
JACKSON, Bendago, 30
Rachel, 30
JACOB, Belinda, 45
George, 29
JACOBS, George, 84, 181
Richard, 84, 181
JAKES, Elizabeth, 101
James Fancy, 81
JAMES L., Billingslea, 18
JAMES, Sarah, 138
JAMESON, Catherine, 168

George, 100
Ruth, 16
Kentucky, 129
KEPHART, David, 174
KEPP, Henry, 28
KERBY, Joshua, 179
KERCHANE, George, 27
Sarah, 27
KERICK, Andrew, 124
Catherine, 124
KERLINGER, Conrad, 125
Jacob, 31, 109, 115, 132, 136,
140, 141, 150, 161, 207, 214, 217,
218
KESSLER, David, 185
Jacob, 185
Peter, 185
KEYES, David, 117
Elizabeth, 117
Keys Industry, 248
KEYS, David, 117
Elizabeth, 117
Samuel, 117
Stephen, 100
KILER, Andrew, 118
David, 118
George, 118
Isaac, 118
Jacob, 118
John (senior), 118
John, 118
Mary, 118
Simon, 118
Susanna, 118
KING, Adam, 119
Eleanor, 3

Elizabeth, 119
Jacob, 119
John, 119
William, 127, 236
KINZER, John David, 68
KIRKER, William C., 156
KIRKWOOD, R. A., 103
Richard A., 12, 222
KIVELY, John, 79
KIZER, Phebe, 122
KLINEDENTS, Catherine, 200
John, 200
KLINEFELLER, George D., 191
Klines Place, 176
KNELLER, Godfrey, 125
KNIPPEL, Barbara, 120
Christopher, 120
David, 120
Elizabeth, 120
George, 120
John, 120
Polly, 120
KNIPPLE, David, 71, 143
KNOCK, Basil, 120
Ezekiel, 121
Honor, 121
Thomas, 120
KNOLE, Rachel, 129
KOONS, Abraham, 121, 174
Benjamin, 121, 122
Catherine, 122
Christena, 122
Christiana, 122
Conrad, 122
David, 123
Edwin, 123

Joseph, 129
Joshua, 73, 130
Lewis J. A., 230
Mary, 230
Moses, 130
Priscilla, 129
Samuel, 129
William Henry, 229
Lammotts Delight, 129
Lammotts Middle of the World, 129
LAMOTT, Abraham, 88
LAMPERD, Mary, 130
LAMPERT, Mary, 130
Susannah, 17
LANDES, Hannah, 212
Isaac, 212
Jacob, 8, 92, 212
Jesse, 102
LANE, Elizabeth, 131, 210
Micajah, 131
LANTZ, Joseph, 90
LAUVER, Frances, 191
Samuel A., 209
LAWRENCE, Dennis Alexander, 132
Henry, 132
Isaiah, 132
John, 132
Lawrence's Industry, 207
LAWSON, Edward, 132
Elizabeth, 132
Jacob, 132
John, 132
Moses, 132
Moses R., 132
Ruth, 132
Sarah, 132

Thomas, 132
LAWYER, John, 147
Sally, 147
William, 3
LEAS, Sophia, 214
LECOMPTE, Samuel D., 87
Lee Castle, 28
LEE, Charlotte E., 133
Elisabeth, 133
Honor, 133
Joshua (junior), 136
Joshua, 136
Maranda, 133
Maria, 133
Robert, 133
Thomas, 133
Thomas L., 133
LEESE, George, 247
Sarah, 152
LEESS, Daniel, 135
Legh Castle, 67
LEGORE, Eliza, 133
Ezra, 133
Jacob, 133
Jesse U., 134
John, 133
Rachel, 133, 134
William H., 134
Lehmans Range, 106
LEIMAN, Jacob, 85
LEISTER, Conrad, 134
Daniel, 135
David, 6, 71, 86, 228
Edward, 64
Henry, 135
Israel, 131

281

John, 140
Juliann, 140
Mary Ann, 140
Samuel, 140
Valentine, 214
MANNING, A., 164, 165
  Elisabeth, 164, 165
  Elizabeth, 165
  Jesse, 77, 137, 164, 165, 167
  Martha, 141
  Nancy, 141
  R., 165
  Rachel, 164, 165
  Richard, 141
  Thomas, 141, 142
MANRO, Catherine, 142
  Charles [slave], 142
  David, 142
  George W., 98
  John, 142
  Nathan, 142
  Squire, 142
  Thomas, 142
Margarets Delight, 40, 41
MARICHEL, Daniel, 73
  Mary, 73
MARK, Peter, 101
MARKER, John, 143
  Susannah, 142
MARSH, Thomas, 54
MARSHALL, James, 6, 74, 141
  John, 103
  Rebecca, 3
MARTAIN, Elizabeth, 77
MARTIN, Ann Catherine, 123
  Barbara, 193

David, 15, 121
Elizabeth, 49
Jacob, 49
Margaret, 15
Mary, 193
Sarah, 83
Thomas Franklin, 121
William, 191
MASONHEIMER, Adam, 205
MASONHIMER, Daniel, 175
  Frederick, 175
  Henry, 188
  John, 175
  Mary, 175
  Peter, 175, 176
  Susan, 175
MATCHEL, Elizabeth, 219, 220
MATHIAS, Catherine, 146
  David, 147
  Elias H., 143
  Eliza, 143, 146
  Francis, 220
  George, 120, 146
  Henry, 145
  Jacob, 1, 7, 16, 46, 56, 147,
  194, 237
  John, 7, 146
  Joseph, 7, 19
  Maria, 143
  Perry, 143, 146, 147
  Priscilla, 146
  Rachel, 120, 143
MATTER, George, 155, 185
  Sarah, 155
MATTERS, George, 186
MATTHEWS, George W., 221

288

Moses, 160
Nicholas, 159, 160
Rachel W., 159
Sarah, 159
Silvester, 159, 160
William, 164
William H., 22
Oggs Discovery, 22
OGLE, John, 52
  Joseph, 52
  Mary Jane, 52
  Thomas, 52
Ohio, 107, 134
OHLER, Catherine, 15
  Christiana, 74
  Thomas, 15
OLINGER, Catherine, 160
  Emanuel, 161
  Henry Eli, 160
  Peter, 160
  Sarah Ann, 161
ORENDORF, David, 7
  Rebecca, 83
ORENDORFF, Joseph, 161
Ormly, 232
ORNDORFF, Anne, 161
  Appolonia, 161
  David, 161
  Elizabeth, 161, 162
  George, 161
  Henry, 14, 162
  Jacob, 161
  John, 161
  Joseph, 161
  Mary, 161
  Peter, 161, 162

Rachel, 161
Rosina, 161
Ruth, 161
Susan, 161
ORRICK, Sarah, 148
OTTO, Catherine, 214
  Herbert, 215
  Sophia, 215
OURSLER, Stephen, 4, 5, 70,
  153, 160, 206
Owens, 170
OWENS, Sarah, 112
Owings Chance, 101
OWINGS, Elizabeth, 46
  James, 46
  Nancy, 238
  Nathan H., 78
  Richard, 46
  Sarah H., 87
OYSTER, John, 83
  Mary, 83
PANABAKER, Cevilla, 163
  David, 162, 163
  Edwin H., 163
  Edwin Henry, 163
  John, 163
  Let [slave], 163
  Levi [slave], 163
  Mary, 162
  Peter, 162
  William, 163
PANEBAKER, Peter, 144
PARISH, James, 139
PARKE, Joseph M., 124
PARRISH, Hellen, 165
  James, 243

John, 164, 165
Johnathan, 164
Jonathan, 111
Moses, 243
Providence, 164
William, 131
PASCAULT, Lewis, 233
Patience Care, 80, 81
PATTERSON, Mary Ridgley, 103
  William W., 107
PAXTON, Esther, 48, 49
  John, 48
  William, 16
PEDICORD, Elisabeth, 165
  Elizabeth, 164
  Humphrey, 164, 165
PENN, Jacob W., 13
  Sarah, 13
  Stephen, 112
  Stewart, 112
PENNINGTON, Owen, 226
PENSIL, Anna Mary, 203
  Jacob, 203
PERRY, Mary, 195
PETERMAN, Daniel, 199, 226
  Elizabeth, 73
  Pruitt, 247
Peters Plague, 35
PETERS, Anne, 166
  Catherine, 166
  Henry, 166
  Jacob, 162, 166, 174
  Lewis, 162, 166, 174
  Rachel, 166
  Veronica, 166
Petersburgh Resurveyed, 5

PETRY, George, 85
PETTERSON, John, 44
PFEIFER, Andrew, 200
  Rebecca, 200
PFEIFFER, Michael D. G., 74
  Sarah, 74
Philipsburgh, 15
PHILLIPS, Samuel, 10
  Uriel, 10, 19
PICKELL, Ezekiel, 221
PICKEN, Thomas, 44
PICKET, Amelia, 78
PICKETT, Aquila, 88
  John, 21
  Nancy, 102
  Thomas, 102
  William W., 88
Pigmans Addition, 19
Pleasant Hill, 163
Pleasant Meadow, 85
Pleasant Spring, 69
PLOWMAN, Joshua, 135, 188
Plowmans Addition, 189
Plowmans Fancy, 189
PLUMMER, Abner, 97, 98
  Ruth, 97
Plymouth, 129
Point Intelligence, 210
Polished Mountain, 178
Polly's Habitation, 21
POMPEY, Henry [slave], 183
POOLE, Aaron, 112
  Mary, 112
PORTER, Elijah, 78
PORTS, Henry W., 129
POULSON, Ann, 166

Cornelius Lee, 166
Rachel, 166
POURTER, Arch, 165
Pourters Delight, 165
POWDER, Andrew, 167, 192
Catherine, 167
Christina, 167
Elisabeth, 167
Henrietta, 167, 246, 247
Jacob (senior), 167
Jacob, 76, 167
John D., 62
Margaret, 167
Mary Elizabeth, 246, 247
Polly, 167
Sally, 167
Susan, 167
POWEL, Esther, 167
Jacob, 167
John, 167
PRICE, Amon, 101
Horatio, 19, 199, 239
Susanna, 89
Property Arnolds Desire, 22
Prospect, 163
PRUGH, Abraham, 17, 22, 45, 168
Caroline, 16
David, 168
Elisha, 22
Eliza Jane [slave], 168
Frederick, 168, 249
Honour, 22
John, 168
Peter, 168
PUSEY, Elizabeth, 168
George, 168

Margaret, 168, 169
Sarah, 168
Thomas, 168
PUTMAN, Bartholomew
(junior), 233
PUTTERSON, Jesse, 159
*Qauled Stocksdale neighborhood,
165*
RAINES, Daniel, 91
RAIT, Basil, 169
Hanson C., 169
John, 169
Margaret, 169
Nathan, 169
RAMALL, Rachel, 99
RAMBY, Elizabeth, 4
Rapho, 178
Raredane Place, 118
RAXTON, Isaac, 37
RAYMOND, James, 1, 87
REAGEL, Henry, 136
Sophia, 136
REAGLE, Mary, 162
William Greenbury, 162, 163
REAVER, Christina, 170
Frederick, 170
John, 170
Joseph, 170
Philip, 170
Ulrich, 170
Ulrick, 170
RECK, John, 215, 244
Red Hills, 119
Red Oak Ridge, 207
REEAD, George, 126, 127
Mary, 126

REED, Frana, 171, 172
George, 172
Jacob, 171
Mary, 171, 172
REES, Andrew, 135
Hannah, 135
REESE, George, 2
Jacob, 19, 30, 157, 231, 239
John, 91
John F., 1
REEVER, Joseph, 170
REID, Alexander Hamilton, 173
Esther [slave], 172
James, 173
Margaret, 172, 173
Mary, 172, 173
REIFSNIDER, Appalona, 248
Catherine, 119
George, 119
Jesse, 7, 239, 248
REIGAL, David E., 205
REIGLE, Lewis, 188
REINDOLLAR, Henry, 185
John, 171, 185
REINECKER, Jacob, 154
REINEDOLLAR, John, 66
Maria, 66
REINEMAN, John, 15
REISZLE, Daniel, 173
John, 173
Margaret, 173
Maria, 173
Michael, 173
Rosina, 173
REMPYONE, Margaret, 214
Resurvey Fathers Gift, 207

*Resurvey on Brothers Agreement,
161*
Resurvey on Flintstone, 178
Resurvey on Lime Pitt, 232
Resurvey on Mackeys Choice, 151
Resurvey on Mill Lot, 41
Resurvey on Small Beginning, 195
*Resurvey on Wells Care Enlarged,
232*
REVER, Samuel, 106
Sarah, 106
RHINEHART, Daniel, 247
RHORBACH, Susanna, 38
William, 38
RHUDULPH, Ann Mary, 100
Peter, 100
RHULE, Barbara, 208
Henry, 208
RICE, John C., 109
RICHARD, Amon, 2
George, 224
RICHARDS, Amon, 73, 153, 242
George (junior), 221
George, 77
John F., 242
Joshua, 186
Rachel, 186
Richard, 189, 231
RIDINGER, Catherine, 173, 195
Peter, 173, 195
RIEVER, Frederick, 101
RIGGS, Augustus, 86
James L., 86
RINEDOLLAR, George, 174
John, 65
Margaret, 174

ROGERS, Hannah, 181
ROHRBACH, Adam, 214
Rome, 129
ROONS, Esther, 56
  George, 56
ROOP, Daniel, 227
  David, 53, 85, 86, 183, 219
  John (junior), 219
  John, 36, 41, 47, 183, 248
  Lydia, 67, 68, 69
  Rebecka, 85, 86
RORBEAUGH, Lance, 55
Ross's Range, 161
ROYER, Amos [slave], 183
  Anne, 182
  Christian, 182, 183
  Ellen [slave], 183
  Emanuel, 143
  Henry Pompey [slave], 183
  Jacob, 183, 248
  Jane [slave], 183
  Jesse, 182, 183
  John [slave], 183
  John, 182, 183, 219
  Lewis [slave], 183
  Mary, 85
  Oscar [slave], 183
  Peter, 182
  Rebecca, 143
  Sevilla, 248
RUBY, John, 249
  Susanna, 77
RUDISEL, Ludwick, 183, 218
  Nancy, 183
  Thomas, 184
  Tobias, 215, 218

  William, 95, 184, 196
RUMLER, Jacob, 249
  Sarah Ann, 249
Rumlers Place, 175
RUNK, Lydia, 249
  William, 249
RUP, Frederick, 184
  George, 184
  Henry, 184
  Jacob, 184, 185
  John, 184
  Mary, 184
  Michael, 184
  Samuel, 184
RUSEL, Jacob, 85, 86
RUSI, Solomon, 24
SADLER, Clarricy, 112
SALTZGIVER, Henry, 104
SAMPLE, Catherine, 105
  John, 105
SANDERS, Betty [slave], 234
  Margaret [slave], 234
SATER, Adonijah, 31
  Anna [slave], 193
  John [slave], 193
  Thomas, 150, 207
SATOR, Thomas, 30
SAUBLE, Amos, 140
  George, 140
  Joseph, 140
  Peter, 140, 141
SAWBLE, Peter, 79, 140
SAWYER, Daniel, 185
  John, 144, 185
  Margaret, 185
  Sally, 144

SHAMER, John, 52
Rachel, 77
SHANER, Joseph, 152
SHANK, Michael, 108
SHARRER, Daniel, 73
David, 208
Joseph, 173
Mary, 208
Susan, 73
SHAUCK, Aaron, 32, 190
Henry, 27, 32, 115, 190
John, 189, 190, 191
Mary, 190
Mary Magdalena, 189, 190
SHAUL, Elizabeth, 29
SHAW, Hugh, 66, 218
Moses, 4, 99, 191
Susan, 82
William, 82, 191
SHEALEY, John, 24
SHEFFER, Jacob, 63
SHEKELS, Temperance, 29
SHEPHERD, Thomas, 102
William, 67, 102, 196
SHERFIGH, Joshua, 49
SHERMAN, Henry, 26
SHILLING, Josiah, 191, 192
Murray, 191, 192
Nicholas, 192
Rachel, 191
Richard [slave], 192
SHIPLEY, Amon, 139
Basil, 120
Denton, 192
Denton R., 193
George, 121

Grove (junior), 243
Hannah, 121
J. S., 192
John Robert, 158
Joshua H., 178, 179
Joshua S., 193
Julia Ann, 120, 121
Lewis Henry, 121
Lloyd, 158
Margaret Ann, 139
Mary Ann, 121, 179
Mary Ann H., 178
Otho, 46, 238
Rachel Ruth, 121
Susannah E., 193
William (junior), 192
William E., 192
SHOCKNEY, Charles, 164
Mary Ellen, 164
Rebecca, 164
Reuben, 164
Sarah, 160
SHOEMAKER, Abraham, 49
Elizabeth [slave], 193
Jacob [slave], 193
John [slave], 193
Magdelane, 49
Mariah [slave], 193
Peter, 193
Samuel [slave], 193
Sarah [slave], 193
SHOEY, Daniel, 194
Henry, 194
Rosanna, 194
SHORB, Catherine, 74
John, 74

SHORT, William, 250
SHOWER, Adam, 218
  George, 200, 218
  Jacob, 208
SHREEV, William, 46, 237
SHREEVE, Levi, 157
  Minerva, 22
SHREEVER, Mary, 208
SHRINER, Abraham, 195
  Jacob, 195
  John, 100, 195, 196, 214, 215
  John P., 195
  Mary, 195, 196
  Matilda [slave], 195
  Peter, 195
  Sarah, 214, 215
  Susannah, 100
SHRIVER, Elizabeth, 108
  Francis, 222, 231
  George, 37, 239
  Isaac, 19, 36, 37, 94, 222
  Jacob, 219
  Maria L., 251
  Mary, 94
  Nathaniel, 108
  Philip, 184
  Susanna, 184
SHUE, Samuel, 73
SHUEY, Catherine, 98
  Daniel, 194
SHULER, Frederick, 63
SHULTZ, Jesse, 30, 186
  John, 73, 126, 136
SHULTZS, William, 73
SHUMAN, George, 109
SHUNK, Aberilla, 196

Benjamin, 82, 122, 134, 143,
  196, 198, 215, 241
Daniel, 196, 215
Jeremiah, 51, 196
Joseph, 79, 196
Mary, 196
Rebecca, 82, 196
SHUSE, Jacob, 117
  Lewis, 117
  Sarah, 117
SIMMONS, Margaret, 245
  William, 245
SINDEL, Goring, 173
SIRE, John, 197
SLAGENHAUPT, Samuel, 185
SLINGLUFF, Charles, 18
  Isaac, 59
  Julian, 212
SLUSS, John, 74
  Susan, 74
SLYDER, Anna Mary, 198
  Catherine, 197
  Frederick, 197
  Henry, 197, 198
  Jacob, 197, 198
  John, 197, 198
  Josiah, 197, 198
  Peter, 197
  Rachel, 198
  Sarah Jane, 197
  William, 197, 198
SMEACH, Andrew, 172
  Elizabeth, 172
SMELSER, David, 128
  John, 50, 128
  William A., 211

Emanuel, 144, 147
Jonas, 16
SPEELMAN, Anna Mary, 205
Spillmans Discovry, 134
SPINDLE, Joshua, 206
Kesiah, 206
Spitters Enclosure, 163
Sportsman Hall, 153
SPRINKLE, Elizabeth, 194
STAGNER, Jacob, 120
Stannors Place, 175
STANSBURY, Caleb, 206
Creasey, 206
Creasy, 207
Cresy, 206
Emanuel, 206
Isaac, 206
James, 217
Jared, 206
John, 30, 101, 186, 206, 207
John L., 206
Joseph, 139, 206
Joshua, 206
Josiah, 206, 207
Mary, 190, 191, 206
Mary Magdalena, 189
Micagy, 117
Micajah, 189, 191
Richard, 1, 206
William, 111, 139, 206
William G., 217
STARY, Christina, 100
George, 100, 193
STEAVIG, John, 115
STEEL , Ann Maria, 57
James Henry, 57

John Thomas, 57
Joseph, 57
Joseph Hays, 57
Joseph Wesley, 57
Mary, 57
Robert, 57
Thomas, 57
William Robert, 57
STEELE, Beck [slave], 207
Hiram [slave], 207
James, 207
James Henry, 207
John Thomas, 207
Joseph, 207
Joseph Wesley, 207
Robert, 207
Thomas, 207
William Robert, 207
STEELL, Daniel, 50
STEFFEE, Christina, 208
Henry, 208
Jacob, 208
Michael, 208
Peter, 208
Unknown, 175
STEFFEY, Henry, 186
John N., 125
STEFFON, George, 205
Magdelina, 205
STEFFY, Heinrich N., 31
STEGNER, George, 199
Peter, 120
STEIFFER, John, 185
STEINCIFERD, Jacob, 232
STEPHAN, John, 205
STEPHENSON, Basil Dorsey, 87

299

STOUFFER, Eleanor, 211
  Eliza, 212
  John, 213
STRALEY, John, 104
  Polly, 104
STREAVIG, John, 34
STREVIG, George, 214
  Jacob, 214
  John, 214
  Margaret, 214
Stullers Place, 239
STULTZ, Abraham, 214, 216
  Ann, 215
  Anne, 216
  Catherine, 215
  Conrad, 214
  David, 214, 215, 216
  Eliza Ann, 215
  Elizabeth, 216
  Ephraim, 216
  Hannah, 214
  Henry, 216
  Margaret, 216
  Mary, 214
  Samuel Franklin, 215
  Sarah Jane, 215
  Susannah, 216
  William, 215
STUMP, George, 15
SULIVAN, Abraham, 216
  Cornelius, 216
  Mary, 216
  Mary Catherine, 216
  William, 216
SULLIVAN, Daniel, 114
  David, 125

Herod F., 217
  Matilda, 14
  Michael, 17, 36, 91, 98, 135,
    163, 172, 189, 197, 204, 205,
    226
  Rebecca, 217
  Unknown, 85
SUMWALT, John, 110
SUNDERGILL, Adaline
  Virginia, 247
  Elizabeth, 246, 247
  John Lewis, 247
  Joshua Hamilton, 247
SWARTBAUGH, John W., 114
SWARTZBAUGH, Barbary, 91
  Edmund, 218
  Elizabeth, 217
  John, 91, 217
  Julia, 91
  Milton, 91
  Peter [slave], 217
  Rosannah, 91, 92
  Sevilla [slave], 218
  Uriah, 91
SWEEDEN, John, 39, 206
SWEIGART, John, 36
SWERMSTEDT, Samuel L.,
  219, 220
SWIGART, John, 228
  Mary, 228
SWINEHART, Jacob, 76
SWITZER, Rudolf, 48
  Sarah Ann, 5
SWOPE, Adam, 218
  Clarissa, 95, 218
  Clarissa A., 218

WAGGONER, Anna, 227
  Elizabeth, 227
  John, 227
  Margaret, 227
  Mary, 227
  Michael, 227
  Rachel, 227
  Sarah, 227
WAGNER, Jacob, 228
  Michael, 227
  Sophia, 227
WAGONNER, Elizabeth, 200
  Jacob, 200
WALCKER, James, 37
WALKER, Catherine, 228, 229
  Daniel, 228, 229
  Elizabeth, 229
  Emanuel, 228, 229
  George, 214, 228
  Harriet, 229
  John, 228, 229
  Joseph, 228
  Maudy, 229
  Noah, 228
  Peggy, 229
  Polly, 229
  Sally, 229
  Susanna, 214, 229
WAMPLER, Abraham, 52, 62, 71, 77, 159 188
  Catherine, 182, 183
  George Edward, 26
  Hannah, 229
WANTZ, David, 143
WARD, Caroline, 230
  Jane, 230

John T., 231
Levina, 230
Richard, 230
Thomas, 230, 231
Washington H., 231
WARE, Richard, 2
WAREHAM, Albert, 233
  Charity, 232, 233
  Conrad, 231, 232, 233
  George, 232, 233
  Henry, 231, 233
  John, 231
WAREHIME, Henry, 146, 147, 163
  John, 214
  Mary, 214
WARFIELD, Alexander [slave], 234
  Alexander, 236
  Davis, 21
  George Fraser, 233
  George W., 32
  George Washington, 234
  Gustavus, 111
  Jane [slave], 234
  Jemima, 234
  Jemima M., 236
  Jesse L., 113, 235, 237
  Joshua, 234, 235
  Levi [slave], 234
  Lewis Marshal, 234
  Lucy Ann [slave], 234
  Mary Catherine, 234
  Sarah, 235
  Sophia [slave], 234
  Susanna, 234

WOOLVY, Solomon, 5
WORKMAN, William, 157
WORMAN, Noah, 91, 92, 194
Worth But Little, 28
WORTHINGTON, John F., 110,
111
John Folly, 111
Mary, 110, 111
Mary Govans, 111
WRIGHT, John W., 132
Nancy, 191
Sophia, 250
YANDIS, George, 108, 169, 194
YEISER, Daniel (senior), 135
Elisabeth, 233
Mary, 233
YINGLING, Benjamin, 192
Catherine, 203, 205
Christian, 154
David, 213
Ellen, 134
Jacob, 31, 81, 154, 203, 230
John, 81, 98, 203
John M., 192, 235, 236
John Murray, 235
Joshua, 17, 19, 57
Louisa, 235, 236
Magdalena, 203, 205
Mary, 135
Ruth, 192
William, 230
William H., 134
YISSER, Essibella, 187
YOHN, Ann Rebecca [slave], 247
Eliza [slave], 247
Henrietta [slave], 247

Jeremiah [slave], 247
John [slave], 247
Mary, 246
Mary Smith, 247
Moses [slave], 247
William, 247
YOHNS, William, 246
YON, Jacob, 76, 212
YOST, Anamaria, 247
Elizabeth, 247
Jacob, 247
Jacob L., 137
John, 247
Margarith, 247
YOU, Barbara, 228
Jacob, 50, 83
John, 228
YOUNG, Elizabeth, 100
Jacob, 143, 176
Samuel, 100
Savilla, 143
Zacharias Lot, 248
ZACHARIAS, Beck [slave], 248
Conrad, 248
Isaac [slave], 248
Jacob, 248
Samuel [slave], 248
Susan, 248
Willy [slave], 248
ZEIMMER, Elizabeth, 152
John, 152
ZENSZ, Peter, 85
ZENTZ, Abraham, 14
ZEPP, Caroline, 249
Catherine, 226
David, 127

George, 226
Samuel, 249
William, 167, 230
ZERBEICHEN, Ulrick, 189
ZILE, Abraham, 89, 249
Barbara, 249
Barbary, 249
Jacob, 249
John, 249
Rachel, 249
ZIMMERMAN, Adam, 249
Christian, 249
Christiann, 249
George, 249
Henry, 32, 249
John, 249
ZIPP, Henry, 197
ZOCCHI, Nicholas, 250
ZOCKEY, Nicholas, 66
ZOLLICKOFFER, Ann Louisa, 251
Annie M., 251
Caroline, 251
Caroline S., 251
Daniel, 10, 47, 48, 251
Henry, 251
William, 251
ZUMBRUN, Jacob, 82, 158, 181

www.ingramcontent.com/pod-product-compliance
Lightning Source LLC
Chambersburg PA
CBHW070556270326

41926CB00013B/2338